DATE DUE

THE JAZZ OF THE SOUTHWEST

The Jazz of
the Southwest

An Oral History of
Western Swing

Jean A. Boyd

University of Texas Press, Austin

First edition, 1998

Requests for permission to reproduce material from this work should be sent to
Permissions, University of Texas Press, Box 7819, Austin, TX 78713-7819.

∞ The paper used in this publication meets the minimum requirements of American
National Standard for Information Sciences—Permanence of Paper for Printed
Library Materials, ANSI Z39.48-1984.

LIBRARY OF CONGRESS CATALOGING-IN-PUBLICATION DATA

Boyd, Jean Ann.
    The jazz of the Southwest : an oral history of western swing / by Jean A. Boyd. —
1st ed.
        p.   cm.
    Includes bibliographical references and index.
    ISBN 0-292-70859-9 (alk. paper). — ISBN 0-292-70860-2 (pbk. : alk. paper)
    1. Western swing (Music)—Texas—History and criticism.   I. Title.
ML3541.B69 1998
781.65'3—dc21   97-33740
                                                                        MN

In memory of Elwyn A. Wienandt
my teacher, mentor, friend
Thanks, El

Contents

Preface

In 1990, when I was searching for a way to combine my musicology and regional Texas music interests, I discovered western swing. I grew up in Texas, so this music was always on the periphery of my musical experience, but I had never paid much attention. Because of my background and training, I began this work with the misconception that western swing was and is country music. I am still amazed that my academic colleagues think that I am writing about country music in Texas.

When I discovered, through listening to the music and interviewing western swing musicians, that western swing was, and is, jazz—swing jazz played on traditional country instruments, with all of the required elements of jazz and some of the best solo improvisation to be heard—I was excited, and then dismayed by the omission of western swing and its artists from jazz history and style books. I decided to bring western swing to the attention of jazz scholars, who will, I hope, complete the work I have begun.

And this book is just a beginning. It does not pretend to be a definitive history of western swing or a complete stylistic analysis of a topic that is as broad as any in the world of jazz. It is an introduction to western swing jazz and those who pioneered it and continue to recreate it. I have based much of the present study on interviews, but it has been physically impossible to interview every living western swing musician. What I present here is a cross section of players and singers from different time periods and numerous western swing bands. There are many similarities in their stories and one common theme: the music they made and continue to make belongs to the mainstream of swing jazz. They were and are in the same league with Benny Goodman, Tommy Dorsey, and many others, not in the "hillbilly" category where they were assigned by record executives who could not decide how to classify improvisation played on string instruments. Western swing musicians have nothing against country music and in fact recognize country music as one of many tributaries of their own music. But "country" is an inappropriate and misleading label for western swing.

Perhaps the time will come when western swing bands and individual western swing musicians will be included in studies devoted to swing jazz. Maybe western swing topics will find a place on the jazz sessions of professional musicology meetings. And, possibly, legendary western swing musicians will one day grace college campuses to perform with jazz ensembles and to direct workshops. When these possibilities are realized, we will learn, once again, that outward appearances do not identify, and certainly cannot limit, the boundless world that is jazz.

I would like to acknowledge the contributions of the more than fifty western swing musicians whom I interviewed and whose insights and memories form the foundation of this study. I would also like to thank the Oral History Institute of Baylor University, and especially Lois Myers and Rebecca Sharpless, who taught me how to conduct interviews, provided me with equipment and research funds, and supervised the students who transcribed numerous interview tapes in an amazingly short time.

To my husband, daughter, and mother, who have accompanied me around the country on my quest for information, helped me with interviews, proofed my writing, and provided endless emotional support, I could not have done this without you. And, finally, I want to express my deep appreciation to my friend Patricia Wienandt, who edited my manuscript and assured me that her husband, my teacher Elwyn Wienandt, would have been proud of my work.

Note to the Reader

Quotations not otherwise identified are from the author's interviews with the musicians, all of which are listed in Works Cited.

THE JAZZ OF THE SOUTHWEST

Introduction: Western Swing and the Texas Mystique

Western swing, like other styles of jazz, evolved from a mixing of cultural and musical elements. Steel guitar virtuoso Tommy Morrell described western swing as an amalgam of "jazz, blues, big band, polka music, country music, Mexican music . . . everything." Because it is a crossroads for diverse cultures, including Native American, Mexican American, Anglo American, German, French, Cajun, African American, Czech, and Polish, Texas was the birthplace of western swing.

Texas also possessed the socioeconomic conditions that nurtured western swing. In the words of Tommy Morrell, western swing began as "prairie music," meaning that its audience consisted primarily of rural folk—farmers and ranchers—who made their living off the land. Texas remained a largely rural and agricultural state until well into the twentieth century. In Texas and Oklahoma, the towns that became centers of western swing activity were basically extensions of the rural countryside. Attitudes in Texas towns did not differ essentially from attitudes in rural areas. Western swing was jazz created by and for country folk.

Rural Texans were plain, hard-working people who belonged to the lower and lower-middle classes of Texas society. Interesting parallels can be drawn between western swing and Texas-Mexican *conjunto* music in that both types of music emerged on the Texas scene at the same time and appealed to similar classes, though different ethnic groups, of people. In his book *The Texas-Mexican Conjunto: History of a Working-Class Music*, Manuel H. Peña argues that the accordion-led *conjunto* ensemble and its repertory of polkas

was the music of the politically disenfranchised, socioeconomically pow-
erless Texas-Mexican working class, that it helped them secure an identity and, to a certain extent, insulated them from extraneous hostile forces
comprised of dominant Anglo-Texans and Americanized, upwardly mo-
bile Mexican-Texans. In a sense, western swing evolved from and responded to a portion of the white Texas population that did not share in
the socioeconomic or political power of the upper class, most of whom
lived in cities and were involved in business and industry. Like its *conjunto*
counterpart, western swing was the poor, rural, working-man's jazz, and
it helped to identify and insulate him from his wealthier, urban neighbors.

Jazz is generally understood to be the product of urban life, but
western swing was devised in an essentially rural setting, in country dance
halls that served farmers and ranchers across one or more counties. Western swing was down-home, earthy dance music that translated the sounds
and techniques of jazz on typically country instruments in a rural, working-class setting. Like *conjunto* musicians, western swing musicians were
of and from the people they served—self-taught musicians who frequently
escaped the drudgery of farm and ranch work through their music. But
they did not abandon the community of folk from which they sprang.
Also like their *conjunto* cousins, western swing musicians, with some ex-
ceptions, did not enjoy the commercial recording success or the historic
recognition afforded other jazz figures.

Texas certainly possessed the venues—the honky-tonks and dance
halls—that promoted dancing and dance music, and, as already noted,
western swing was jazz designed to accompany dancing. Texas was a
prime location for honky-tonks after the repeal of prohibition in 1933,
because Texas was one of the states that allowed for county-by-county
local-option elections to determine the legality of liquor and beer sales.
County-line taverns sprang up along the lines between wet and dry counties all over the state. Even though economic times were hard and salaries
low, many Texans owned cars in which they could escape to local honky-
tonks, especially on Saturday nights, to relax and drink away their Depression era troubles. Some honky-tonks catered to families and advertised more wholesome atmospheres, but most were dives with dance
floors. Jukeboxes provided the music for dancing during the week, but on
weekends many honky-tonks featured local bands, making the Texas
honky-tonk scene a breeding ground for western swing and other types of
popular dance music.

Texans also promoted dancing through dance clubs, still called German clubs even after 1900 because German immigrants to Texas had first established organized dance societies. So popular was dancing in the state that dance entrepreneurs built large dance halls capable of accommodating hundreds of couples. One of the longest-lasting of the German clubs was the San Antonio German Club, founded in the 1880s and chartered by the State of Texas in 1936 as a benevolent society dedicated to the promotion of fellowship, goodwill, and the social welfare of the citizens of Bexar County. Other old dance clubs were the German Club of Kerr County and the Germania Farmers Verein, founded in Anhalt, Texas, in 1860 and still active in 1908, when members constructed a new dance hall. For many years the Farmers Verein sponsored special Mayfest and Oktoberfest celebrations at which as many as 2,000 people danced to bands playing traditional German dance music.[1]

In West Texas, where ranches incorporated thousands of acres of grassland in order to maintain large herds of cattle and horses, the ranch dance became an extremely important social institution, drawing entire families and ranch hands for many miles. Some of these ranch dances became organized functions that occurred regularly at specific times and places, such as the Matador Ranch Valentine Dance, held every Saturday night beginning in the 1890s at one of the large ranches—Matador, Pitchfork, Moon, or McAdams. Some communities assumed the role of dance promoters, as in the case of Crider's, located originally in a field west of Hunt, Texas. Beginning in 1925 and continuing for a number of years, dances were held here after rodeo performances.

The short list of legendary Texas dance halls, some of which are still in operation, is a long list indeed: Austin's Double Eagle and Broken Spoke; Monahans's Green Lantern; Grand Prairie's Old Sadie Hawkins; Comfort's El 87; Helotes's Floore's Country Store; Fischer's Fischer Hall; Bandera's Cabaret; Luckenbach's Luckenbach Hall; Abilene's Ponderosa Ballroom; Longview's Rio Palm Isle; Lubbock's Red Raider and Cotton Club; El Paso's Caravan East; Amarillo's Caravan Club; Goliad's Schroeder Hall; Gruene's Gruene Hall; Fort Worth's Pickin' Palace, Billy Bob's, Gateway, and Cowtown U.S.A.; Dallas's Longhorn Ballroom and Palms Danceland; Pasadena's Gilley's; Kerrville's Long Branch; Anhalt's Anhalt Verein Hall; Mexia's Cowboy Club; and Waco's Terrace Club. Add to these more famous halls all of the local SPJST halls, Sons of Herman halls, Veterans of Foreign Wars halls, Knights of Columbus halls, and many more, and Texas emerges as the land of a thousand dance halls, most of which have featured swing bands at one time or another.

The many cultures, the socioeconomic climate, and the abundance of dance venues in Texas certainly contributed to the birth and growth of western swing; but the spark of life for this music came from something more subliminal and harder to describe—a certain Texas mindset, or as some would call it, mystique. T. R. Fehrenbach begins his book *Seven Keys to Texas* by acknowledging this mystique and showing why it is seldom appreciated by non-Texans.

> While no one denies that there is such a thing as a Texas mystique, the very notion offends many Americans who in this time and place can accept any form of ethnicity except the Old American wrapped up in a sense of territoriality. But there is a true Texas ethnicity, American to the core, American in its origins, American in its intense patriotism—but in some ways divergent from the American mainstream. And at the same time it can be argued that while Texas is constantly changing under the pressure of American society and government, Texans are also influencing the nation as a whole.
>
> The fact is that some Americans happen to be Texans in much the same way that some Britons are Scots and some Germans are Bavarians. Although Texans have been caught up in the same flaccid commercial cosmopolitanism that pervades America coast to coast, and like the Scots and Bavarians, swallowed up by broader nation-states and cultures, they have retained an essential identity.
>
> Texans, in fact, have occupied something like the position of the Scots within the British empire: provincials who have provided frontiersmen, entrepreneurs, and adept politicians to the greater society while remaining basically provincial. A Texan who goes to Washington or New York may make his [or her] mark on the nation, but he [or she] remains a Texan. And like Scots, Texans have been both admired for their qualities and despised as barbarians.[2]

Texans have a powerful sense of who they are, of time and place, and of their past. Few states in the union possess as colorful and intense a history as Texas. Texans are imbued with and shaped by their history, both the good and the bad of it. This strong sense of the past causes Texans to be traditionalists, conservatives, and proud of it. But there is also a contradictory strain of adventurous individualism that runs through the character of the native Texan, and an adamant belief in the sanctity of privacy. That no government, state or federal, should infringe upon the rights of the individual in the privacy of his or her domain remains the inviolable belief of most Texans.

Western swing "became" because of the Texas mystique, with its contradictory streams of traditionalism and individualism. Western swing musicians kept the traditional country instruments and some of the traditional repertory that were part of their musical past, but they screamed their individuality through the adventurous jazz improvisation that was the essence of their present. Western swing music thrived in Texas during the 1930s and 1940s and migrated throughout the nation, as Texans did, because it was the native dance music of Texas.

ONE

Western Swing: Description and Development

ecord company executives of the 1930s and 1940s did not
know how to classify improvisation created by country string
bands, so they labeled it "hillbilly." But western swing musicians viewed themselves as jazz performers. One of the oldest
western swing societies in the United States, located in Sacramento,
California, publishes a monthly newsletter that often includes the
following statement: "Western swing music is a division of the American phenomenon known as jazz. Many elements of musical roots
are combined to form western swing music, including blues, Dixieland, ragtime, big band, swing, country, pop, and breakdowns."[1]

Jazz is not a type of music, as the Italian Renaissance madrigal
is a type of music, but rather an approach to making music that in-
volves personal interpretation, improvisation, and a unique rhythmic method. Jazz interpretation may include sounds that are not
considered correct or polished, by classical music standards, but
that allow performers to individualize compositions. Improvisation
is the art of spontaneously creating new music based upon existing
melodies, chords, or scales; and the integrity and interest of an improvisation are dependent upon the intelligence, experience, and
emotion of a performer. The rhythmic language of jazz derives from
African and African-American usage of multiple layers of distinctive but interlocking rhythm patterns (polyrhythm) and a difficult-
to-define concept called swing. Swing occurs when musicians accent
slightly ahead of or behind a well-established pulse; when swing is
not present, jazz becomes static. Western swing musicians have been
involved in all of these aspects of jazz, so why have they been ignored as jazz musicians?

Western swing suffers from the same mindset that plagued all jazz created in the Southwest in the 1920s and 1930s, when record companies did not view the region as a fertile jazz-producing area. Thus, many fine southwestern groups made relatively few recordings. Since jazz historians depend upon recorded evidence as primary source material, the paucity of recordings of jazz bands from the Southwest has led to the mistaken notion that jazz was insignificant to this part of the country. Western swing bands have suffered the added disadvantage of being labeled "hillbilly," which further precluded them from investigation by jazz historians.

An outstanding jazz historian himself, Gunther Schuller has spoken to the fact that western swing has simply been overlooked by the jazz community. He is on target when he provides the following description of western swing: "[It] was the most pervasive southwestern music of all, especially on radio, . . . with featured guitarists playing improvised single-note lines. These players also pioneered the electric or amplified guitar but have never . . . been given credit in any jazz-writing either for their jazz leanings or their efforts on behalf of guitar amplification. Players like 'Zeke' Campbell, Bob Dunn, and Leon McAuliffe were very much in a jazz groove and by the mid-thirties certainly far removed from any of the older guitar, mandolin, banjo vertical 'finger-pickin' country styles." [2]

Western swing was a jazz style formed by the fusion of various ethnic musical elements found in the Southwest, predominantly in Texas. Western swing was, from the outset, dance music designed for the numerous dance facilities that dotted the landscape of Texas and Oklahoma. Western swing, like its Mexican *conjunto* cousin, was rural music, played in rural settings or for transplanted rural people in urban venues. Western swing rarely assumed fixed forms but varied from band to band, soloist to soloist, and region to region.

Western swing pioneers inherited a basic string ensemble and a traditional repertory of tunes (fiddle tunes, breakdowns, blues) that had served generations of rural southwesterners as dance music. Even when horns were added in the late 1930s, western swing bands coalesced around their nucleus of strings—fiddle, guitar, banjo, bass. It was this basic instrumentation that caused record company executives to classify western swing bands as "hillbilly."

But western swing musicians, though they played country instruments and even included some oral tradition tunes, did not play or sing in a "hillbilly" manner. Western swing was played and sung in a manner consistent with popular music and jazz that was current in the late 1920s and early 1930s; and this was the music that was heard even by rural folk on phonographs and the radio. In its adaptation of a basically urban musical style, western swing was an indicator of socioeconomic transformations occurring in the Southwest. Two of the factors that contributed to the emergence of western swing were urbanization and widespread dependence on the radio for entertainment. Urbanization came late to the Southwest and in Texas was propelled by the oil boom of the 1920s and 1930s. Where oil was discovered, villages became cities and cotton fields sprouted boom towns overnight. Many rural Texans migrated to towns in search of job opportunities. For these displaced Texans traditional music assumed greater meaning as a source of stability in an otherwise unstable and foreign environment. But traditions had to evolve to satisfy the new context, which for music meant updated lyrics and modifications in rhythm and instrumentation. String bands playing in honky-tonks had to compete with noisy crowds and jukeboxes, so performance practice had to adjust accordingly. Guitarists exchanged the vibrating open chords of country music for the crisp bar chords of jazz, strumming all six strings energetically so as to be heard over the din. Bass players raised the bridges on their instruments in order to increase the volume of sound of the strings rebounding off the fingerboard, and they either plucked the strings aggressively or slapped them for emphasis. In some bands, drums and piano were added to underline the dance beat.

Another factor that influenced the birth of western swing was the radio, which became a primary source of musical sounds and ideas for musicians all over the country. The radio began to increase in popularity among Americans during the 1920s as the number of radio stations and their broadcasting capabilities multiplied significantly. Radio stations appeared more slowly in the South and Southwest than in the more urbanized North, but they did appear. Of the 510 stations in operation by the end of 1922, 89 were located in the South. Texas was at the center of broadcasting in the southern United States with 25 stations. Since most of the radio stations were in the northern states, radio programming was dictated from the North, and even southern program directors followed the lead of their northern counterparts in featuring urban popular music, sacred music, semiclassics, and some jazz. As a result, rural southerners and southwesterners received a steady diet of new and basically northern music that began to influence listeners' tastes and performers' styles. Eventually program directors in the South and Southwest opened time slots for local musical talent, but not before the transformation process had begun to effect changes in traditional music.

The first powerful radio station in the South, and possibly the first to include shows of traditional southern music, was WSB in Atlanta, which was owned by the *Atlanta Journal*. This station first began broadcasting in March 1922 and within a few months was featuring traditional folk performers like Fiddlin' John Carson. Radio station WBAP in Dallas produced the first radio barn dance show in the United States in January 1923, more than a year before Chicago's WLS aired its National Barn Dance and three years before Nashville's WSM began broadcasting the Grand Ole Opry. Like most radio stations at the time, WBAP had a policy of programming only popular music, sacred music, semiclassics, and some jazz, but the weekly square dance hosted by old-time fiddler and Confederate veteran Captain M. J. Bonner proved extremely popular with listeners. Guests on the program included Fred Wagner's Hilo Five Hawaiian Orchestra and the Peacock Fiddle Band out of Cleburne, Texas. WBAP was one of the strongest stations in the Southwest and could be heard as far away as New York, Canada, Hawaii, and Haiti. It is reasonable to assume that WBAP's square dance show was the prototype for other barn dance programs that appeared on other stations in the Midwest and South in the 1920s. WBAP's management was so pleased with the success of the barn dance that the station began to schedule other traditional music acts and by 1927 was offering its listeners a live country music broadcast every Saturday night.[3]

The popularity of WBAP's traditional music programming encouraged other southwestern radio stations to attempt similar shows, and soon listeners in Texas, Oklahoma, Missouri, Arkansas, Kansas, and New Mexico could listen to "down home" music early in the morning before leaving for the cotton field, the oil field, or the factory; again during the lunch hour; and one last time at the end of the work day. Local musicians were not paid for performing on radio, but they received free air time in which to advertise their upcoming dances. Thus, the radio became extremely important for the success of southwestern dance bands. In fact, the broadcast range of a given radio station was the main factor in determining the scope of a band's dance circuit and the size of the crowds in attendance. The radio also provided a means for local musicians to exchange ideas and learn from one another, as well as from the various programs of popular music and jazz that filled the airways. Bands that could not afford to buy stock arrangements could recreate and reinterpret the numbers they heard on the radio and on recordings. The radio made the repertory of popular music and jazz a universal repertory among all manner of dance bands, including southwestern string bands.

In the summer of 1930, a West Texas fiddler named Bob Wills and his guitarist-partner Herman Arnspiger won a fiddlers' contest sponsored by the Fort Worth station KFJZ, which netted them fifty dollars and a chance to audition for the station. When Wills, Arnspiger, and vocalist Milton Brown performed for assistant program director Al Stricklin, who was also a ragtime pianist, Stricklin thought their music comical, but unique, and assigned them a broadcast time from 8:00 to 8:30 each morning. Listeners liked the trio, and later that same summer the more powerful WBAP in Dallas offered them a show sponsored by the Aladdin Lamp Company. They became the Aladdin Laddies and enjoyed the increased success and circulation that WBAP provided them. In order to reach a broader audience, they modified their musical offerings to include, besides fiddle tunes, popular songs and some jazz material.[4] The Aladdin Laddies were still a country fiddle band, but the transformation to western swing had begun for these three musicians.

Because of what they heard on radio and recordings, fiddlers in the Southwest lost interest in traditional fiddle tunes and breakdowns; they wanted to play the popular material and jazz they were hearing. And when two or more fiddlers played in the same band, they could emulate a harmonizing brass section. Guitarists, both standard and steel, as well as bass players and banjo pickers, found models among the ranks of jazz musicians. Traditional playing and singing styles were modernized; sound and performance practices changed. Fiddlers assumed the role of trumpet players, embellishing melody lines and sometimes even incorporating trumpet phrasing and hot licks. Guitarists learned a new vocabulary of chords and strummed more percussively to enhance the dance beat. The steel guitar could play single-line melody or imitate an entire section of winds. The addition of piano and drums completed the metamorphosis from fiddle band to western swing band. And some western swing band leaders went so far as to add horns, but never to the detriment of the strings.

With all of the traditional material they had in their backgrounds and all they were learning via radio and recordings, western swing bands were extremely versatile in their repertory. The same band could play numbers as diverse as "Ida Red," "Dark Town Strutters' Ball," "Stardust," and

"South." As the 1930s progressed, most western swing bands gravitated more to the popular and jazz tunes and retained only a scant few of the older fiddle tunes. Like all jazz musicians, western swing performers emphasized reinterpretation of compositions through improvisation. Perhaps because many western swing musicians did not read music, the written score was never as sacred for them as it became for some of the large horn bands. Some western swing musicians never advanced beyond basic chord charts and had to rely upon their imaginations; and some band leaders insisted that their sidemen constantly recreate the music on their play lists. For example, Bob Wills made it a condition of employment that when he pointed his fiddle bow, the designated player was to improvise something entirely new, no matter how many times he or she had taken a solo chorus on the same number; to fail at this was to be looking for another job. Even the few western swing musicians who could read music quickly learned that feeling mattered far more than arrangements.

Whether played by horns or strings, all swing jazz took on certain characteristics of melody, harmony, and rhythm, with melody emerging as the most important element of a performance for most audiences in the 1930s and 1940s. Swing was the most popular music of the time, not because it was jazz, but because it offered memorable tunes to people seeking escape from the stresses of economic depression and war. Most swing arrangements followed a pattern that fulfilled audiences' demand for familiarity and musicians' need for creativity: first, the entire ensemble played the main melody, followed by a vocalist singing one or more verses and then individual instrumentalists taking off on solo choruses that might diverge sharply from the melody. At the end of the arrangement, the singer and ensemble would restore the original tune.

The harmonic vocabulary of jazz became more complex during the Swing Era through the addition of more chord structures, advanced methods for altering chords, and the use of key changes to lend greater harmonic variety. Perhaps because they played and sang by ear rather than by notation, some western swing musicians were quite adventurous in their chord changes. Guitarist Eldon Shamblin transformed the sound of the Bob Wills band with his huge, modern chords. And pianist Skeeter Elkins remembers a harmonic experiment that involved himself and several guitarists in the Wills band.

We were in Los Angeles. Bob hired a bunch of guys there. He hired Jimmy Wyble. He hired a guy from Spade Cooley's band. Billy

Wright, fiddle player. Billy Bowman played steel. We were trying to get the thing together to present the same sound different, and—just for fun. We sat there in the motel and I helped them get some great big chord things. And they were taking two and three parts apiece. Jimmy Wyble playing two or three. The other guitarist played two or three parts, and then Billy Bowman played two or three, and those chords were stretched out like a big orchestra. It was a great, fine-sounding song.

Such harmonic and textural experimentation was not rare in the more proficient western swing bands. The string orientation of western swing bands presented another interesting problem, especially for wind players, because the string players were accustomed to playing in sharp keys and horns in flat keys; when strings and horns were combined in western swing bands, it was the horns rather than the strings that had to adjust.

Swing is actually a rhythmic concept, and swing jazz came into existence when musicians abandoned the 2/4 meter common in ragtime and Dixieland in favor of a looser, freer swing-four. Though they rarely receive any credit, southwestern jazz bands participated in this rhythmic transformation. There are differences, however, between horn swing bands and string swing bands. Because western swing bands played primarily for dancing, in large dance halls or honky-tonks and without public address systems, western swing rhythm sections were more forceful and dominant than those of most horn bands. In fact, Larry Willoughby, in his book *Texas Rhythm, Texas Rhyme*, compares western swing to rock and roll in terms of the foreground prominence of rhythm.[5] To some people western swing rhythm sections were rough-sounding and unsophisticated, but their aim of generating an easily heard dance beat for large groups of noisy people dictated their playing approach.

Another reason western swing rhythm sections tended to play more forcefully than those of wind bands stemmed from their continued use of 2/4 meter for ensemble choruses, though they generally adopted the more laid-back swing-four for backing soloists. Rhythm also helped to distinguish western swing bands originating in different parts of the country from one another. For example, some listeners separate Texas swing from West Coast swing on the basis of the more driving, energetic rhythms in Texas swing.

Western swing shared many characteristics of melody, harmony, rhythm, tone color, performance practice, and even repertory with the big horn bands of the era, but managed to maintain their distinctiveness as a separate jazz development. As with most styles of jazz, it is difficult to make an unequivocal statement about how and when western swing actually began. Even the Sacramento Western Swing Society wrestles with this issue, as demonstrated in their newsletter: "The history of western swing music can be endlessly debated. However, our research concludes that the art form was rooted in and around Texas and Oklahoma. In its early developmental stages, it took on a consistent and uniform sound, pioneered by Bob Wills, Milton Brown and their many associates during the 1930s."[6]

Before Wills and Brown made their impact on western swing, there were numerous lesser-known fiddle bands that bridged the gap between traditional music and western jazz. One of these was Prince Albert Hunt's Texas Ramblers out of Terrell in East Texas. Hunt was a superb breakdown fiddler who performed traditional country fiddle tunes, but with improvised melodic variations that resulted in a jazzlike fiddle style. Hunt learned the art of improvisation from black musicians in his hometown. His band was quite popular in Dallas from the late 1920s until his death in 1931.

Another transition group was the East Texas Serenaders, led by left-handed fiddler Daniel Huggins Williams from Tennessee. The Serenaders consisted of fiddle, tenor banjo, guitar, and bass. It was the bass player Henry Bogan who added the jazz element to this Texas string band with his improvised bass figures played on a three-string cello. The Serenaders recorded for Brunswick and Decca from 1927 to 1934 and enjoyed a large following around their hometown of Lindale, Texas.[7]

Prince Albert Hunt's Texas Ramblers and the East Texas Serenaders were but two of the best examples of the grassroots fusion of traditional country music and jazz affecting most Texas fiddle bands in the 1920s. The first full-fledged western swing band was the creation of pop singer Milton Brown from Fort Worth. Brown met fiddler Bob Wills and guitarist Herman Arnspiger in the spring of 1930 at a Fort Worth house dance where Wills and Arnspiger were playing. When Wills heard Brown sing, he invited him and his younger brother, Derwood Brown (guitarist), to join the band. Calling themselves the Wills Fiddle Band, they began to play every Saturday night at Eagles' Fraternal Hall in downtown Fort

Worth. They spent much of their spare time at Kemble Brothers Furniture Company, where they listened to the latest pop and jazz record releases and expanded their repertory.

In the summer of 1930, Wills, Arnspiger, and Brown won the fiddle contest that got the Wills Fiddle Band on the air, first at radio station KFJZ, then on the larger Dallas station WBAP, where they performed as the Aladdin Laddies. WBAP increased the band's exposure, and soon they were playing dances at the Crystal Springs dance hall and swimming pool near Fort Worth. To increase their volume of sound for the Crystal Springs job, Wills hired tenor banjoist Clifton "Sleepy" Johnson and a second fiddler, teenager Jesse Ashlock, who became Wills's protégé.

In late 1930, Wills, Arnspiger, and Brown, with the help of furniture company owner Ed Kemble, convinced Burrus Mills to sponsor the band on a KFJZ program. Since Burrus Mills produced Light Crust Flour, the band assumed the name Light Crust Doughboys. They broadcast for the first time in January 1931. The general manager of Burrus Mills, W. Lee O'Daniel, was not interested in the band but rather in the amount of manual labor they produced at the mill as employees. But when he observed that the sale of Light Crust Flour had increased because of the radio personality of the band, he took over as band manager and emcee, making all of the performance arrangements, appearing on the radio broadcasts, and even writing song lyrics and inspirational speeches.

On February 9, 1932, the Doughboys, consisting of Sleepy Johnson (guitar/banjo), Derwood Brown (guitar), Bob Wills (fiddle), and Milton Brown (vocals), recorded two sides at the Jefferson Hotel in Dallas on the RCA Victor label. The two songs released, "Sunbonnet Sue" and "Nancy Jane," were traditional and did not sell well, but the Doughboys were undaunted. At this point the Light Crust Doughboys was not a western swing band, but rather a group of musicians in transition from traditional fiddle band to western jazz ensemble.

Seeking more recognition and a wider audience, O'Daniel moved the Doughboys to WBAP, where they were given a prime-time slot at 12:30 P.M. After six months on WBAP, they were also broadcasting over stations WOAI (San Antonio) and KPRC (Houston) and on Southwest Quality Network stations KTAT (Fort Worth) and KOMA (Oklahoma City). The show was so popular that O'Daniel built a state-of-the-art studio at Burrus Mills and raised each musician's salary to twenty-five dollars per week, a small fortune during the Depression. But when he demanded that the Doughboys restrict their playing activities to the daily broadcast and personal appearances and that they not play for any dances, Milton and Derwood Brown bolted.[8]

Milton Brown was disgusted by the restrictions O'Daniel placed on the Doughboys, and he had an idea for a musical sound that required the freedom of his own band. In September 1932 he organized the Musical Brownies and molded them into the first western swing band. The initial Brownies band consisted of Jesse Ashlock (fiddle), Ocie Stockard (tenor banjo), Wanna Coffman, who slapped his bass fiddle for a bigger sound, Derwood Brown (guitar), and Milton Brown (vocals). In March 1992, Kevin Coffey, columnist for the *Fort Worth Star Telegram*, assessed Milton Brown's talent and background: "a smooth pop singer from a family of string band musicians. His father fiddled; brother Derwood picked guitar; Milton merged these with heavy doses of jazz and blues . . . and occasional touches of mariachi and Tin Pan Alley cowboy."[9]

Brown revolutionized Texas string band music and created a western swing band that other Texas ensembles emulated. He added the first pianist to a string band—Fred "Papa" Calhoun, who brought jazz improvisation to the Brownies. Early in 1933 he hired formally trained violinist Cecil Brower, and thus created the first example of harmonizing twin fiddles. And then in 1934, when Milton took the unprecedented step of adding jazz-oriented electric steel guitarist Bob Dunn, he had put together the prototype western swing band, consisting of two fiddles, guitar, banjo, bass, steel guitar, and piano, to which he added his melodious pop vocal styling and occasionally some scat-singing.

Brown also defined the essence of western swing, as Coffey explains: "The Brownies were a string band that played pop music. It was jazz-based music for dancing and the key was improvisation. Though the music was not known by its present name until the 1940s, Roy Lee Brown (youngest brother of Milton Brown) says, 'Western swing is not western swing without jazz improvisation' and a jazz dance beat, and the Musical Brownies were likely the first band to incorporate take-off solos." Coffey further asserts that Brown established the typical repertory of western swing, though much of what western swing bands today play has been reduced to songs written by or associated with Bob Wills. "The Brownies played pops, both current and standard, as well as heavy doses of jazz and pumped-up blues. A cowboy song or a sentimental waltz would crop up occasionally, but the Brownies were essentially a young, hard-driving band." Of Milton Brown as a singer, Coffey writes: "Milton Brown had an expressive and versatile voice . . . that could move effortlessly from the lovely 'My Mary' to the wicked hot jazz of 'I'll Be Glad When You're Dead, You Rascal You.' In fact, Brown ranks among the top white jazz vocalists of his era, though his association with 'hillbilly' music prevents him from receiving serious consideration as such." [10]

Milton Brown and His Musical Brownies became the most popular and influential dance band in Texas between 1932 and Milton's untimely death in 1936. They had a large and avid following of people who attended their dances and bought their records. And they were the first to record western swing—in 1934 on the RCA Victor/Bluebird label. In 1935 and 1936 they recorded for Decca and, in the brief two-year period from 1934 to 1936, released one hundred tunes. Had Milton Brown not died at the age of thirty-three, he would have achieved the national prominence that was later afforded to Bob Wills, Spade Cooley, Tex Williams, and others who built on his model.

Milton Brown created the standards for instrumentation, rhythm, improvisation, and repertory that distinguished western swing from traditional fiddle band music, and hundreds of southwest fiddle bands followed his lead. Some of these followers achieved remarkable success with Brown's formula; one of them was Bob Wills. In August 1933, eleven months after Milton Brown left the Doughboys, Bob Wills did the same. Wills felt a similar personal and musical repression under O'Daniel and, like Brown, had musical ideas floating through his mind that could not be realized with the Doughboys. Vocalist Thomas Elmer Duncan and steel guitarist Kermit Whalin left the Doughboys with Wills, and the three musicians traveled eighty miles south to Waco, where Everett Stover, radio manager of WACO, had promised them a 12:30 P.M. broadcast spot. While in Waco, Wills added two more musicians to the band—his brother Johnnie Lee (tenor banjo) and Kermit Whalin's brother June (rhythm guitar). It was also in Waco that Wills began calling his band the Texas Playboys. Like Brown, Wills directed their radio show primarily to popular dance music so that they appealed to a wider audience. They began to get dance jobs in and around Waco, and then W. Lee O'Daniel cast his shadow over the Playboys by filing a lawsuit against Wills for using as part of the band's identification the phrase "formerly of the Light Crust Doughboys." Though the case against Wills was dismissed, he decided to put greater distance between himself and O'Daniel. So in January 1934 Wills moved the Playboys to Oklahoma City and radio station WKY.

The Playboys band that moved to Oklahoma City consisted of Wills (fiddle), Tommy Duncan (piano/vocals), Kermit Whalin (bass/steel guitar),

Johnnie Lee Wills (tenor banjo), June Whalin (guitar), Don Ivey (piano), and Son Lansford (fiddle/guitar/bass). They began broadcasting on WKY in February 1934, and within days O'Daniel was proving himself once again a menace to their success. O'Daniel got the Playboys kicked off the air by promising to bring his better-known Doughboys to that station. The Playboys moved to station KVOO in Tulsa, where they found a manager willing to stand up to O'Daniel; they made KVOO their radio home for the next decade. Within a month of their arrival in Tulsa, the Playboys were playing a dance somewhere every night except Sunday. In the fall of 1935 Wills negotiated a contract with Red Star Milling Company, a subsidiary of General Mills, to sponsor the radio show and produce Playboy Flour, the wrappers of which contained pictures of various band members and their favorite recipes. The Texas Playboys were on the road to becoming one of the most recognized and popular dance bands in the country.

The band Wills took to Oklahoma was not the band of his dreams; it was rough and unpolished in its sound. And it was not a swing band like Milton Brown's because it was not made up of jazz musicians. But Wills knew precisely the sound that he wanted and began to reshape his ensemble accordingly. Pianist Don Ivey left to form a string band called the Alabama Boys. Guitarist June Whalin joined an NBC network show in New York, and steel player Kermit Whalin joined a band in Ohio. Longtime friend and musical associate Herman Arnspiger rejoined Wills as guitarist. From the Doughboys Wills acquired Sleepy Johnson and a young steel player named Leon McAuliffe. After Milton Brown's death, Wills hired Brown's fiddler, Jesse Ashlock, whose idol was jazz violinist Joe Venuti. Then he enticed stride pianist Al Stricklin away from his teaching and playing jobs in Fort Worth. With the strings well in place, Wills began to build the horn component of his dream band.

Wills had always favored horn bands, and by the late 1930s he had added so many horns to the Playboys that he had two separate front lines—one composed of strings and the other of horns. In the mid-1930s Wills began building his horn section with trumpeter Everett Stover, former announcer for the Playboys. Then he added Robert "Zeb" McNally on clarinet and saxophone and New Orleans–style trombonist Art Haines. The string players in the band learned jazz licks from the horn players, and Wills's Texas string band was gradually transformed into a Dixieland-style jazz band. The addition of William "Smoky" Dacus on drums further enhanced the Playboys' Dixieland sound and made their insistent dance beat even more prominent.

This was the thirteen-piece Playboys band that made its first recordings on the Brunswick label between September 20 and 25, 1935: Bob Wills (fiddle/vocals), Jesse Ashlock (fiddle), Johnnie Lee Wills (tenor banjo), Son Lansford (bass), Herman Arnspiger (guitar), Sleepy Johnson (banjo/guitar), Leon McAuliffe (steel guitar), Everett Stover (trumpet), Zeb McNally (clarinet/saxophone), Art Haines (trombone/fiddle), Al Stricklin (piano), Smoky Dacus (drums), and Tommy Duncan (lead vocals). They cut twenty sides, some of which featured fiddles playing more traditional music, such as "Maiden's Prayer," and others in a New Orleans Dixieland vein, like "Osage Stomp" and "St. Louis Blues."

A year later, September 29–30, 1936, the Texas Playboys were in Chicago to record again for Brunswick. Art Haines had left the band to form the Ragtime Rascals in Shawnee, Oklahoma, and Son Lansford had gone out on his own to front a band in Amarillo that he called the Sons of the West. Replacement musicians included Joe Frank Ferguson, a pop ballad singer with a sweet tenor voice and some ability to play bass, and jazz saxophonist Ray DeGeer. This session produced no fiddle music but rather a large collection of jazz numbers, many in a Dixieland style, including "She's Killing Me," "Weary of the Same Old Stuff," "Basin Street Blues," "Back Home Again in Indiana," "Fan It," "Bear Cat Mama," and "Swing Blues No. 2." The best-selling record to come out of the session was Leon McAuliffe's own "Steel Guitar Rag."

In June 1937 the Texas Playboys were back in Dallas to record twenty-eight tunes, fifteen of which were jazz, including "Old Jelly Roll Blues," "Thirty-First Street Blues," and "Dallas Blues." A year later, in May 1938, they were in Dallas again, this time recording for Columbia, which had acquired Brunswick. A new guitarist, Eldon Shamblin, set a new harmonic direction for the band. Ray DeGeer had left Wills to play with swing bands in Chicago and was replaced by Charles Laughton (saxophone/trumpet). Though the Playboys band that recorded in 1938 continued to play blues numbers, including Bessie Smith's "Down-Hearted Blues," it was moving in the direction of modern swing, as evidenced by the inclusion of arrangements of "Don't Stop Loving Me," "Oh Lady, Be Good," and "Moonlight and Roses." As if to appease their more rural clientele who bemoaned the modernization of the Playboys, Wills was back in the Dallas studio in November 1938 to record fiddle tunes such as "Spanish Two-Step," rearranged into "San Antonio Rose," "Silver Bells," "Beaumont Rag," and "Don't Let the Deal Go Down."

For the next decade fiddle tunes and even blues took a back seat to big band swing arrangements; the Texas Playboys could compete with the big bands of Benny Goodman, Tommy Dorsey, Glenn Miller, and others. In fact, with two front lines—strings and horns—the Texas Playboys were more versatile than the other big bands. Horns and strings were well integrated in the Wills band; brass and reeds shared melody lines with strings, took jazz choruses, filled in breaks behind other instruments or singers, and sometimes played duets with fiddles or guitars. And on some tunes only the horns were used, whereas on others only the strings.

By 1940, Wills had five saxophones, two clarinets, and two trumpets, along with a full contingent of strings, and the band's sound was polished and refined, thanks in part to the scores provided by Granville King, who was hired primarily for his arranging skills. Recordings released by the Texas Playboys were outselling all others on the labels on which they were signed—Vocalion, Okeh, Columbia. Art Satherley, A & R man for Columbia, estimated that Bob Wills's records were playing on 300,000 jukeboxes and being heard by millions of Americans daily. The band was also drawing extremely well at dances, averaging 1,000 to 1,500 people on the road, 700 to 800 on Thursday nights at Cain's Academy in Tulsa, and 1,200 to 1,500 at the same club on Saturday nights. By 1940, the Texas Playboys was the most popular swing band in the Southwest, and Bob Wills was the best-paid bandleader in the country.[11]

The band Wills fronted in the early 1940s was one of the largest in the business, with eighteen pieces: Wills (fiddle/vocals), Ashlock (fiddle), McAuliffe (steel guitar), Shamblin (electric guitar), Arnspiger (rhythm guitar), Johnnie Lee (tenor banjo), Lansford (back on bass), Louis Tierney (fiddle/saxophone), Stover (trumpet), Tubby Lewis (trumpet), Wayne Johnson (saxophone/clarinet), Zeb McNally (saxophone), Tiny Mott (saxophone), Ferguson (saxophone/vocals), Don Harlan (saxophone), Stricklin (piano), Dacus (drums), and Duncan (lead vocals). Most of the horn players came to Wills from big horn bands and gravitated to the Playboys because Wills paid better. Other horn players who passed through the Texas Playboys between 1930 and 1942 were trumpeter Benny Strickler, who had worked with Joe Venuti and had turned down a job with Artie Shaw to go with Wills; trumpeter Danny Alguire; clarinetist Woody Wood, previously with the Red Nichols band; trumpeter Alex Brashear, who had worked for both Charlie and Jack Teagarden; trumpeter Jamie McIntosh, formerly of the Ben Pollack Orchestra; saxophone players

George Balay and Granville King; and saxophonist/trombonist Neil Duer. Among the Playboys' all-time greatest hits were two that featured horns: "New San Antonio Rose," a Wills tune with lyrics added by several band members, and the hot swing number "Big Beaver."

"New San Antonio Rose" in particular vaulted Bob Wills and His Texas Playboys into national prominence and probably convinced Monogram Pictures to offer Wills and a few of his string players a contract to make a movie with cowboy star Tex Ritter. The title of the movie was *Take Me Back to Oklahoma*, and it added the western image to the Texas Playboys. They played some cowboy ballads, but in an updated swing style. George T. Simon, author of the book *The Big Bands*, editor of *Metronome* magazine, and jazz critic for the *New York Herald Tribune*, described the Playboys as "a compromise that resulted in thousands of dedicated West Coast fans, attracted by the sight of cowboy-attired musicians who sounded more like city slickers." [12]

Bob Wills and His Texas Playboys had a following on the West Coast even before they went out to make the movie because hundreds of thousands of hard-hit farmers and ranchers from the Depression and Dust Bowl areas of Texas, Oklahoma, Kansas, and Missouri had migrated to the fertile San Joaquin and San Fernando valleys of California. Thus, Wills found in California a ready-made audience that already appreciated his music. Film work increased the dance business both in California and back home in Tulsa.

In July 1941 Columbia Pictures hired Wills and his entire big band to appear in *Go West, Young Lady*, starring Glen Ford, Penny Singleton, Ann Miller, and Charles Ruggles. While working on the film, Wills took twelve of his musicians, predominantly horn players, into the studio for a Columbia recording session. Intent on featuring horns, Wills did not even unpack his fiddle until Satherley convinced him that the people bought records to hear Wills. This was only one of many times that Wills was told that the Playboys was just another good swing band, nothing unique or special, without his fiddle and his homey vocal interjections.

The United States' entry into World War II played havoc with the Texas Playboys, as it did with most of the big swing bands. Vocalist Tommy Duncan was the first to leave the band to join the service, followed by Al Stricklin, who went to work in a defense plant in Fort Worth. By Christmas 1942, the old band was history. In fact, when Wills signed a contract with Columbia Pictures to do eight western movies with actor Russell Hayden, he had to borrow musicians from the band of his brother

Johnnie Lee. The nucleus of the Wills band for the movies consisted of Wills, Joe Holley (fiddle), McAuliffe, Harley Huggins (guitar/vocals), Bob's younger brother Luke Wills (bass), and Millard Kelso (piano). Before the Playboys could finish the eight movies, Wills received his draft notice and had to seek a month's deferment. In early October 1942, Wills was back in Hollywood to finish the Hayden movies. He decided to play some dance jobs and opened at the Venice Pier Ballroom in Venice, California, to crowds that totaled 15,000 people over a three-night period. Since the band that played both for the completion of the movie contract and at Venice Pier was a small string ensemble, with no horns, the message was finally brought home to Wills that people came out to see him and his fiddle; but Bob Wills could not be satisfied musically without the big band.

Wills went into the army in December 1942 and was released six months later, July 1943, because he was physically unfit for military service. He decided to make California his headquarters, and in September 1943 he bought a home in the San Fernando Valley, began broadcasting on radio station KMTR in Los Angeles, and made regular appearances at the Mission Beach Ballroom in San Diego. He also started work on another movie for Columbia Pictures, *Cowboy Canteen*, and hired Music Corporation of America (MCA) to manage the band.

By early 1944, Wills had assembled his largest band ever, consisting of four fiddles, three guitars, bass, piano, four saxophones, four trumpets, four trombones, drums, and two singers—in all, twenty-two musicians. This band lasted only seven months and never recorded, but it was Bob Wills's dream band. Times were changing, however, and the big band Swing Era was gradually winding down. The horn players did not care for Wills's folksy managerial style and wanted to work by musicians' union rules. For all its size, talent, and versatility, this twenty-two piece band had lost its distinctive Playboys sound. And the American people, weary of war, wanted to hear a simpler, more spontaneous music that could be played just as well by a few strings. Sadly, Wills disbanded his big group, never again to have a complete horn section. From late 1944, the Texas Playboys featured jazz fiddlers playing hot choruses, and fiddle players like Jesse Ashlock, Louis Tierney, Joe Holley, Johnny Gimble, and Keith Coleman gave the band its distinctive character. Guitarists, too, assumed greater importance in the post–World War II Playboys band, with stars like Junior Barnard, Cameron Hill, and Jimmy Wyble incorporating trumpet and trombone licks into their improvised choruses. The steel guitar gained even more prominence, and Wills often combined guitars, amplified steel, and amplified mandolin to simulate a large horn section.

Life for Wills and the Playboys in California consisted of frequent recording sessions, dance engagements, movie making, and a national tour that took up most of the winter of 1944–1945. A September 4, 1946, Columbia recording session included no horns and a rather broad repertory—fiddle tunes, blues, pop songs, guitar instrumentals. Like pop music and jazz in general, Bob Wills was coming back to his musical roots. In October 1947 Wills left Columbia to go with MGM Records, and the band's MGM recording session for October 30 through November 12 was heavy on the blues. Also in 1947 Wills purchased the Aragon Ballroom near Sacramento and converted it to Wills Point, complete with a swimming pool, amusement park, dance hall, and bungalows for the band members. Wills Point could have been a profitable venture if Wills could have avoided national tours and remained at home to manage it, but Wills Point ultimately failed.

In the summer of 1949 Wills decided that California no longer offered a favorable climate for the Playboys and began moving the band from place to place, always trying to recreate the glory days in Tulsa before the war. The Playboys headquartered in Oklahoma City (1949); Dallas (1950), where Wills built and lost the largest dance hall in the Southwest, the Bob Wills Ranch House; Houston (1952); Amarillo (1953); Abilene, Texas (1957); and finally Tulsa (1957). There were frequent returns to California, to live, record, and perform, and national tours that continued to prevent Wills and the Playboys from establishing a permanent home.

By 1959, Bob Wills and the Texas Playboys were appearing in Las Vegas and Lake Tahoe so frequently that they made Las Vegas their base of operations. Even when they moved back to Tulsa in 1961, they continued to play frequent engagements in Las Vegas. Largely for economic reasons, Wills was traveling with a small string band, but in mid-1963 he assembled a big band for a California tour and a recording session with Liberty Hill Records. The personnel included five fiddlers—Wills, Louis Tierney, Billy Armstrong, Gene Gassaway, George Clayborn; Gene Crownover on steel guitar; Billy Wright on viola; Johnny Patterson on electric guitar; Tommy Allsup alternating between guitar and bass; Casey Dickens behind the drums; Gene Graf at the piano; Luke Wills on bass; and six different singers—George Clayborn, Vicki Carr, Luke Wills, Clifford Crofford,

Buz Cason, and Billy Mize. But Bob Wills himself did most of the vocals, and the album bore the title *Bob Wills Sings and Plays*.

In October 1963 Wills, who had suffered a heart attack and grown weary of the stress of life on the road, sold the Texas Playboys to Carl Johnson of Fort Worth and went to work for Johnson for a salary. He suffered a second heart attack in 1964 and never again fronted his own band. Rather he would perform with other bands or hire pickup musicians for recording sessions or single performances. It is estimated that over 600 musicians passed through Bob Wills's band, many of them staying for only a brief time or appearing as pickup musicians for specific occasions.

In 1968 Bob Wills was inducted into the Country Music Hall of Fame, an honor he never expected to receive because he never thought of himself as a country musician. Wills's biographer, Charles Townsend, writes:

> It would appear difficult to exclude Wills entirely from the tradition of rural or country music. In terms of origin, his music was certainly not urban. In the beginning, Jim Rob [Bob] and his father played the fiddle at West Texas country or ranch dances. This fiddle tradition was always part of Bob Wills's music. Nevertheless, he added jazz and swing idioms, even drums, brass, reeds, and piano, so that essentially he was playing non rural pieces, in non rural style. Wills generally made an effort to get away from his country roots. Mainstream country music has remained relatively close to its rural and folk origins—and if this ever ceases to be the case, the term "country music" will become a meaningless commercial hybrid. Many people in Nashville and elsewhere who love country music fear it will lose its identity if it loses its country origins. This accounts, in part, for the determined effort many artists make to sound "country," that is, more natural and less affected. Bob Wills, by contrast, feared he would sound country and therefore made a determined effort to sound like popular dance bands.[13]

Western swing was not country music, though some of its roots can be traced to such rural traditions as Texas fiddle style and string band music. But those folk music traditions were melded first with Dixieland jazz and then with swing to become western swing. Milton Brown was the originator of western swing; but because of Brown's premature death, Bob Wills became the principal disseminator. Other big swing band musicians thought Wills's band sound, and Wills himself, too folksy; and some scholars could argue that his entire approach was derivative.

Townsend admits that sometimes Wills's music was

> not creative at all . . . especially when he was copying jazz and swing bands. In these cases, only his occasional folk yell distinguished his music from the music of those he was emulating. Yet even during that short period when he could perform like the traditional swing bands, between 1939 and 1942, he was also playing music that sounded like what he heard in West Texas between 1913 and 1929. He used instruments generally associated with rural and country music, and in a continual effort to produce the sounds of swing and of jazz and popular dance bands, blended them with reeds and brass and drums and piano. This was experimental, creative, and original; it was eclectic in that he was borrowing from both rural and urban musics. Much to Wills's chagrin, most of the swing bands he admired . . . would never accept his musical hodgepodge and what to them was musical heresy. They called him a hillbilly and thought he was corny. They never could understand and certainly never appreciated, how he could outdraw them and why his career lasted twenty-five years beyond the Swing Age. Of course, he was not a hillbilly, and he certainly did not play the kind of music the Grand Ole Opry and Nashville were making so popular.[14]

Bob Wills died on May 13, 1975, after lying in a stroke-induced coma for eighteen months. His last major appearance before his stroke was a tribute concert held at the Tarrant County Convention Center in Fort Worth on March 6, 1972, which brought Wills and many of the former Texas Playboys together again. Though confined to a wheelchair, Wills had lost none of the old charisma, and the packed house went just as wild for Bob Wills and the Texas Playboys as before. Over a forty-four-year career, Bob Wills released 550 record sides and created an undeniable legacy that continues to influence western swing as well as commercial country music and even rock and roll. As late as July 1948, Bill Haley, of early rockabilly fame, was billing his band as Bill Haley and the Four Aces of Western Swing.

Western swing first took root as the popular dance music of the Southwest in the 1930s and 1940s and migrated to California with the multitudes of southwesterners fleeing Depression and Dust Bowl conditions. Bob Wills was well established in California by early 1944 because he was playing to displaced homefolks. But the West Coast ultimately developed its own brand of western swing, distinct from the music coming out of Texas and Oklahoma. Besides Bob Wills, the two leading figures in West Coast swing were Spade Cooley and Tex Williams.

Donnell Clyde "Spade" Cooley was born in poverty near Pack Saddle Creek, Oklahoma, on December 17, 1910. When Donnell was only four years old, he moved with his family to Corvallis, then Salem, Oregon, where a family friend noted that the boy was making and playing folk fiddles. When Donnell turned seven, this same friend gave him a few fiddle lessons. Young Cooley attended the Chemawa Indian School because he was one-quarter Cherokee, and it was at the school, as a result of his poker playing, that he acquired the nickname "Spade." It was also at the Chemawa School that Cooley received his first serious music lessons, but as a cellist in the school orchestra rather than as a fiddle player. Cooley took to the cello and practiced faithfully. He also studied with one of the leading music teachers in the area, a German immigrant named Hans Von Sietz.

In 1930 the Cooleys moved to a farm in Modesto, California, and twenty-year-old Spade escaped the drudgery of agricultural work by playing his fiddle at every opportunity. Starting as part of a duo with a blind fiddler,[15] he went on to work as a sideman in many local bands, until finally, about 1942, with the management assistance of Bert "Foreman" Phillips, the foremost western music producer in Los Angeles, he formed his own band. America's entry into World War II transformed Los Angeles and all of Southern California into a center for the defense industry, so there were thousands of workers, from disparate parts of the country, living and working in Los Angeles and needing entertainment and relaxation. The music these people had known and loved back home was played in numerous dance halls and clubs, which provided a great deal of work for musicians. Cooley's band included himself playing fiddle, Tex Williams (vocals/bass), Gene Hass (guitar), Dick Roberts (steel guitar), Happy Perryman (rhythm guitar), and Vic Davis (piano). They opened at the Venice Pier Ballroom in late 1942.

When Phillips took Happy Perryman and a couple of Cooley's other sidemen to create a second band to play at the Riverside Rancho, near downtown Los Angeles, Cooley hired new musicians who helped him devise a distinctive Spade Cooley band image and sound—Smokey Rogers (guitar/banjo/songwriter) and Deuce Spriggens (bass/vocals/comedian). Rogers composed the song "Shame, Shame on You," which launched the

Cooley band into stardom. With Deuce Spriggens and Tex Williams, Rogers also formed the comedy trio "Oakie, Arkie, and Tex," which contributed to the popularity of the Cooley band.

In late 1943 Spade Cooley ended his business relationship with Phillips and moved his band to the Riverside Rancho. He also signed a recording contract with Art Satherley of Columbia Records and increased the size of his band with the addition of Cactus Soldi and Rex Call (fiddles), Joaquin Murphy (steel guitar), Johnny Weiss (guitar), Eddie Bennet (piano), Warren Penniman (drums), Pedro DePaul (accordion), and Spike Featherstone (harp).[16] This was an innovative band in several ways, the most obvious being instrumentation, for accordion and harp were not standard in western swing bands. Cooley was also featuring a front line of three to four fiddles, all of them played by reading musicians. Cooley was a competent arranger and had two other fine writers in Pedro DePaul and Smokey Rogers; the three of them created brilliant, complex band scores. The Cooley band rehearsed long hours to produce a sound that was remarkably polished and refined, though every member of the band was capable of playing intense improvised jazz choruses.

During the two years that Spade Cooley's band played at the Riverside Rancho, the crowds outgrew the hall. Cooley leased the largest dance hall in the area, the Santa Monica Ballroom, where former Cooley band member Deuce Spriggens was fronting his own group. Spade Cooley was a domineering leader who had to be in control, and shortly after he moved to the Santa Monica Ballroom he absorbed Spriggens's band into his own and fired Spriggens.

The situation with Spriggens was just the beginning of internal conflict in the Spade Cooley band. When Tex Williams was approached by Capitol Records to sign a solo recording contract, Cooley was offended by Williams's audacity in pursuing independent business negotiations, and Cooley and Williams parted company. Most of Cooley's musicians left with Williams to form the Western Caravan, and Cooley was left to rebuild his band. Cooley's response was to create a large horn section grouped around a small nucleus of strings. For a brief time Bob Wills had fronted such a band, but Cooley experienced greater success with this kind of musical organization, perhaps because he was a formally trained, reading musician and thus able to communicate with horn players. People who knew Bob Wills reported that he seemed uncomfortable in the midst of a large group of music-reading horn players, though he thrived on their music. Cooley did not exude the folksy personality that Wills did, and his managerial style was more businesslike.

Spade Cooley and his reorganized band continued to thrive with dance jobs, radio broadcasts, record releases, song writing, and finally their own television show. Cooley started with the *Hoffman Hayride* in mid-1947, which in a short time was billed as *The Spade Cooley Show*. On the air for six years, *The Spade Cooley Show* was one of the most successful programs on California television. A survey made at the high point of this six-year run indicated that of 1,500,000 television sets in operation in Southern California, 1,355,000 of them were tuned to *The Spade Cooley Show* every Saturday night.[17] Much of the credit for the success of the show went to the tireless efforts and unbounded energy of Cooley, as he was constantly writing, rehearsing, perfecting his band, and booking outstanding guest acts.

On the West Coast, Spade Cooley was the "King of Western Swing." Possibly to prove that he really was top of the hill, Cooley booked a national tour that was to culminate in a performance at Carnegie Hall in New York City. The band drew capacity crowds as long as they remained west of the Rockies, but once they crossed over into the Midwest and Southwest, they had to compete with well-established territory bands and with the Wills influence. East of the Mississippi River, no western swing band, no matter how good, could survive. Spade Cooley returned to Southern California where money and success were constantly at his fingertips.

Cooley suffered his first heart attack in 1949. In 1951 he saw his television program driven off the air by the *I Love Lucy* show. He invested heavily in a real estate venture to be called Water Wonderland—a golf course, hotel and motels, restaurants, a complete western town, and a huge dance hall—located in Antelope Valley, California. With his personality and business acumen, Cooley probably could have made Water Wonderland a profitable endeavor; but there was another side to Cooley's life that overshadowed all of his success. On April 3, 1961, convinced that his wife was unfaithful, Spade Cooley tortured and murdered her in the presence of their daughter. He was convicted and sent to prison. During the trial he suffered two more heart attacks, but he survived nine years in prison. Cooley was released from prison in November 1969 and immediately booked an appearance with Chill Wills. The audience was receptive as always, and Cooley's career seemed back on track. But after the show he suffered a fatal heart attack.

Spade Cooley was to West Coast swing what Milton Brown was to Texas swing; both were originators, with Brown defining Texas swing and Cooley creating the West Coast sound. West Coast swing bands included instruments such as accordion and harp, which were almost never found in Texas bands; and they incorporated more reading musicians, written arrangements, and polished performances. West Coast swing rhythms also tended to be smoother and less syncopated and energetic than those in Texas swing.

Tex Williams assumed a place in West Coast swing similar to that of Bob Wills, as duplicator, eclectic synthesizer, and primary disseminator. After Williams separated from Cooley, taking many of Cooley's musicians with him, he essentially reformed the Cooley string band, while his former boss went on to experiment with horns. Sollie Paul "Tex" Williams was born on August 23, 1917, in Ramsey, Illinois, the tenth child of Thomas and Tillie Hill Williams. The elder Williams was a blacksmith, a grist mill operator, and a good breakdown fiddler; and it was from his father and an older brother that Tex acquired his interest in music. By the age of five, Tex was playing the banjo and studying the guitar. Around 1930, he made his radio debut on station WJDL of Decatur, Illinois. In late 1934 Tex joined his first professional band, Peggy West and Her Rocky Mountaineers. But the worsening Depression made financial success difficult for the hundreds of small local bands like Peggy's. In 1938 Tex and his older brother, Mennifee, moved to Washington State to work as apple pickers, and within a few months Tex was appearing with local bands. He joined a fairly competent touring cowboy band fronted by George McCormick, but there were far too many no-name traveling bands. As one West Coast swing historian explains,

> During the thirties and forties there were numerous small groups
> touring the country, appearing on local radio without pay, in order
> to plug their local dances. If fortunate, the fellows could almost
> make enough money to survive. Some of these groups were luckier
> than others, but the successful bands such as those of Otto Gray,
> Dude Martin, Stuart Hamblen, and Bob Wills were certainly
> the exception. Tex recalls that on more than one occasion, the
> McCormick band members slept in McCormick's old Hupmobile
> and at times washed dishes for their meals. Feeling he could starve
> just as well on his own, Tex broke off after a few months, finding
> work in the Silver Dollar Tavern near the site of the booming Grand

Coulee Dam project. Tex recalls that the tavern owner, Whitey, befriended him and he spent a pleasant year there.[18]

From the Silver Dollar, Tex went on to play with his first good band, Cliff Goddard and His Reno Racketeers, which circulated primarily in Oregon and Washington. He remained with this group a little less than a year, singing and playing rhythm guitar; then he joined a well-established country band called the Colorado Hillbillies, with whom he appeared in a few B-rated western films. When the bandleader's brother decided to go out on his own, Tex left with him, which seems to have been a good choice, as the two men found jobs appearing in a Tex Ritter movie.

Early in 1942 Tex moved to Los Angeles, where he was quickly recruited to be the featured vocalist for the Spade Cooley band. When he left Cooley in mid-1946, taking many of Cooley's sidemen with him, he formed a commonwealth band (Western Caravan) in which the players shared equally in the band's profits. This could have been a strong inducement for Cooley's players to leave with Williams. Tex Williams and His Western Caravan opened on July 4, 1946, at the Redondo Barn and then began playing five nights a week at a converted roller rink called the Palace Barn. They featured three fiddles—Cactus Soldi, Rex "Curly" Call, and Gibby Gibson. They also used the comedy trio consisting of Williams, Deuce Spriggens, and Smokey Rogers that had first entertained as part of the Cooley band. Vocals were provided by Williams, Rogers, and Spriggens, and the lead guitar work came from the talented Johnny Weiss, also formerly of the Cooley band. Accordionist Pedro DePaul created arrangements for the Western Caravan, as he had for Spade Cooley; and harpist Spike Featherstone and steel guitarist Joaquin Murphy added their own special touches to the new band, as they had to the old. To this nucleus of former Cooley sidemen Williams added Ozzie Godson at the piano and vibraphone and Muddy Berry behind the drums.

The Western Caravan made its first recordings for Capitol at Capitol's Hollywood studios on July 24, 1946. These first releases were only moderately successful. The number that finally catapulted the band into stardom was their recording of a Merle Travis song, "Smoke, Smoke, Smoke That Cigarette," which sold over a million copies. With this hit, the Western Caravan reached the same pinnacle of national recognition enjoyed by Bob Wills and Spade Cooley.

Late in 1947, Tex Williams and His Western Caravan began a five-year engagement at the mecca of West Coast swing, the Riverside Rancho.

During this period they also made national tours, broadcast over the radio, and appeared on television. In 1949 Williams was approached by Universal Studios to do a series of feature films and musical shorts; though reluctant at first due to a physical handicap related to a childhood bout with polio, Williams eventually worked on some two dozen movies.

By 1951, Tex felt that the Caravan had outgrown Capitol Records and moved to RCA Victor, but Victor was even less able to market the group, so in 1953 Williams signed with Decca. The major record companies were increasingly unable to sell western swing bands because of the growing popularity of rock and roll, so in 1957 Williams disbanded the Caravan and continued as a solo act.[19]

Spade Cooley and Tex Williams developed a West Coast sound that was recognizably different from that of Texas swing; but even Texas swing was diverse and regional in its sources and sounds. Western swing musicians in the Houston-Beaumont area of southeastern Texas were heavily imbued with blues and were aware of the Cajun musical styles emanating out of southwestern Louisiana. Thus, the Texas Wanderers, with jazz fiddler Cliff Bruner and blues pianist Moon Mullican, featured earthy blues numbers interspersed with Cajun favorites like "Jolie Blon" as well as popular ballads and their own renditions of big-band swing arrangements. In San Antonio, which was a center of both Hispanic and German cultures in the state, Adolph Hofner, beginning his musical career in 1935, incorporated German polka and waltz music into his particular mix of western swing. North Texas bands—Milton Brown and His Musical Brownies, the Light Crust Doughboys, and others—were more influenced by traditional fiddle tunes and by northern popular music and commercial jazz. Growing up in West Texas and then living and working for a time in New Mexico led Bob Wills to compose his "Spanish Two Step," which was inspired by Hispanic dance music. Eventually this tune was revised into "San Antonio Rose" and was recorded by Wills's big horn band. On the West Coast, western swing acquired greater polish, refinement, and complexity in the hands of Spade Cooley, Tex Williams, and others, who depended more upon written scores played by music-reading musicians.

Regionalism was significant to the creation of western swing sounds and styles of performance. Thus, western swing, like all other forms of jazz, is not easy to define. Although there are western swing performance practices—for example, the use of two fiddles and a heavy dance beat as well as a core repertory of tunes, including "San Antonio Rose" and

"South"—there is no single correct method of making this music. Because the vast majority of western swing musicians read little musical notation, the essence of western swing is improvisation, not written arrangements. As Larry Willoughby so eloquently explains,

> There appeared on the Texas plains and prairies in the late 1920s and early 1930s a new and innovative form of American popular music—an improvisational mix of country, jazz, blues, ragtime, folk, and a style to be known twenty-five years later as rock 'n' roll. It was the dance music of the Southwest, western swing. Western swing incorporated all of the ethnic influences prevalent in Texas: the country sound of the southern string bands, the rhythms of the blues-and-jazz-oriented black culture, and a flavor of Mexican folk and mariachi music. It was a music characterized by experimentation and bound by no limits in style or direction. As an entertainment form, western swing introduced the evolving rural Texas dance band tradition to the growing cities of the Southwest.[20]

Like other big swing bands, western swing groups suffered a decline in the 1950s and 1960s because of the emergence of rock and roll and because inflated prices made traveling with large ensembles unprofitable. But swing jazz made a comeback in the 1970s, a musical era known for its emphasis on nostalgia. Western swing musicians and audiences who had been swept into the background during the twenty years of rock preeminence emerged enthusiastically to greet both returning old-timers and new proponents of their favorite jazz. The audience for western swing has grown in the past twenty-five years and includes a large number of young people. The youthful element in the audience can be explained by the fact that well-established commercial country stars have incorporated western swing music into their acts. Popular artists like George Strait, Charlie Daniels, Waylon Jennings, Willie Nelson, and Merle Haggard have retrieved old western swing arrangements and scored hits. Former Texas Playboys fiddler Johnny Gimble has emerged as a western swing icon who never fails to draw large, enthusiastic audiences. In Austin, Alvin Crow's band has kept western swing alive and well, even when it was not popular music. And possibly the best newcomer western swing band, Asleep at the Wheel, continues to compile record successes and to draw large crowds.

Asleep at the Wheel was formed as a country band by three eastern urbanites in the early 1970s. The three original members, Ray Benson,

Leroy Preston, and Reuben Gosfield, escaped the big cities of the North to search for a more traditional music in the rural hills of West Virginia. They began appearing in concerts in the Midwest, performing both traditional country music and their own songs. As they traveled and performed, they picked up additional musicians, one of the most significant being singer Chris O'Connell, whose unique renditions of slow ballads gave a distinctive flavor to the band.

A stay in San Francisco in 1972 marked a change in the band, especially when they hired jazz pianist Floyd Domino. They assumed the trappings of a swing band, and when they recorded Bob Wills's "Take Me Back to Tulsa" in 1973 and discovered that there was a large audience for western swing, their course was set. In February 1974, Asleep at the Wheel relocated to Austin, the new hub of western swing activity in the state, which has remained their home to the present. While the group has undergone numerous personnel changes, they have built an outstanding western swing band, boasting twin fiddles, lead, rhythm, and steel guitars, swing bass, drums and piano, horns, and outstanding vocals.[21] Their repertory includes both older western swing tunes and newer compositions, and all of the old-timers agree that Asleep at the Wheel is a fine, contemporary western swing band.

Asleep at the Wheel can be successful today not only because of a tendency among people living in these difficult times to be nostalgic, but also because jazz never really grows old or out of touch. Music that is always the same, yet always different, entices and enthralls audiences today as it did in the past. Thus, "Right or Wrong" played by Asleep at the Wheel will not sound exactly as it does when played by Playboys II, or any other pioneer western swing band, but it will be just as full of energy and life because it is being reinterpreted and reimprovised in the context of the constantly changing musical process that is jazz.

TWO

Western Swing Fiddlers

L abels can pose serious obstacles to open-minded discussion of many topics, including western swing music and its fiddlers. The terms "fiddle" and "fiddler" suggest a style of playing and a repertory that are not consistent with western swing; but because of the rural origins of the music, western swing players consistently have been referred to as fiddlers rather than violinists. Country fiddlers often alter and retune their violins to facilitate playing the breakdowns and fiddle tunes that constitute the majority of their repertory; and the fiddler's approach to playing the instrument varies significantly from that of the classically trained violinist. A western swing fiddler will probably not file down the bridge of the violin, or retune it, or hold it against the chest or in the crook of the arm; and rather than play standard breakdowns in repetitive patterns, the western swing fiddler will improvise on the melodies and supporting chord structures of a variety of pieces, new and old, folk and popular. The western swing fiddler is more accurately a jazz violinist in a swing band.

Because violins are poorly heard on early recordings, modern jazz audiences fail to understand the significance of violins to early jazz bands. Violins were commonly used as solo instruments in ragtime and society orchestras in the 1890s and early 1900s. In fact, most orchestral ragtime arrangements include parts for at least one and often two violins, which are given the same melodic and structural significance as clarinet and trumpet.[1] Vaudeville pit orchestras featured violins. One of the more successful vaudeville and dance band leaders in New York City in the late 1890s and early 1900s was Will Dixon, whose band, the Nashville Students, included a violin, along with banjos, mandolins, guitars, saxophones, drums, trumpets (or cornets), and acoustic string bass. A picture of the Nashville Students reprinted in Frank Tirro's *Jazz: A History* shows New Orleans jazz violinist Armond J. Piron seated on the front line among the other melody instruments.[2] In May 1912 the most influential black bandleader in New York, James Reese Europe, conducted an orchestra of some 145 players in a concert at Carnegie Hall; this extraordinary aggregation included mandolins, bandoras (large lute-shaped guitars), harp-guitars (a guitar with a harplike structure attached to its body instead of a neck), banjos, violins, saxophone, tuba, cellos, clarinets, baritones, trombones, cornets, tympani, drums, basses, and ten pianos.[3]

From 1918 to 1928 Armond J. Piron led his Novelty Orchestra, consisting of trumpet, trombone, alto saxophone, tenor saxophone, clarinet, piano, banjo, and drums and featuring himself on solo violin at Tranchina's Restaurant at Spanish Fort on Lake Pontchartrain near New Orleans. Another early New Orleans bandleader who included violin as a front-line melody instrument was cornetist Peter Bocage.[4] Clearly our understanding of the typical early jazz band instrumentation—trumpet or cornet, clarinet or saxophone or both, trombone, banjo or guitar, tuba or string bass, piano, drums—must be expanded to include the violin as featured lead instrument. In fact, in the South and Southwest, dance bands were string bands; so when early jazz accompanied dancing, strings could be expected in the ensemble. Some of the large northeastern dance bands of the mid-1920s included violin sections, most notably Paul Whiteman's orchestra, whose string section was led by Matty Malneck.[5]

One of the most sophisticated and highly visible bands in the Southwest during the late 1920s and early 1930s was the Alphonso Trent Orchestra, which was the regular house band at the Adolphus Hotel in Dallas and broadcast nightly over radio station WFAA. The orchestra's personnel, at various times, included the incomparable Leroy "Stuff" Smith on violin and vocals. A little remembered but at the time greatly respected territory jazz band out of Oklahoma, Andy Kirk and the Clouds of Joy, featured violinist Claude Williams on its Brunswick recording sessions of 1929.[6] In time the violin, except for a few outstanding soloists, disappeared from the basic jazz ensemble because it could not compete with the louder brass and woodwind instruments. In early bands, however, there existed ample precedent for the use of violin in jazz.

Southwesterners did not need jazz to appreciate the violin, for the instrument was completely entrenched in the musical traditions of the region from Spanish colonial times. The violin was also the lead instrument in the indigenous instrumental ensemble of the South and Southwest, the fiddle band (string band), used to accompany dancing. Typical fiddle bands consisted of one or two violins and banjo, or violin, banjo, and guitar. These native fiddle bands were the forerunners of western swing bands and jazz in Texas. Western swing violinist Carroll Hubbard, speaking of his own musical background, emphasized that he learned a great deal from his father and grandfather, both of whom were traditional breakdown fiddlers. Swing rhythm and improvisation were basic and natural to old-time Texas fiddlers. Hubbard remembers that his grandfather often played solo fiddle for dancing and that his playing was in full, toe-tapping swing. Hubbard also recounts how his father taught him to vary breakdowns. "I've played in a lot of different ways—lots of breakdowns. That's the way I grew up. Daddy said, 'Play it different—paint a different picture every time.'" For Texas country fiddlers, then, the test was not in being able to play a breakdown accurately from memory, but in being able to vary its tune and make its beat contagiously danceable. The jazz story in Texas has been written so as to exclude violinists like Carroll Hubbard and the fiddle tradition from which they sprang. The evidence indicates that these fiddlers, really jazz violinists, were in the thick of jazz innovations in Texas, and that their rhythmic and improvisatory approaches were inherent in traditional Texas breakdown fiddling. Texas was the birthplace of western swing because Texas was home to a thriving fiddle tradition, which was the foundation of jazz violin in the state, and of string bands that formed the nucleus of western swing bands.

The violin is to the western swing band what the trumpet or lead reed instrument is to a horn band—the lead melody instrument. Some western swing bands revolve around a single violinist whose role is to improvise on the principal melody and its underlying chords. Other bands use two or more violins—a section of violins, like a section of trumpets or reeds. In the latter context, one violinist provides the melodic lead while the others improvise countermelodies above and below the main melody, thus filling out the harmony.

Western swing violinists form a tight fraternity with many shared experiences and ideas. Most began playing when they were quite young, and the story told by Cliff Bruner of his picking out tunes on the violin when he was five is not at all unusual. Nor is it an oddity that Carroll Hubbard won a fiddlers' contest in Weatherford, Texas, at the age of nine, or that eleven-year-old Curly Lewis took first place at a fiddling contest in Stigler,

Oklahoma, at which Bob Wills was a judge. They began playing young and working young. Clyde Brewer recalls that he was playing house dances at the age of nine and that when he first began playing in bands during World War II, he was too young to be in the honky-tonks where they worked. During the intermissions he would go sit in the car until called to play the next set. Most western swing violinists had similar experiences.

Western swing violinists also shared the rural background in which musical instruction was largely unavailable. They learned by listening, watching, and doing, and improvisation was essential to their playing because they did not read musical notation. Many came from folk fiddle backgrounds, but diverged from the standard breakdown repertory. Cliff Bruner explains: "I had a cousin who could play breakdowns; that's all he could play. But I didn't like breakdowns; never was too good at it because that wasn't what I liked. I liked the pretty tunes or the popular tunes back then." As with other jazz musicians throughout the country, recordings and radio were the main sources of current musical information for western swing violinists. Bruner remembers the wind-up Victrola and the half-dozen recordings by Jimmie Rodgers with which he grew up. "These tunes would come out and I'd just improvise on them and play them. I'd set my own style; there were many different fiddle men who would set a style of playing."

The recording industry grew steadily in the 1920s, both in the number of recordings issued and the number of companies issuing them. The depression of the 1930s curtailed recording activity but also forced the surviving companies to explore a broader spectrum of American music in order to open new markets. Recordings of small and large jazz bands, popular singers crooning "Your Hit Parade" numbers, blues artists, country singers and pickers, gospel shouters, and much more found their way onto the record players of emerging Texas jazz violinists and provided a current repertory upon which to work their own improvisatory magic. Says Cliff Bruner, "We learned to just improvise, and still sticking with the melody, we'd doctor it up a little bit. I think it puts a lot of beauty onto a tune. I don't care of it's a breakdown or 'Stardust,' it still comes from the heart and you're just ad-libbing, and you're doing something different that somebody else is not doing. You're playing it from your own thinking."

During the Depression era, the radio proved to be a more pervasive and convenient source of current musical information for all jazz musicians. The music was literally in the air, making the radio the most important single factor in the development of western swing. Each western swing musician interviewed for this project stressed the importance of the radio as a source and as a vital vehicle for furthering his or her own career.

In Texas and Oklahoma, western swing bands were being heard regularly on local radio stations by the mid-1930s. Band members were not paid for appearing on the radio; rather they exchanged their talent for free advertising: they were allowed to publicize their upcoming dance engagements. Prime times for western swing broadcasts were 6:00 A.M., before farmers and ranchers started to work; 12:00 noon, while rural folk were eating lunch; and 6:00 P.M., when the rural workday was winding down.

The transmission capability of a radio station was crucial to the success of a band because it established the boundaries of the band's ability to book dance jobs. Every western swing musician tells stories of rushing to get back in time for a radio broadcast. Violinist Bobby Bruce describes one such occasion when he was working for Luke Wills and His Rhythm Busters out of Fresno, California.

> We had a daily radio show on KOTV Fresno at six-fifteen in the morning, and another one at noon, and then we'd take off and work up and down the San Joaquin Valley. And I remember that we'd just make it in, like if we were working in some town up or down the Valley like Bakersfield . . . we'd work until two in the morning. We'd get back to Fresno after packing the bus and driving in, and it would be four-thirty, quarter to five. At six-fifteen you have a radio show, so we'd sleep in the parking lot for forty-five minutes and then get on into the building, and we had this radio announcer. He had this enthusiasm, and here we are bleary-eyed, and we had slept for forty-five minutes in the parking lot, and we would go in to do this show with toothpicks to hold our eyes open. And he would say, "It's the music of Luke Wills and His Rhythm Busters." And we could hardly keep our eyes open or keep our heads up, and we'd try to play. The announcer had obligated us to play our tails off. It didn't matter what time it was.

And play with gusto they did because the daily radio programs were extremely important to their continued success as dance bands.

Recordings and radio made it possible for jazz violinists to be heard, and a few emerged as models for the rest. Like their counterparts elsewhere in the country, western swing violinists were especially interested in the styles and techniques of Joe Venuti, Stephane Grappelli, and Stuff Smith. A few western swing violinists attained local prominence equal to the national prominence of Venuti, Grappelli, and Smith and influenced several generations of western swing violinists. This group included Cliff Bruner, J. R. Chatwell, and Cecil Brower.

Philadelphia-born Joe (Giuseppe) Venuti (1898–1978) was a well-trained violinist and a gifted jazz artist. His intonation was precise, and his violin tone was round, warm, and replete with overtones. His technique was flawless, and even in his seventies he could compete with younger players. He was also an innovator, with such novel bowing techniques as removing the pin from the frog of the bow, wrapping the bow hair around the strings, and dropping the bow stick below the body of the instrument in order to sustain three- and four-note chords. Venuti was recognized for his harmonic refinements and for his highly developed rhythmic sense.[7]

Venuti worked and recorded with some of the best white jazz musicians of the 1920s and 1930s, including Bix Beiderbecke, Frank Trumbauer, Benny Goodman, and Jack Teagarden. But it was the duet recordings he made with his lifelong friend, guitarist Eddie Lang, that earned him a prominent position among jazz musicians of his generation. One of these, "Wild Cat," illustrates the salient features of Venuti's unique violin styling. He utilized the full range of the violin, from low rich tones to the high, ethereal sounds near the bridge. His phrasing was free, never boxed in or predictable, and yet his sense of timing was perfect. The melody of the popular song "Wild Cat" was completely transformed through Venuti's ingenious improvisation on its underlying chord structure. Venuti's tone was controlled, but warm and inviting; his articulation of pitches precise, but still full of feeling.

One of the European jazz violinists who was influenced by Joe Venuti, and who in his turn touched the styles of other American jazz artists, was French native Stephane Grappelli. Grappelli made his reputation as a member of the most highly acclaimed jazz ensemble in Europe in the 1930s, the Quintette du Hot Club de France, where he met and worked with famous jazz guitarist Django Reinhardt. Like Venuti, Grappelli slipped into an undeserved oblivion in the 1950s and early 1960s, but was rediscovered by the jazz community through his appearances with Joe Venuti at the Newport Jazz Festival in 1969. Grappelli's most recent recording effort occurred in 1993, when he appeared with Mark O'Connor on the *Heroes* album released by Warner Brothers.

Award-winning fiddler Mark O'Connor traveled to Paris to record with Grappelli because Grappelli was a major influence for O'Connor. They cut two numbers together, "This Can't Be Love" and "Ain't Misbehavin'." Grappelli introduced "This Can't Be Love" in his most romantic vein, with a slow, long, sweet phrase full of warm vibrato. Then the tempo doubles and the two violinists engage in rapid-fire improvisations that never clearly state the melody. Grappelli's phrases grow out of one another and build subtle layers that reveal his intelligent grasp of musical design. Finally, at the end of the performance, after a series of creative variations, the two violinists restate the original melody.

Grappelli remembers playing "Ain't Misbehavin'" in a band led by its composer, Fats Waller, at a London club in 1938. He begins this 1993 version with O'Connor by stating the melody slowly, expressively, and with little elaboration, after which Grappelli and O'Connor explore the tune and its chords in a series of improvised double-time choruses. Grappelli in 1993 had lost none of his technique or charm.

Grappelli's style differs from Venuti's, and he has probably been less of an innovator; but he is every bit as creative in his improvisations. Grappelli tends to concentrate on lovely, unadorned melodies and to produce a rather sweet, pure tone. He plays delicately rather than aggressively, but he can swing with the best.[8]

The jazz violinist who probably exerted the greatest influence on western swing fiddlers was Hezekiah Leroy Gordon "Stuff" Smith (1909–1967) from Portsmouth, Ohio. Smith played in the excellent Alphonso Trent Orchestra out of Dallas, then briefly in Jelly Roll Morton's band in Chicago before moving east to perform with his own quintet at the Onyx Club in New York City. In 1943 Smith took charge of Fats Waller's band after the pianist's death. But fame eluded him until he relocated to Copenhagen in 1965, where he remained active until his death.

Smith was a different kind of jazz violinist—less refined and more exciting. Jazz violin historian Matt Glaser observes: "Smith was an innovative musician. He played violin in a raucous style and with a sense of swing that was of unequaled intensity. Harmonically his work was extremely adventurous, and he evolved radical techniques to accommodate his wildly inventive ideas. Wide vibrato, hoarse tone, expressive intonation, and rhythmic creativity are all hallmarks of his style. Dizzy Gillespie has cited Smith as a profound influence upon his playing."[9] Smith was also the first violinist to amplify his instrument electrically, thus making its sound more equal to that of the horns.

Smith's rendition of the popular ballad "After You're Gone," made in the late 1930s or early 1940s with sextet instrumentation, reflects the influence of Louis Armstrong both in Smith's violin playing and his singing. Smith plays an introduction that rises up the scale in triplets before trumpeter Jonah Jones plays the melody. Then Smith sings a verse of the song before taking off on two wild choruses during which his fingers execute rapid runs, triplets, slurs, bends, and double and triple stops, all in a driving, electrifying, swinging rhythm. Smith was not a delicate stylist like Grappelli, nor did he coax a full-bodied, warm tone like Venuti's. His sound was biting, coarse, emotional, explosive, and he was a technical genius.[10]

Joe Venuti, Stephane Grappelli, and Stuff Smith were jazz violinists of great ability who eventually earned international reputations. In the Southwest, and especially in Texas, there were jazz violinists of equal talent who did not achieve such recognition but who greatly influenced several generations of southwestern jazz violinists. Cliff Bruner belongs at the head of the list of western swing violin pioneers.

Bruner was a rural jazz stylist who was aware of other players—for example, Joe Venuti—but created his own unique approach. "I never tried to copy anybody's style, never in my life. I created my own and I had to live with it, good or bad, but I never copied fiddle players, intentionally." Bruner plays with great emotion and rhythmic energy. His violin sound is full, somewhat like that of Joe Venuti, but his rhythmic drive and swing relate more to the playing of Stuff Smith.

A recent compact disc on the Rhino label, *Texas Music: Western Swing and Honky-Tonk*, includes Cliff Bruner and the Texas Wanderers performing "Milk Cow Blues," recorded in San Antonio in 1937 for Decca. "Milk Cow Blues" was a standard played by every western swing band, but I agree with John Morthland's comment that Bruner's version is "the funkiest."[11] Bruner plays the first verse of this slow, twelve-bar blues, beginning low in the violin range and climbing upward, building emotional impact as he goes. While Leo Raley sings two verses, Bruner harmonizes a fitting countermelody, a perfect duet with the vocalist.

Bruner's solo chorus is a new variation on the tune, complete with double stops, runs, and blues inflections. Even though this is a moderately slow blues, Bruner's violin line conveys a sense of rhythmic drive, of swing; he rarely plays anything on the steady beat provided by the rhythm section. Cliff Bruner was a powerful jazz violinist whose earthy, grassroots musical language identified him with Texas and made his style easy for younger Texas violinists to understand and emulate.

A different kind of fiddler was West Texan J. R. Chatwell, whom Cliff Bruner introduced to the western swing fiddle fraternity. Like Bruner, Chatwell played his violin to escape the drudgery of the cotton fields; and also like Bruner, he was a western swing pioneer who influenced many younger players, including Johnny Gimble, who called Chatwell "a gut-bucket violinist." Chatwell played much like Stuff Smith—explosive, exciting, raucous. In 1937 Chatwell was working with a rather nondescript string band, the Saddle Tramps, which recorded several sides in Dallas for the Vocalion label. One of these sides, "Hot As I Am," features Chatwell's frenzied violin.[12] Chatwell dominates from the beginning, playing variations on the riff tune while scaling the entire range of the instrument and incorporating several fiddle styles—breakdown, blues, and hot jazz licks—in the process. His tone is bright and brittle, and his unrelenting rhythmic drive energizes the entire band. This Texas fiddler knew how to swing! J. R. Chatwell deserves more credit than he normally receives for pioneering Texas jazz violin.

Cecil Brower was a trained violinist who participated in the transition from fiddle band music to western swing. Never a country fiddler, Brower was one of the first jazz violinists to play with a Texas string band, and the band of which he was a part—Milton Brown and His Musical Brownies—originated the jazz string style that is today identified as western swing. After Brown's death and the demise of the Musical Brownies, Brower played and recorded with other western swing groups, including Roy Newman and His Boys and Bob Wills and His Texas Playboys. Brower's solo chorus on "Taking Off," recorded by Milton Brown and His Musical Brownies on the Decca label in Chicago in 1935,[13] is the product of a jazz musician who has worked on bands with jazz horn masters. His solo line, though idiomatic for the violin, is phrased like a horn solo. Brower's playing has rhythmic drive, swing, and syncopation. His tone is light, clear, and refined. He was the classically trained violinist in full mastery of jazz improvisation.

A Few Good Violinists Talk about Western Swing

CLIFF BRUNER was born in 1915 in Texas City, Texas. His father, a longshoreman on the Houston docks, dreamed of being a farmer and, according to Cliff, would periodically leave the docks to sharecrop or lease a farm, spend all of his money, and return to his longshoreman job to earn a living. It was during one of these forays into farming that the elder Bruner moved his family to Arkansas, where he worked a tomato farm for a couple of years. Cliff was about five years old. As he recalls, he was playing in their farm house when he discovered a violin under a bed. "I got the thing out and I was sawing on it and my grandmother, who was living with us at the time, said, 'That sounds like a tune that I've heard before.' So I did the same thing over and over again. That's when I started playing. I was playing fiddle before I could talk good."

From that moment Cliff Bruner was a fiddler. When the tomato farm in Arkansas failed, the Bruners returned to Texas City and Mr. Bruner to the docks. As a young boy Cliff began to demonstrate his gift for the violin, first to family members, then to the broader public. He won an amateur talent contest in Houston and played his first professional jobs when he was just a boy. His brothers frequented house dances, and on one occasion, when the fiddler did not show at one of these, they hurried home and pulled young Cliff from bed.

> I didn't want to go. I was bashful. But I played the fiddle, but without any rhythm. Usually there was one in the crowd that could beat tempo with sticks . . . about the size of a pencil, and they'd beat on the neck of your fiddle. While you played the fiddle, they'd pound that neck with those sticks. I played "Arkansas Traveler" or "Eighth Day of January." I knew a lot of those old tunes. They took up a collection; I got five or ten dollars. It was good money for me. I'd go to a show for a nickel and the streetcar cost a nickel, and hamburgers, a nickel. I'd have a good time on a quarter and get some change back.

The only formal music training Cliff received was with a Mexican-Texan musician who could not speak English and played only Mexican music. Cliff admits that he probably learned something from this man, though he did not like his violin playing or his repertory. But Cliff was exposed to one of the distinctive threads of Texas musical culture that was woven into Texas jazz.

When Cliff was in his teens, the family moved to a farm outside the tiny country town of Tomball, Texas. At the Tomball public school Cliff met another talented musician, Jasper Heaton, and the two teamed up to play twin fiddles. All through high school Cliff escaped the drudgery of farm work by finding places to play his fiddle, sometimes with his friend Jasper. "We'd come into Houston playing the parks. We'd pass the hat and get money. We'd play for the country dances." In the summer, after school was out, the two boys would hop a freight train going north. "I was trying to get anywhere, didn't make a difference where, if I could get a chance to play my fiddle. And to make a long story short, we always ran into some fellows that felt just like I did, and we were always trying to start a band and looking for the rainbow to get us off the farm and we just nearly starved to death." Cliff worked in bands in East Texas, Amarillo, and San Antonio during the late 1920s and early 1930s. Times were hard and money scarce, but musicians could earn more than most people. Cliff remembers working sixteen-hour days in the blistering heat on the farms around Tomball for a dollar a day, then going out as a musician and earning ten or fifteen dollars in one night.

Cliff's break came when he was eighteen and was invited to join Milton Brown's Musical Brownies. Cliff was living in Houston at the time and claims that he did not know much about the Musical Brownies; but when he received a telegram from Milton Brown, the bass player in the band in which he was playing urged him to go on and join the "greatest band in Texas."

Milton Brown was the first Texas bandleader to use twin fiddles, and Cliff was paired with Cecil Brower for the next several years. Cliff notes that not only did Milton Brown have the top-rated Texas band at the time, but he also paid extremely well—one hundred dollars per week during the depression of the 1930s. Cliff recorded forty-eight sides with the Brownies on the Decca label. The future looked bright for Milton Brown and His Musical Brownies. There was talk of a New York booking for a performance at the World's Fair and of ongoing movie negotiations. But in 1936 Milton Brown fell asleep at the wheel of his car; the serious injuries that he suffered in the crash claimed his life several days later. Cliff admired Milton Brown. "He was the most wonderful bandleader that I ever worked for. If he was still living, I'd still be in his band. I'd never want one, and I'd be much happier than I would having my own band because he was that kind of guy."

After Milton's death his brother Derwood tried to keep the Brownies together, but the group disbanded. Cliff returned to Houston. He was twenty years old and once again intent on forming his own band, modeled after Milton Brown and His Musical Brownies. The result was Cliff Bruner and the Texas Wanderers, a seven-piece ensemble that included the usual strings plus saxophone. Like Milton Brown, Cliff started his band with twin fiddles, though he later preferred to work only with his own solo violin. In the beginning, Cliff's second violinist was J. R. Chatwell, whom Cliff had met and befriended while still playing with the Brownies. The first Wanderers band included a tenor banjo player, Joe Thames, though Cliff would later replace the banjo with drums. Cliff hired ex-Brownie Papa Calhoun to play piano, and the Texas Wanderers had recorded some fifteen sides for Decca by late 1936. The recording sessions took place at the St. Anthony Hotel in San Antonio, and Cliff remembers meeting the widow of Jimmie Rodgers and young Ernest Tubb at one of those sessions.

> She was promoting him. He was down on his luck at the time. And didn't know anybody. She had met him and was trying to get him started. She said, "I wonder if you would mind going with us up and introduce us to the man that's in charge?" I said, "I sure will." She had given Jimmie Rodgers' guitar to Ernest Tubb. It was a little Martin with "Jimmie Rodgers" in pearl on the neck. We went up there and they borrowed my bass man and my guitar man, nearly everybody. And we made six or eight sides. And the doggone things hit; they started playing.

Back in Houston and recording at the Rice Hotel, Cliff and the Texas Wanderers made several hit records of their own, including a version of Floyd Tillman's "It Makes No Difference Now." Cliff intuitively knew that "It Makes No Difference Now" was going to be a hit for the Texas Wanderers. He explains, "They pressed that record day and night for two full weeks and released it. And it sold millions of copies all over the world . . . in eight different languages." Because the musicians and songwriters had little legal protection in those early days of recording, the producer and recording company made most of the profits. But Cliff Bruner and the Texas Wanderers did gain wide public exposure from the release of "It Makes No Difference Now," which enabled them to book more dance engagements at better prices.

In fact, the Texas Wanderers were so popular and commercially successful that Cliff could entice players from other bands, including Bob

Wills's Texas Playboys. Offers began coming in from the West Coast. One promoter wanted to move the band out to California and feature them on a dance circuit that ran from Venice Pier in the Los Angeles area to San Francisco. There were also talks of movie contracts. But Cliff's wife was ill, and he decided to remain in South Texas and continue with his dance circuit and radio program.

The Texas Wanderers broadcast daily on station KXYZ in Houston. One of Cliff's successful business ventures involved renting the large Eagle Hall and initiating a regular barn dance, to which thousands of people flocked on Saturday nights. There were many reasons for the success of the Texas Wanderers, including Cliff's violin playing, the general togetherness of the band, and the powerful dance beat created by the rhythm section; but the Wanderers also had a star personality in the person of mandolinist Leo Raley, the first mandolin player to electrify his instrument. Raley's mandolin could not be heard at first, and the other members of the band wanted Cliff to fire him. But Cliff stuck by his sideman and found a way to make him audible.

> I said, "Bob Dunn made him a homemade pickup on his guitar and called it a steel guitar." He had a great big magnet that came out of a T-model Ford. He'd carry it everywhere he went to magnetize his strings before this pickup would pick up what he was doing. I looked all over Houston for somebody that could wind a magnet for a mandolin, and we found a guy that said he would make us one. We hooked it up to that mandolin, and Leo outsold everybody on the band. We nicknamed him Aunt Nellie, and everybody wanted to know where Aunt Nellie was. He was a comedian anyway, and he was the most popular member of my band.

Cliff moved the band from Houston to Beaumont when they were fired from station KXYZ because Cliff would not turn over control of the Wanderers to the station owner. Because of Cliff's refusal to sell his band, other Houston radio stations and dance halls closed their doors to the Wanderers. Without any job prospects in sight, the band members boarded their bus and headed for the neighbor city of Beaumont. Cliff went immediately to the powerful radio station KFDM and persuaded the station owner to give the Wanderers an audition. "We went in there about one o'clock and we stayed on the air all afternoon. I did my own announcing. I said, 'Friends, we're here and have been thinking about moving over here. Call if you'd like for us to stay.' We clogged the lines in

Beaumont." The Texas Wanderers quickly found a home in Beaumont. They played on the air thirty minutes in the morning, an hour at noon, and later in the afternoon as well. They also packed the city auditorium for a live show every Saturday night, and their dance circuit extended north to Lufkin and east to Lafayette in southwestern Louisiana.

Cliff formed several different bands during his long career, most of them called the Texas Wanderers, and he also played with other groups, including those of Governors W. Lee "Pappy" O'Daniel and Jimmie Davis. The Texas governor's race of 1938 was quite colorful, and the results hinged in large part upon O'Daniel's profile as a bandleader. The authors of *Texas, the Lone Star State* explain:

> About a month before the election it became evident that W. Lee O'Daniel of Fort Worth was reaching more people than all other candidates combined. He applied to the race for governor the same tactics he had used in selling flour by radio: popular music interspersed with comments and an occasional short, informal speech. Whether it was the promise of a businesslike administration, the castigation of professional politicians, the music, the candidate's homely philosophy, or the promise of pensions that drew the voters has not been determined; it is only known that for the first time since the Texas primary law was adopted did a candidate for governor, making his first race, poll more than half the votes.[14]

O'Daniel's band, the Hillbilly Boys, certainly helped him win both this election and his second race for governor in 1940. During his terms as governor, and even when he won election to the U.S. Senate in 1942, O'Daniel managed his band. He secured regular day jobs for the band members, set up a rehearsal schedule, and booked the band to play at various locations that would prove advantageous for O'Daniel. During the brief time that Cliff played violin in O'Daniel's band, he worked in the adjutant general's office. The band rehearsed twice a week and played an hour-long program every Sunday morning from the Governor's Mansion. Cliff never received any pay for his band work, and when he grew tired of playing for free, he quit the band. O'Daniel retaliated by having him fired from his job with the adjutant general's office.

Cliff's experience with Jimmie Davis was quite different. Davis was a recording artist by the time he ran first for railroad commissioner and then for governor of Louisiana. Like O'Daniel, Davis used his music and his own band to help him win elections. One of his opponents in the governor's race protested that it was impossible to defeat a song, in this case, Davis's recording of "You Are My Sunshine." [15] Davis was governor of Louisiana from 1944 to 1948 and again between 1960 and 1964. Cliff went to work for Davis immediately after leaving O'Daniel's Hillbilly Boys, during Davis's campaign for railroad commissioner. Thus began a long and fruitful association between the two musicians. Cliff explains, "I spent all those many years with Davis. And Jimmie used to use my band on nearly all his recordings when I had a band in Houston."

Cliff worked off and on for Davis for a number of years, often leaving to restart his own band. On one occasion he left Davis for a year to try his luck in Chicago. Cliff took a few of his musicians and hired others when they reached Chicago. They found employment in a western-style club called the Corral Club, where Cliff advised the owner on interior design and music. The club was frequented by gangsters, and Cliff recalls, "About every two weeks you'd see these guys walk in the club, and Big Syd, the manager, would go over and just lock the door so nobody could get in and nobody could get out. They'd first come and throw a hundred dollar bill at the band. So we'd play for them so much overtime; that was just extra. They'd put all their drinks, everything they had, free for everybody in the club. But nobody else could come in or go out. And they'd give us more money. We played all night sometimes."

Cliff rates the Chicago club band among the best he ever fronted, but he got homesick and decided to rejoin the Davis organization in Louisiana. His stay with Davis was cut short by another effort to form a band, this time in Port Arthur, Texas, with his friend and associate, blues pianist Moon Mullican. The Showboys, as they were called, was the kind of jazz combo Cliff favored—violin, steel guitar, two acoustic guitars, drums, upright string bass, and piano. The Showboys were enjoying both musical and commercial success in South Texas when Jimmie Davis, who was running for governor, attempted to entice Cliff and Moon to return to his band. Though Davis's monetary offer was substantial, Cliff decided that they could make more by staying with their own band in South Texas. Moon Mullican's infamous roving disposition led him to leave the Showboys, however, and sign with Davis. In Mullican's place Cliff hired Mancel Tierney, and the Showboys continued to thrive in South Texas and to record on the Decca label. But the association between Cliff and Moon was not yet over.

We were going to New York to record and the guitar man said, "Cliff, I heard that Moon's down there playing on the river in New Orleans. Let's go by there on the way to New York." I said, "No sir. He left." He had broken our contract and I felt sold out. The guitar man said, "He's playing in some joint down by the river. I wonder why?" I said, "No sir." But I was like Milton Brown; after I'd get tired, I'd go to sleep in the bus. I woke up and the bus driver had gone to New Orleans, and I could hear Moon playing. I thought I was dreaming. He was just playing that piano in that big old joint. It was about three or four o'clock in the morning. Somebody went in there and told him I was outside; he jumped up and left the piano and came out there, and threw his arms around me. "Oh, Cliff, I'm so glad to see you," he said. "Where are you going?" I said, "We're going to New York to record." He said, "Let me go with you." "Well, Moon, if you want to go, get in the bus and let's go." And he got in the bus and went. And so Moon and I went back together again.

When Cliff's wife died, leaving him with two small children, he turned the band over to Mullican and began searching for a more stable occupation, something that would allow him to stay home. He eventually went to work for the Prudential Insurance Company and retired some years later from his own agency. He has continued to perform and to record with pickup bands and with other western swing organizations. Cliff Bruner is a living legend among Texas violinists.

CARROLL HUBBARD was born in Dallas in 1919 and grew up around Weatherford and Fort Worth. He credits his father with starting him on his musical career. "My daddy ordered a U.S. School of Music correspondence course for my sister and me. That's how we started in music; our daddy helped us. We had finger exercises that were illustrated in the book. We'd go into breakfast and do our finger exercises while we were having breakfast. And Daddy helped us." When they first began to study music, Carroll was learning piano and his sister violin, and Carroll feels that the time spent on the piano improved his music-reading skill significantly. Eventually Carroll's sister tired of playing violin, and the two children switched instruments.

When the family moved to Fort Worth, about the time Carroll was ten years old, Mr. Hubbard found music teachers for his talented children. Marius Thor taught classical violin in Fort Worth, and Carroll became one of his pupils. By this time Carroll had already won a fiddling contest in Weatherford. "I was about nine years old. They had all sorts of fiddlers. I was the youngest fiddler there, and I played a breakdown Daddy taught me. Being so young, I couldn't accept cash. So they gave me a pocket watch." When he was fifteen, Carroll began supplementing the family income by playing in dance bands around Fort Worth. It was from the guitar and piano players with whom he worked that Carroll learned about improvising on the underlying chord structures of tunes.

In 1936, when he was seventeen, Carroll went with W. Lee O'Daniel's Hillbilly Boys as lead fiddler. The band was based out of Eagle Pass in South Texas, convenient to the powerful station XEPN across the border in Piedras Negras, Mexico, from which they played a daily broadcast. It was O'Daniel's habit to assign each band member a nickname, and he dubbed Carroll "Little Caesar the Fiddle Teaser." O'Daniel was fond of young Carroll and invited him to live with the O'Daniel family so that he could help sons Mike and Pat O'Daniel with their music. When O'Daniel ran for governor of Texas in 1938, the Hillbilly Boys hit the campaign trail with him. And when he won the governor's race, they moved to Austin, where they broadcast every Sunday morning from the Governor's Mansion.

When O'Daniel won a U.S. Senate seat in 1941, he transplanted his Hillbilly Boys to Washington, D.C., and found them all jobs so that he did not have to pay all of their expenses. Carroll worked in the senator's mail office, stuffing envelopes; and like the other musicians in the band, he became discouraged with the lack of actual playing they did. "I guess the allure of going to Washington to be there with the senator was something. So that's why we went. It was a good little experience for as long as it lasted . . . just a few months. I got enough of stuffing envelopes."

The United States was at war in 1942, when Carroll left O'Daniel and enlisted in the military. Like many fine musicians, Carroll served his country as an entertainer rather than a combat soldier. He was stateside for over two years before being shipped overseas. He met a fellow serviceman, an accordion player, and they teamed up to perform at officers' clubs. They also formed a dance band for larger jobs. "When we went overseas we thought we were going to have to be litter-bearers, but we got out of that. We just did traffic control and prisoner-of-war duty. Then over there we played at the officers' clubs. And when the war with Germany was over, I was invited to go to Guildhall School of Music in London for a refresher course. So they flew me to London to do that. And that was an enjoyable thing."

Carroll spent several months studying classical violin in London and was preparing to perform the difficult Second Concerto in D Minor, op. 22, by the famous Polish violinist Henry Wieniawski (1835–1880) with the Guildhall Symphony Orchestra when he was shipped home. Back home Carroll found ample opportunity to play his violin. He joined the Light Crust Doughboys band, which was still sponsored by Burrus Mills in Fort Worth. For ten years Carroll traveled and recorded with this pioneer western swing band.

> It was quite a stint. Smokey Montgomery [banjo player] ramrodded this now. Burrus Mills would send us on the road. We stayed at the best places. We'd eat the best food. We all weighed 190 pounds and over. We did a regular broadcast on WBAP radio, which was housed in the Medical Arts Building in Fort Worth. Zeke Campbell was a great guitar player! And Knocky Parker was a great piano player! Parker was really a character. He would hobo around the country. He was a professor. He got his Ph.D. He taught at the University of Florida. We did these regular radio shows, and Burrus Mills would send us out to play concerts; they used to call them play dates, not concerts. And we played dances.

Carroll worked with other western swing bands in the Fort Worth–Dallas area, including Bill Boyd's Cowboy Ramblers. And the same musicians who played in the Doughboys and recorded with the Cowboy Ramblers formed the nucleus of the Big D Jamboree band, the Country Gentlemen. The Big D Jamboree aired from Dallas every Saturday night and was a starting place for quite a list of talents, including Elvis Presley, Tex Ritter, and Ray Price. While working on the Jamboree band Carroll gained a new stage identity and a theme song. His stage persona involved a comic routine acted out as he played "Chicken Reel," and his theme was his rendition of "Listen to the Mockingbird."

When Carroll grew tired of doing the same act every Saturday night, he headed for Tulsa, where he was hoping to find a job with Bob Wills and His Texas Playboys.

> Curly Perrin and I hitchhiked to Tulsa. We were going to set the world on fire. We went up to see Bob Wills. And we got there and Bob Wills told us both, "Well, I've got my own band going. I don't

have any room for you. But I'm gonna set my brother up with a band." So he got us two long black Cadillacs and hired a bunch of musicians. And we'd go out from Tulsa and play a dance and come back in the wee hours of the morning and sleep a couple of hours and get up and play the *Oil Night Show*. And then we'd take off again out of state and go play another dance. Two black Cadillacs would be rolling down the road. We would be smoking those big black cigars and go play a dance.

The two Wills bands were closely associated and sometimes exchanged musicians. Carroll recalls that all of the players from both bands would meet at the Cimarron Ballroom in Tulsa to discuss business. Carroll enjoyed the freedom of playing for Johnnie Lee Wills. Like his brother Bob, Johnnie Lee would point to a musician on the bandstand, indicating that the designated individual should take a solo chorus playing any fitting ideas that came to mind, in true jazz fashion.

When Carroll returned to Fort Worth after his time with Johnnie Lee Wills, he found a new occupation as musical coach for Les Neuf (The Nine), a female string ensemble from the Dallas Symphony Orchestra. They played popular song arrangements and light classics for wedding receptions and private parties. Ezra Rachlin, conductor of the Fort Worth Symphony Orchestra, heard Carroll play his trademark song, "Listen to the Mockingbird," and hired him for the symphony. Because of his classical violin training, Carroll fit well into the symphony orchestra, where he played for three years. During the time that he played violin in the orchestra, he also participated in Zelman Brunoff's Dallas Symphony Society Orchestra, which played society gigs. Carroll traded in his western clothes for a tuxedo and dropped out of western swing for a time.

During Lyndon Johnson's presidency, Carroll and his violinist wife, Ora Mae, participated in the federally funded Project Muse, which sent musical groups into the public schools. Their string quartet traveled a ten-county area in Texas, appealing to children's natural interest in music. Carroll's famous "Listen to the Mockingbird" was renamed "Tweety Bird" and became a valuable key to winning over the children and preparing their minds for more serious music.

Throughout the 1960s and early 1970s the Hubbards were called frequently to play at recording sessions and dance jobs by a number of artists, including Ray Price. On one such occasion in the mid-1970s, they were playing a concert with Price at the Dallas Apparel Mart when he announced that he was going back on the road and wanted both Carroll and Ora Mae to join his regular band, the Cherokee Cowboys. The lure of the road and the quality of Price's band enticed the Hubbards into a five-year stay with Price. Ora Mae assumed the role of band manager, hiring and firing, booking concerts, procuring instruments, and arranging with local musicians' unions for pickup players. At first they traveled to jobs on chartered private jets, and when that became too expensive, on commercial airlines. After the commercial airlines lost track of their reservations and luggage on numerous occasions, Price bought a bus, and everybody was content. By the 1970s, Price had relinquished his image as a honky-tonk singer and returned to country-pop. It was, as Carroll puts it, the "Urban Cowboy era."

The Ray Price Show was a repetitive affair, the same every concert, but the Cherokee Cowboys was a swinging aggregation led by steel guitar player Buddy Emmons. They appeared with Price—in Las Vegas, Reno, on the television programs *Nashville Now* and *Austin City Limits*, in little towns and big cities in the United States and Canada—and always drew high praise.

The illness of Ora Mae's father forced the Hubbards to leave the Price band in 1980, but in 1983 Price called them again to appear with him at the Roy Clark Theater in Branson, Missouri, thus initiating another three-year association that saw the Hubbards spending a great deal of time with Price on the West Coast, where he had a tremendous following. Both Carroll and Ora Mae finally decided that the time had come to settle down and enjoy a homelife, but as Carroll puts it, "It gets in your blood. You get out there on stage and all those people applaud and love you and want your autograph and put you on a pedestal and you're there." And Ora Mae adds, "Then you get off the bus and say, where are we?" In 1985 they left the Ray Price show permanently.

The Hubbards did not leave music, however. In fact, they returned to Weatherford and opened the Weatherford Conservatory of Music, through which they provided private instrumental and vocal instruction to children and adults. With a staff of eight teachers, they taught banjo, piano, violin, voice, theory, and Kindermusik to a student body that sometimes numbered one hundred. If a student wanted to learn an instrument other than that available on the regular curriculum, the Hubbards would procure adjunct faculty from Fort Worth. The conservatory was a successful addition to the community until General Dynamics, the main employer in the area, laid off thousands of workers, bringing economic hard times to Weatherford and an end to the Weatherford Conservatory of Music. Carroll and Ora Mae continue to teach privately, to record, and to play various western swing shows and society jobs, and Carroll tunes pianos and arranges as well.

Carroll was influenced by some of the great jazz violinists. He places classically trained, jazz-oriented Cecil Brower of the Musical Brownies at the top of his list. "I didn't copy. I learned from Cecil as far as improvisation." He admires and was influenced by Johnny Gimble, with whom he has "swapped a few licks." He adds, "I really appreciate good fiddle jazz. There are not too many fiddle players who can play the true swing jazz, like the old standard tunes." One who still can, and who quickly comes to Carroll's mind as a positive force in his own playing, is Stephane Grappelli. But Carroll reserves the place of greatest honor for his own father, who would encourage his improvisational creativity by telling him to "play it through once and play it again, but don't play it the same way."

Like Cliff Bruner, Carroll insists that he was swinging and improvising before he knew what he was doing. "I had an understanding of chords. A lot of players don't have that knowledge. There are different ways to improvise. A lot of players will just play around the lead without paying any attention to chords. They hear what they want, what sounds right to them, but they don't know that it's right. I understand chords, what's coming next. And so I look ahead and know what to do."

Carroll's approach to playing the violin is similar to that of Stephane Grappelli. Rarely aggressive or raucous, he plays tastefully, with a controlled, delicate touch and little vibrato. His tone is light, at times ethereal. Slides, growls, bends, and even double stops are used sparingly—for effect. Seldom does Carroll bluntly state a melody but rather weaves a filigree of notes all around a tune and its underlying chord structure, always building his improvisations on anticipations of upcoming melodic and harmonic material. Carroll swings, but not with the hard-driving abandon of Stuff Smith. His rhythmic sense, like his tone color, is controlled and tight to the beat.

BUDDY RAY was born in Waco, Texas, in 1920. His entire family was musical, and Buddy's first playing experience was with the family dance band, in which his mother played piano, a brother played guitar, and his sister sang. Buddy was a classically trained violinist. At the age of eleven he began studying with the National Institute of Fine Arts, and he participated in the Waco public school string program during his junior high and high school years. But it was playing in dance bands that most appealed to Buddy.

Immediately after high school graduation, seventeen-year-old Buddy and his nineteen-year-old brother drove a Model A Ford to California. The year was 1937, the Depression was grinding on, and California held much allure for Texans, Okies, and Missourians trapped in Depression poverty. "There wasn't any money to be made anyway. It was just a way to keep from working. And we liked to play. That was the main thing, to play. We always knew that the streets were paved with gold in California. Everybody went to California. Boy, if you'd been to California and back, you were really something. There weren't many jobs anywhere. It was just the idea that if you were going to starve, you just want to starve in a nice place." The Ray brothers nearly did starve in Los Angeles, playing honkytonks for a dollar a night plus tips and all they could drink. But when they returned to Texas, they had the distinction of having earned their living as musicians in the magic world of California.

Buddy's first job after returning from Los Angeles was with a Shreveport band called the Modern Mountaineers, which he remembers as a "pretty good little dance band." They had a popular noon radio show and played dances in the Shreveport area. They also had a recording contract with the Okeh label of RCA Victor. Buddy recalls traveling to San Antonio in 1937 for a recording session, and he notes that neither the band musicians nor the songwriters made money; but they did earn the distinction of being recording artists, which helped promote their dance jobs.

When the Mountaineers disbanded, Buddy joined a band in Houston that was under the direction of Dickie McBride, formerly of Cliff Bruner's Texas Wanderers. Cliff had moved his band to Beaumont, and McBride remained in Houston with another aggregate of players, which he called the Village Boys. Buddy played violin with the Village Boys for several years during the 1940s and remembers them as a good, versatile band. "We had a vocal quartet. We must have had a repertory of over a thousand tunes, maybe two thousand. We had vocal trios, quartets . . . that sang all of those Sons of the Pioneers tunes, and all of the popular songs. And we played all of the Benny Goodman sextet tunes. We played a lot of Duke Ellington tunes, Louis Armstrong tunes. We also played hoedowns. Ted Daffan was writing some tunes, Floyd Tillman was writing a few, and we'd record them."

With such a wide variety of music to both sing and play, the Village Boys could fill any bill and were quite a popular band in South Texas and

Louisiana. They broadcast three times a day on a powerful 50,000-watt radio station in Houston, recorded on the Decca label, and regularly packed the Roseland Ballroom in Houston.

Despite the fact that the Village Boys was a quality western swing jazz band, the Houston musicians' union classified it as a "hillbilly" band and was reluctant to grant union membership to its players. The problem was that only union members could broadcast on the radio station for which the band worked. The situation was finally resolved, but not before Buddy's eyes were opened to the ways of the commercial musical world with regard to western swing musicians. "They didn't consider us musicians. We were hillbilly pickers and had old instruments. The band was a jazz band. That's what we liked to play and we had more requests for ballads and things that Andy Kirk and Duke Ellington wrote and the singers like Billy Eckstein and these guys were singing."

In 1943 Dickie McBride and the Village Boys moved to California. Besides Buddy, there were two other exciting musicians on the band at that time—pianist Millard Kelso, who played for Bob Wills for some time, and guitarist Jimmy Wyble, one of the best to every play the instrument.

Shortly after his arrival in Los Angeles, Buddy went to work for Bob Wills, who was reorganizing the Playboys. The year was 1944, and a number of Playboys had been drafted into military service. Wills had a radio show on station KMTR and a regular dance circuit. The six months that Buddy spent as a member of the Texas Playboys were not among his happiest; he was assigned the job of reading harmony lines. Buddy felt that he had little to play and few options in the Wills organization. After Buddy left the Playboys, Wills reduced the number of fiddles and hired Jimmy Wyble on guitar and Noel Boggs to play steel. Buddy considers this Playboys band—with Wyble and Boggs—the best Bob Wills ever had.

From the Texas Playboys, Buddy moved to Oklahoma City to join Merle Lindsey's top-rated eleven-piece western swing band. "We were using trumpet and tenor trombone, three fiddles, and steel, two rhythm guitars, and lead guitar. Big sound, and real swinging. Merle was a fiddle player like Bob Wills, played the same kind of tunes. But he just fronted the band like Bob. He was a great front man . . . the personality, and hired good musicians, and we did our own arrangements. The band really swung. He had one of the good western swing bands of the day."

Buddy returned to California after his stint with Merle Lindsey and lived the life of a freelance musician, playing at various times in different dance bands and show bands and, between jobs, leading his own pickup jazz bands at various nightclubs. He worked for about a year at the River-side Rancho in the band of T. Texas Tyler, and when Merle Travis formed a band, he hired Buddy to play fiddle. Other California bands with which Buddy played from time to time included those of Jimmy Wakefield, Roy Odell, and Tex Williams.

Buddy supplemented his rather uncertain income by sidelining on some fifty movies, pretending to play various instruments from violin to clarinet. The music was prerecorded so that all he had to do was panto-mime playing. He particularly enjoyed the time he spent on the set of *The Benny Goodman Story*, which starred Steve Allen as Benny Goodman.

> That was really a fun job because I grew up playing Benny Good-man songs. They don't tell you what the job is. The studio manager just wanted to know if I could come to work. He said, "You have to have a guitar." I said, "I'll find one." I went out there and was walking around the studio and the first guy I ran into was Teddy Wilson, the pianist. I didn't know what to do. I just went up to him and told him, "I sure like your playing!" And then Gene Krupa was on the job. Lionel Hampton was there for a while. Stan Getz sat right beside me in the band. He was practicing all the time. Buck Clayton, trumpet player with Basie so long, he and I got to be real good buddies. I took him deep-sea fishing.

After twenty-five years in Los Angeles, Buddy tired of the pressures and uncertainties. He moved up the coast to San Francisco and managed a swank billiards club for about a year. Then he returned to Texas. He was planning to settle in Dallas and find playing jobs there, but he received a call from Ray Price. For the year that he worked for Price, Buddy resided in Waco and traveled to Dallas to meet Price's tour bus. This was the last steady band job that Buddy had. He now resides in Fort Worth and plays occasionally.

Buddy Ray's violin playing is an interesting mix of jazz styles. He claims that the explosive Stuff Smith exerted the greatest influence on him. "He was my best friend for about fifteen years out in Los Angeles. He's the world's greatest! Stuff did an album with Dizzy Gillespie, and did one with Nat Cole. He did an album with Ella Fitzgerald. And of course he did a lot of his own albums. He's the one that influenced me. What Stuff was doing was pretty far out. He cut those records in 1934, and they're still far out."

Buddy has spent his professional life avoiding the screech and whine associated with country fiddling. He prefers a true, rich violin sound, and in order to preserve that sound in a band, he uses an amplifier. "You know, I ran into a lot of trouble like that with bands. A lot of them really didn't like the sound I was getting because it didn't sound like a fiddle."

Having spent many years playing in western swing bands on the West Coast, Buddy is competent to compare the stylistic differences between Texas and West Coast swing. Texas was and remains a nonunion state, meaning that Texas bands worked on a percentage plan. The band generally took sixty percent of the gate, and the management got the other forty percent. Of the sixty percent that was the band's cut, the leader usually took double, and the remainder was split equally among the sidemen. In this system, where a band was not really paying a player's salary, it was more difficult to fire someone. Buddy explains, "You didn't get fired in Houston. When you got on a band, you were there the rest of your life if you wanted to stay. You were just one of the band, and whatever happened just couldn't be helped. You weren't making that much money." Without union control, Texas jazz musicians could earn well above union scale, but they could as easily fall far below it.

Even in the early 1940s, when Buddy moved to California, the state was unionized, which assured higher salaries and, subsequently, higher living expenses. Union musicians were hired and paid salaries on dance bands, show-tour bands, and television and movie studio bands. With the salary came greater power for managers and greater pressure for players. There was no tolerance for a poorly played job.

Unionization brought an entirely different slant to musical life in California and may partially explain the arrangements and the cleaner, more rehearsed sounds typical of the Spade Cooley and Tex Williams bands. Texas jazz bands, especially those from South Texas, were more freewheeling, less rehearsed, and more likely to play from head arrangements. Buddy Ray could work in either atmosphere because he was a superb jazz violinist. He liked the stability and higher pay scale of the union situation but preferred the freedom and spontaneity of the Texas jazz scene.

JIMMY THOMASON (b. ca. 1919) was a contemporary with Buddy Ray at Waco High School. Jimmy began doodling on guitar and mandolin about 1931, while he was in junior high school. But when he entered Waco

High in 1933, he noticed that Waco was a hub of fiddle band activity, and switched from mandolin to fiddle. Jimmy had his first lessons from his friend Buddy Ray, about whom he said: "He played legit. He could read everything. I taught him fiddle music, and he taught me how to read and to hold the fiddle." Jimmy also took a few lessons from a local violin teacher but otherwise learned by watching, listening, and doing. Before long he was playing in local dance bands in the Waco area. Jimmy was influenced early by fiddle player Cotton Thompson and mandolinist Leo Raley, who worked for Doc Tate's Medicine Show in Waco before going on to greater fame in excellent Texas jazz bands. While he was still in high school, Jimmy spent time in Houston working with Cliff Bruner, from whom he learned "the finer parts of fiddle playing. I was kind of a band boy. I was band boy, doorkeeper, doorman, roadie, whatever you want to call them. He's kind of like my father. He's quite a player."

Jimmy's first professional break occurred quite accidentally, because he was a member of the musicians' union at a particularly critical moment. In the late 1930s the union persuaded the various record companies to use only union musicians at sessions. Texas was not a strong union state, but the ban on nonunion musicians still affected sessions in Texas. Because he was a union member, young Jimmy Thomason was hired by Decca for a three-day recording session. One of the groups with whom he recorded was the Shelton Brothers out of Shreveport. Jimmy described the Sheltons as a show band rather than a dance band. Their personnel for this recording session included Bob and Joe Shelton, Bruce "Rosco" Pierce, and, on twin fiddles, Jimmy Thomason and a diminutive Louisiana fiddler whose small stature belied the power of his violin playing, Preacher Harkness.

Recording artist Jimmie Davis was at that three-day session in Dallas and approached Jimmy afterward. "'What are you doing in Waco?' he asked. Jimmy said, 'I'm trying to go to school. I want to go to Baylor, but I don't have the money.' And he said, 'Well, I got a job for you. Do you want to go with me?' And Jimmy said, 'I'd love to.'" Davis took young Jimmy Thomason back to Shreveport and found him a job making sixty dollars a month working in the state fingerprinting division. Thus began a long association between Jimmy Thomason the violinist and Jimmie Davis, the singer and politician. While living in Shreveport, Jimmy also played with other bands, including the Shelton Brothers. Jimmy was with Davis as he worked his way up through various lesser elected positions and eventually into the governor's mansion.

Louisiana law prohibited a governor from succeeding himself, so when Davis's first term ended in 1948, he moved to Palm Springs, where he owned a supper club. Many of the Davis band members, including Jimmy, moved to California with him. The Davis band did not work much together as a band in California, so Jimmy was on the lookout for a job when he happened into a bar in Bakersfield, mainly to hear the band play. He sat in with the band and afterward was approached by several men who operated a radio station in Bakersfield. They invited Jimmy to organize a band to broadcast every Saturday night from the Beardsley Ballroom. The band Jimmy built was a western swing band, a "throwback to Milton Brown, Bob Wills." Besides the Saturday night broadcast, Jimmy and his band were featured on the radio each morning from six to seven, in the afternoon from twelve to one, and every night from six to seven and nine to midnight.

They moved from radio to television, performing on the first television show in Bakersfield in 1953. Jimmy later regretted rejecting an offer to go with a syndicated network that would have taken him to San Francisco and Hawaii, but at the time he did not want to be away from his family. Instead, he accepted an invitation to return to Waco and help create *The Home Folks Show* on station KWTX, featuring Jimmy and his wife, Louise, another Texas fiddler, Johnny Gimble, and steel guitarist Cotton Ward. The Thomasons had grown to love California, however, and soon returned to Bakersfield, where Jimmy became immersed in radio and television work again. Jimmy became involved in station management, specializing in salvaging foundering radio stations by reformatting their programming, and in 1964 he took on the responsibility for a television show that ran for nearly ten years. Health problems forced Jimmy out of the tense life of radio and television, and he began teaching a course on the history of country music at Cal State Bakersfield. He presented guest lectures at UCLA, LSU, and other university campuses. Jimmy also worked for the city of Bakersfield in its alcohol and drug counseling program. Jimmy Thomason died on June 1, 1994, after a five-year fight with cancer.

Jimmy reached his musical maturity in the middle of the shift from fiddle to western swing jazz bands. As Jimmy remembered, the fiddle bands that he heard around Waco had good rhythm sections that could sustain a good dance beat, but their country fiddlers could play only breakdowns. People loved the sound of the fiddle, but their musical tastes demanded hot jazz numbers.

As a fiddle player, I didn't want to learn to play "Wagoner" or any of those hoedowns—"Boil the Cabbage." What I wanted to learn was—I was listening to Django Reinhardt and Stephane Grappelli, and I was listening to Joe Venuti and Eddie Lang and Stuff Smith. That was who I was copying my stuff off of. I know that when I went to work with Cliff Bruner as a band boy, I'd find Bruner with Benny Goodman records and Artie Shaw. And I remember Moon Mullican developing a piano style and trying to copy after Teddy Wilson, with the right hand of Teddy Wilson. This is what I remember in these bands, and they gave me my first lesson in western swing, with Milton Brown and with Bruner. And they studied the stuff. On Bruner's band there was a vocalist that copied pop artists. His name was Dickie McBride, and he was a wonderful vocalist. They would listen to Louis Armstrong, and Bruner would go to copying a diminished lick that Armstrong would hit in his vocals, and Bruner would practice that on his fiddle. And this is where I began to learn this stuff and then I could go back and listen to Joe Venuti and Stuff Smith and it made more sense to me.

By listening Jimmy also developed his ear for jazz horns. He credited Jimmie Davis as the first fiddle bandleader to use a trumpet on a recording; the trumpet player was Sleepy Brown out of Shreveport. Bob Wills at one time employed a complete horn band along with his strings, and in his Bakersfield bands Jimmy always had either trumpet or tenor saxophone, and sometimes both.

As something of a western swing historian, Jimmy recounted the sequence of events that gave rise to western swing. But Jimmy's sense of history derived from his recollections because he was there. He remembered that Bob Wills was in Waco about 1933 with a fiddle band that could not draw a crowd, while Milton Brown was already formulating his distinctive western swing music and becoming the most popular bandleader in the Fort Worth area. And he insisted that Brown recorded some six months before Wills. Most important, he recognized at the time that Milton Brown and His Musical Brownies were jazz artists, not country musicians. Jimmy also insisted that Milton Brown invented the beat pattern that made western swing so danceable. "They called it that Fort Worth Beat. They even wrote tunes about it. It's just strictly a two-beat with a push. Most of your beat is 2/4 and you've got a bass playing 4/4." This superimposition of 2/4 against 4/4 contributed to the driving swing that characterized Texas swing, and that differentiated Texas swing from the West Coast variety that Jimmy heard during his many years in California. Jimmy pinpointed the essence of West Coast swing when he said, "It's mechanical. One of the finest showmen I have ever seen front a band was Spade Cooley. But to listen to Cooley, even with his three and four fiddles, all doing parts and this, that, and the other, it was all written out. So, if we're asking that a group come and join us in a jam session, what are they going to play? Nothing from the heart."

Jimmy Thomason was a humble man who focused on the contributions of others while glossing over his own. He played jazz violin with some outstanding performers, including Jimmy Wakely, Tex Ritter, Cowboy Copas, Moon Mullican, Cliff Bruner, and Jimmie Davis. As a promoter and radio and television personality, he kept swing at the forefront of his listeners' minds. And as a historian, he kept the record straight and all of the pioneers in the spotlight.

JOHNNY GIMBLE is, in the minds of many people, the quintessential western swing violinist—in fact, the only western swing violinist they know. Voted five times "Instrumentalist of the Year" by the Country Music Association, named eight times "Fiddler of the Year" by the Academy of Country Music, and nominated for three Grammy awards, Johnny Gimble is the most frequently heard swing violinist in the United States.[16]

Johnny was born in 1926 on a farm about six miles from the East Texas town of Tyler. His was a large family—six boys and three girls—of whom several became musicians. Johnny's father began bringing home instruments and encouraging the older boys to play; there was a guitar for brother Jack and a fiddle for brother Bill. Bill was the first to teach younger brother Johnny to fiddle. "None of us read music. We just learned what we could from around the neighborhood and around Tyler. When I was about twelve years old, we got our first radio and our first record player. We listened to string music because that's what we played. We just tried to play what we heard. We learned a lot of songs wrong but we played them the easiest way."

Johnny remembers that Huggins Williams, who in the 1920s and early 1930s had recorded with the East Texas Serenaders, patiently helped the Gimble boys learn a few fiddle tunes. There was also the high school band in which Johnny played alto saxophone and his brother Gene played clarinet. But as Johnny recalls, "I lost my book, and I just played by ear what the guy next to me was playing."

Like the majority of western swing fiddlers, Johnny learned by watching and listening, and the radio was a major factor in his music education. The Gimbles tuned in to the Light Crust Doughboys radio show, which aired daily from Fort Worth. "They were playing on strings, but they played everything from 'Ida Red' to 'Stardust,' so we tried to do that, too. We'd hear the hit parade tunes . . . and we'd try to learn them if there weren't too many chords in them." They heard other bands on records and radio, but Johnny remembers that the most influential recording he ever heard was Cliff Bruner's "Draggin' the Bow" and "When You're Smilin'." Bruner and other members of the Texas Wanderers band exerted a powerful influence on Johnny. "Bob Dunn played jazz on the steel. Moon Mullican was playing blues and jazz on piano. Bruner never did have two fiddles in his band. He'd play solo, and when he would play the melody he never did play it exact; he'd play it with a lot of syncopation, a lot of swing. He could swing a melody."

Those recordings by Cliff Bruner and the Texas Wanderers introduced Johnny to the freedom of jazz improvisation. "The dance bands, the string bands would play one chorus through of the melody and maybe have a vocal. But the solos were all jazz. You were free to play whatever you felt like. And that's what I still like to do."

In 1943 seventeen-year-old Johnny Gimble graduated from high school. He knew that the draft was inevitable as soon as he reached the age of eighteen; but in the interim he wanted to play his fiddle. Because of the war and the resulting paucity of experienced musicians, Johnny was hired by the Shelton Brothers. "I got to play with guys who had the experience and I learned a lot from them." The Shelton Brothers had a daily broadcast on radio station KWKH in Shreveport, played shows and dances, and entertained at schools, clubs, and honky-tonks. When Jimmie Davis ran for governor of Louisiana, a few of the Shelton Brothers band, including Johnny Gimble, joined Davis's campaign band. Johnny played tenor banjo on the Davis band.

When Johnny turned eighteen, he was drafted and his musical career temporarily placed on hold. Though military service did not offer Johnny a job playing his violin, it did expand his musical horizons, for it was during this time that he began listening to the big swing bands—Benny Goodman, Glenn Miller, Tommy Dorsey, Harry James—that were broadcast regularly on Armed Forces radio. While stationed in Vienna, Johnny grew to appreciate the waltzes, especially those of Johann Strauss, that were played everywhere in the city. Johnny still possesses a special touch for playing waltzes that he undoubtedly acquired in Vienna, the waltz capital of the world.

After his discharge from the army, Johnny returned to Texas with the intention of getting work in a dance band. His opportunity came in 1949 when he was invited to join the Roberts Brothers Rhythmaires out of Corpus Christi, Texas. The Rhythmaires broadcast a daily show on a 50,000-watt radio station, which gave them a large area of coverage. They could easily travel the 150 miles across the King Ranch to play dances at locations in the Rio Grande Valley, and they could work as far north as Austin.

Not long after he joined the Rhythmaires, fate placed Johnny Gimble in the right place at the right time, and he got the chance of a lifetime. The Rhythmaires opened for the Texas Playboys in Corpus Christi, and Tiny Moore, who was managing the Playboys band, heard Johnny play. Moore was impressed and invited Johnny to audition for Bob Wills. Two weeks later Johnny auditioned and was immediately hired.

This was a difficult time for Bob Wills and the Texas Playboys, as they were on the road constantly, playing one-nighters from Texas to California, up and down the West Coast, then back to Arkansas, Kansas, and finally Tulsa for an extended stay with the Johnnie Lee Wills band on station KVOO and on their dance circuit. When touring became too strenuous for Wills, he sold all of his property in California in order to build the Bob Wills Ranch House, a huge dance hall, in Dallas. But financial mismanagement on the part of Wills's business associates forced Wills to sell the Ranch House and take to the road again. Johnny had had enough of touring, and after two years with Bob Wills and the Texas Playboys, he left the band.

Johnny and his family settled in Dallas, where he attended barber college in order to "support my music habit." One of the playing jobs that occupied Johnny in Dallas was the Big D Jamboree. He also played in a band organized by Dewey Grooms, owner of the Longhorn Ballroom, formerly the Bob Wills Ranch House. While he was playing at the Longhorn Ballroom in the early 1950s, he met Don Law, a producer for Columbia Records, who gave Johnny some studio work. Among those stars Johnny backed in live performance and in the studios in Dallas were Lefty Frizzell, Marty Robbins, and Ray Price.

Johnny was also introduced to television during his stay in Dallas. Jim Boyd, younger brother of cowboy movie star and western swing musician Bill Boyd, was hosting a weekly television show with the Cowboy Ramblers, a band which Bill and Jim had formed in the early 1930s. As a boy, Johnny had learned to play "Under the Double Eagle" and "Over the Waves" by listening to Cowboy Ramblers recordings. Now some twenty years later he was playing violin on a weekly television program with this pioneer western swing band.

In 1955 Johnny moved to Waco to appear with his former band partner from the Jimmie Davis band, violinist Jimmy Thomason, on *The Home Folks Show*, broadcast on the television station KWTX. Johnny remembers this as a "country music show that featured anybody who wanted to be on TV." When Jimmy Thomason moved back to California, the station manager put Johnny in charge of the show, which he hosted for three years. Television could be used exactly like radio as a means of advertising upcoming dances. Life for the Gimbles in Waco was steady and secure, but the lure of Nashville, which was fast becoming the music capital of the nation, proved too strong.

Nashville in the late 1960s was not particularly kind to fiddlers. Rock and roll had changed the complexion of commercial music, and even country music producers demanded a more rocklike sound. The fiddle, regardless of how it was played, was associated with an older style of hillbilly music. The Gimbles lived on savings while Johnny kept himself available for session work. Eventually he began to get calls for studio work, earning a good living as an "A" string musician in Nashville, where he lived and worked from 1968 to 1978.

Though Johnny Gimble was a Texas jazz violinist, he succeeded in Nashville by playing country fiddle, backing such popular artists as Willie Nelson, Merle Haggard, Charley Pride, Chet Atkins, Porter Wagoner, Dolly Parton, Conway Twitty, Loretta Lynn, Johnny Rodriguez, Connie Smith, George Strait, Tammy Wynette, Mel Tillis, even Joan Baez and Paul McCartney. Johnny has also recorded several albums of his own, on which he presents a rich musical fare including sweet waltzes, big band tunes, hot jazz numbers, powerful blues, and aggressive ragtime. He has appeared frequently on television, as the staff fiddler on *Good Ole Nashville Music*, as a member of *Hee Haw*'s Million Dollar Band, on the show *Nashville Now*, and more performances on *Austin City Limits* than any other artist. He also has movie credits, having worked in *Nashville*, *Songwriter*, *Honeysuckle Rose*, and as Bob Wills in Clint Eastwood's *Honkytonk Man*.[17]

Several of Johnny's own albums have been nominated for Grammy awards. His *Fiddlin' Around*, recorded with Chet Atkins in 1974, lost the Grammy to *Dueling Banjos*; and then his *Texas Fiddle Collection* from

1975 was beat out by an album put out by Chet Atkins. Johnny's latest Grammy nomination—for his 1988 MCA release, *Still Fiddlin' Around*—presents the greatest irony of all, as Johnny explains: "It was nominated, and it got beat out by Asleep at the Wheel, and I played on their album that won."

Johnny is a western swing violinist in the tradition of Cliff Bruner and J. R. Chatwell. His *Still Fiddlin' Around* is a quintessential collection of western swing. Johnny plays fiddle and mandolin and sings. His trademark song, "Fiddlin' Around," is full of slides and slurs and double stops. He can make the violin laugh, talk, sing, and even scream, but never screech, for he is fully in control. "Nellie Gray," which sounds like it wants to become "Faded Love" at any moment, is a full-bodied, Cliff Bruner–like violin sound with great emotional depth. The swing is always there, both in the rhythm section and Johnny's violin playing; and the melody line is a skeleton on which Johnny and the other players—Maurice Anderson (steel guitar), Curle Hollingsworth (piano)—weave their own intricate designs. "Mandolopin" is a special treat revealing Johnny as a technical giant on the mandolin, and when he puts down the mandolin and picks up his fiddle, the ideas flow uninterrupted. "Blue Again" follows the traditional pattern of stated melody followed by a series of improvised variations and concluding with a restatement of the original tune. "Pretty Palomino" sounds like a swinging, jazzy, funky, old-new breakdown and shows Johnny for the fusion artist that he is.[18]

Mark O'Connor recognized this fascinating mixture of styles in Johnny's playing when he invited him to be on his 1993 Warner album, *Heroes*; they played a duet version of Johnny's own "Fiddlin' Around." O'Connor writes in his liner notes: "Johnny plays with such a commanding knowledge of the style that there has never been an equal to him. It is fascinating how his fiddling joins country and jazz right square in the middle. The fusing of these two styles is yet another American musical treasure we can be proud of. One could draw a comparison between Gimble's fiddle and a Dixieland clarinet: wonderful note choices; big fat tone; and Dixieland phrasing. Yes, it sure does swing!"[19]

BOBBY BRUCE is the only one of the violinists interviewed for this project who does not come from Texas or Oklahoma. He was born in Chicago in the early 1920s and grew up in a musical and theatrical family. A precocious child, Bobby began studying violin at an early age and also made his theatrical debut as a child. With his piano-playing sister and his beautiful mother, Bobby performed in an act called "The Personality Kids" on the Keith Orpheum Vaudeville Circuit around Chicago. "We did tap dancing, acrobatics, singing, and then I had my fiddle, and I'd be playing some of the current tunes and sing them. When you hear a million songs by the people who come before you on Vaudeville and the people who come on after you, you hear a million songs and a million styles, and you love it all." Bobby made such amazing progress in his violin playing that he earned a scholarship to the Chicago Musical College, where he studied with some of the best teachers in the area. His vast musical repertory included the classics as well as popular and show tunes; but his real love was jazz, and his musical hero was Stuff Smith, whom he later came to know as a friend. Bobby was only sixteen when he lied about his age, joined the musicians' union, organized a jazz band, and began playing in clubs around Chicago.

World War II caught Bobby at draft age, and he joined the Marine Corps. His three-year hitch in the Marines took him to Guam, Saipan, Iwo Jima, and most of the Pacific Island battles, and he always went ashore with a violin strapped to his back. In quieter moments Bobby entertained his fellow Marines from his foxhole. Word of Bobby Bruce the fighting violinist filtered back to the Pacific high command, and when the military decided to stage a show for the soldiers on Guam, Bobby was placed in charge of writing the musical arrangements and directing the orchestra.

Bobby's first band job after the war was with Luke Wills and His Rhythm Busters out of Fresno, California. Like most bands of the time, the Rhythm Busters had a daily radio show and played a regular dance circuit throughout the San Joaquin Valley. After a year with Luke Wills, Bobby got a call from Leon McAuliffe, who, having left the Texas Playboys, had his own outstanding jazz band operating out of Tulsa. Bobby describes McAuliffe's group as a "modern" band. "He had an appreciation for better chords and good taste. I just loved his idea of what good music is. Leon would get a whole fistful of notes to play, like a section of saxophones with a steel guitar. He'd bar those chords. We had a saxophone and a trumpet and a couple of fiddles, and we'd each get some good notes to play and do it right with Leon, and it sounded like a big band. When you've got a real driving beat going, the people adored it."

Bobby was the principal arranger during the five years he was on the

McAuliffe band, and he remembers how naturally talented these non-reading western swing musicians were.

> A lot of people in Leon's band couldn't read a note. I'd make these intricate little four- and five-part harmony things, and then each one had a certain line. Any one line might sound like chop suey until you put them all together and then they sounded pretty good. So what I had to do was take each person aside after I'd written it and they would memorize their line, and having great ears, these musicians, although they couldn't read a note, once they heard it, they never forgot it.

Leon McAuliffe's band was highly visible and well recognized in a five-state area, and even appeared on a pioneer Tulsa television program, *The Helen Alvirez Show*. Bobby's years with McAuliffe were professionally good years, but he and his wife grew homesick for California. Word of their impending return preceded them, and Bob Wills had a job waiting for Bobby when he arrived. Bobby was a member of the Texas Playboys for about six months and also played with Jimmy Wakely on his weekly CBS radio show and on personal appearances. He appeared occasionally with the Spade Cooley and Tex Williams bands.

After six months of band work in California, Bobby decided that his reputation as a violinist was sufficiently established that he could go freelance and have plenty of work. The jobs have never stopped coming for Bobby Bruce, and his list of studio, television, and movie musical credits is amazing. Almost immediately after leaving Wills, Bobby went to work for television station KTLA as the concertmaster of the orchestra on *The Oran Tucker Show*. Tucker was a big band leader who had a one-hour show with Roberta Lynn; for this job Bobby called upon his classical musical training. For his next television job, *Country America*, Bobby exchanged his tuxedo for jeans and a country fiddle style. The show attracted all of the top country performers, and Bobby handled all of the musical arranging for the show's guests.

Over the years Bobby drew on his encyclopedic knowledge of violin styles for the various television shows on which he worked, including *The Ray Anthony Show*, *The Barbara Mandrell Show*, the western series *Paradise*, starring Lee Horsely, *Roseanne*, *Green Acres*, *Bewitched*, *Little House on the Prairie*, and *Highway to Heaven*. Bobby's reputation for versatility also won him movie jobs. Henry Mancini called Bobby to perform the "wild fiddle" playing on the movie *Oklahoma Crude*. "Whenever Henry [Mancini] would have a concert, he had me playing in the violin section; but then he'd bring me out, and underneath my tuxedo coat I wore a leather vest, and I'd take off my bow tie, and my tux coat, and then I'd just have shirt sleeves and a leather vest, and I'd do this "Oklahoma Crude Theme," get everybody stamping their feet and clapping. They loved it."

Bobby worked with Quincy Jones on the score for *Roots*. He did all of the fiddling for Lou Gossett, who played a character called the Fiddler. In fact, Bobby wrote and played the tune that the Fiddler played as he lay dying. For their work on *Roots*, both Quincy Jones and Bobby Bruce won Oscars. Bobby did all of the fiddle work on the movie *Jeremiah Johnson*, with music written and directed by John Rubinstein, son of the famous pianist Arthur Rubinstein. Bobby recalls, "It was a different kind of a film. It was really primitive, rough. They didn't want anything sophisticated because Jeremiah Johnson was a mountain man." Bobby called upon much of his arsenal of different violin styles for the movie *Funny Girl*. "We had to do some small group playing, and one of the eras was in 1914 for the first world war. Another one was in the 1920s like flapper times, and another was in the forties for the second world war, the swing era of jazz. So we had three of these things. It was three different flavors in the music. When they say 1914, 1922, 1940, 1960, 1980, as a kid I was working the Keith Orpheum Circuit doing Vaudeville, so I picked up a lot of different styles."

Bobby's ability to play well in different styles has kept him busy in Los Angeles for over forty years, recording movie and cartoon tracks and working on television. He can put on his tuxedo and play classical and society music; he can change to jeans and be a country fiddler; he can fiddle the roles of black slaves or wild mountain men; and he can concoct sound effects for cartoons. But Bobby's first love was jazz, and so it remains. Playing in swing bands is for Bobby an ideal situation for creativity and for working with some extraordinary jazz musicians, like pianist Paul Smith, guitarists Barney Kessel and Jimmy Wyble, and steel guitarists Noel Boggs, Joaquin Murphy, and Herb Remington. Bobby is aware that many jazz critics and historians overlook western swing. "You just put a ten-gallon hat on it, but it is jazz. When we're out there with the Cowboy Symposium [Ruidoso, New Mexico] every now and then, Tommy Allsup will start playing some of the better chords and everybody, their radar will go up and they'll catch on to it, and pretty soon they're kicking the hell out of it—playing jazz!"

CURLY LEWIS was born on a farm near Stigler, Oklahoma, in 1925, the fifth of nine children. The Lewis family was musical, and their father procured instruments for all his precocious children. Curly learned to play several instruments—fiddle, guitar, mandolin, bass, tenor banjo—but the fiddle quickly became his favorite. Curly received his first fiddle when he was nine, and by age eleven was competing in fiddle contests. He has special feelings about winning the Bob Wills fiddling contest in Tulsa in 1936, where he met Bob Wills for the first time and beat sixty-seven older fiddlers from seven states to win the first prize—one hundred dollars. A quiet, unassuming man, Curly credits his win to his size and youth rather than talent.

As a boy Curly began performing professionally in a family trio supervised by his father. They played in Tulsa beer joints for tips, thus earning a little money to supplement the family income during the bleak years of the Depression. There was no extra money for music lessons, and Curly recalls: "My dad wanted me to play fiddle. One day he came home with a fiddle, and he had an old friend that played fiddle. He used to come over and stay all night with us and he would play the fiddle and I just picked it up. I just started playing. Nobody taught me; I didn't have any lessons." Although there were no formal music lessons, there were heroes to emulate. "My favorite jazz outfit was the Hot Club of France—Django Reinhardt, Stephane Grappelli; he was my favorite fiddle player, and actually still is."

After high school, Curly got a job playing fiddle for bandleader Billie Walker, who worked the Tulsa area. After six months with her, he was hired to play guitar with the Johnnie Lee Wills band. The year was 1945, and Curly had just turned twenty.

> I went to work for Johnnie Lee playing guitar. I played guitar for about a year before I started playing fiddle. His guitar player came back from the army, so there went my job playing guitar. Then he put me to work as a vocalist. Then his vocalist, Leon Huff, came back. So to keep my job, I had to start playing fiddle. I knew how to play, but I didn't play anything except breakdowns. Henry Boatman helped me out. He said, "You've got to stop playing

that breakdown stuff. Play that part you've been singing, and that's all you have to do."

Curly was with Johnnie Lee Wills altogether nearly ten years. For at least part of this ten years, Johnnie Lee fronted a large twelve-piece ensemble that included trumpet, three saxophones, and the strings. The horn parts were written out, but the string players improvised freely.

Musicians moved with some frequency between the Johnnie Lee and Bob Wills bands. "This was a kind of stepping stone. Every time a real good musician came to work for Johnnie Lee, Bob needed one and he gave him a call. Johnnie Lee would always give them the option of staying or going, and nine times out of ten, they'd go."

Curly got his chance to go with Bob Wills when he left Johnnie Lee's band to travel out to California. "Bob was playing the Townhall party out in Long Beach, and I just happened to go down there, and I was out in the audience and Jack Loyd, the singer, came out in the audience and I got to talking to him and he went back and told Bob I was out there. Bob got out of their bus and asked me to go with him. He had a fiddle player at the time who was leaving, Billy Wright was his name. And that's really how I started playing in his band."

Bob Wills had an excellent band at this time in the late 1940s; it included jazz guitarists Billy Bowman, Jimmy Wyble, and Earl Finley, the keyboard wizard Skeeter Elkins, Monte Mountjoy on drums, and two popular vocalists, Jack Loyd and Darla Darrett. Curly played twin fiddles with Bob Wills for six months, then Wills disbanded for a time, and Curly returned to Johnnie Lee's band in Tulsa.

In 1955, Curly joined Hank Thompson's Brazos Valley Boys, which was a new experience, even for a seasoned veteran. "I didn't know you could travel as much as we did." The Hank Thompson show toured the entire country in the late 1950s. Rock and roll had eclipsed country music and western swing, but Hank Thompson's honky-tonk-flavored music could still elicit responses from misplaced, middle-aged people who felt alienated by changes in American society and music. Though Thompson was primarily a country singer, his band was a rip-roaring, hard-improvising, western swing, Texas jazz band.

In 1957, after over two years of incessant touring, Curly left the Thompson organization and returned to Tulsa to work for Leon McAuliffe's Cimarron Boys. Curly considered McAuliffe's band to be one of the top western swing bands in the business. This was probably due to the fact that McAuliffe was a perfectionist and spent a great deal of time rehearsing his band; but he never doused the creative fire of his musicians when it came to solo improvisation. At the time Curly went to work for McAuliffe, there were three fiddlers on the band—Curly, Gene Gassaway, and Keith Coleman, all three previous Texas Playboys. Gene Gassaway left and Jack Loyd came on board playing clarinet and singing. Curly explains that he and Loyd would take turns playing melody and harmony on certain tunes. McAuliffe's band played dances and concerts and often appeared at the Golden Nugget in Las Vegas.

After four years with Leon McAuliffe, Curly returned to the Hank Thompson band, which toured frequently in Europe, the Far East, and Africa between 1963 and 1970. Thompson continued to draw large audiences, especially at the U.S. military installations around the world where he liked to book jobs.

With the exception of his brief stay with Bob Wills and the Texas Playboys, Curly had a habit of remaining on the same band for a long time—ten years each with Johnnie Lee Wills and Hank Thompson, four with Leon McAuliffe. After some twenty-five years of road work, he settled down in Tulsa and played jobs as he got calls, while working for the city's parks department. Playing opportunities are always available for Curly at western swing festivals, Texas Playboy reunions, cowboy symposiums, and recently jazz festivals. Just two months before this interview Curly was part of a western swing pickup band calling itself the San Antonio Rose Band, which scored a success at the Shasta Jazz Festival in Redding, California. And why not? You can't take the jazz out of western swing even when you take western swing out of its normal habitat, the dance hall.

CLYDE BREWER was born in 1930 in Luling, Texas, a small town about fifty miles east of San Antonio. His mother was a church musician and Clyde's first teacher. She started him on mandolin when he was six because all Clyde wanted to do was sit and listen to the old Philco radio. The bands he heard on the radio were among the top swing bands out of San Antonio and Fort Worth—Adolph Hofner, the Tune Wranglers, the Shelton Brothers, and, of course, the Light Crust Doughboys. By the time he was nine, Clyde's hands were large enough to handle the guitar, and he was playing guitar and mandolin at neighborhood house dances.

When World War II began, the Brewer family moved to Beaumont, where young Clyde's musical career really began. There were numerous bands in the Beaumont area, most notably those of Cliff Bruner and Moon Mullican, and, like so many other Texas violinists, Clyde fell under the spell of the master Texas swing fiddler, Cliff Bruner. "Cliff was the stylist and individualist, soloist-type fiddle player who played the good hot licks, we used to call them."

Music began to come together for Clyde when violinist and songwriter Shelly Lee Alley arrived in Beaumont and married Clyde's mother. When Alley formed his own band, Shelly Lee Alley and His Alley Cats, young Clyde went to work for him. Alley assumed the role of mentor to Clyde, when Clyde would slow down and listen. "Shelly used to say, 'Slow down and let me teach you.' 'No, I don't have time for that.' I wanted to learn this chord or that lick, or whatever." Alley had a great deal to teach Clyde because he had been a professional musician for a long time. During World War I he had conducted a well-respected military orchestra in San Antonio. After his discharge, Alley had moved to Dallas where he led several small orchestras and was the first bandleader to broadcast with his band over infant radio station WFAA. Alley's later KRLD Jazz Orchestra was recognized as one of the most popular dance bands in the Southwest. Alley was also a songwriter whose tunes had been picked up and recorded by various artists, including Jimmie Rodgers, who cut two of Alley's songs, "Travelin' Blues" and "Gambling Barroom Blues."

His recordings with Jimmie Rodgers and his radio exposure gave Shelly Lee Alley a considerable following in Texas, so his swing band, the Alley Cats, was quite successful through the 1930s and 1940s. The Alley Cats played in nightclubs and dance halls around southeast Texas and southwest Louisiana. World War II was on, and the Beaumont–Houston–Port Arthur area was booming with defense plants, shipyards, and refineries, all essential to the war effort. Clyde remembers, "There were bands everywhere, and on weekends there would be seven or eight dances just in Beaumont, with every band drawing a large crowd. The work was plentiful."

In 1946 Alley retired from the band business, and Clyde, age sixteen, began to learn to play the violin. His mandolin-playing experience had prepared him for fingering the violin, but handling the bow took a little time. The Alleys were living in Houston when Shelly Lee retired, so Clyde went to work for a small band that played several nights a week at a club on Shepherd Drive. From this unnamed group, Clyde went on to play mandolin, guitar, and a little fiddle with a Beaumont band called the Bluebonnet Playboys. In 1947 Clyde was hired by one of his heroes, jazz pianist Moon Mullican, to play fiddle in his band. Mullican was a hot item with a relatively new label, King Records, and there was about to be a recording ban called by the musicians' union. "King Records sent their A & R man, Sid Nathan, down to Beaumont where Moon was playing, to record him real quick, get all the records made up that you can because they've got to abide by this record ban. So we went in the radio station there at KRIC and we did twelve sides for King and we got through just a few minutes before midnight, then the record ban came on."

The ban lasted for a year and brought significant changes in the way songwriters and sidemen were paid; but it was an interesting year because only vocalists and harmonica players were free to record, singers being exempt from union membership and harmonica players discounted as nonmusicians. It was a year for duet, trio, and quartet recordings, with background harmonica accompaniment.

Moon Mullican and the Showboys played regularly at the Forest Club in Beaumont in addition to their recording sessions and out-of-town appearances. Life with Moon Mullican was always an adventure, as Clyde recalls.

> Moon got real popular nationwide off a song called "Sweeter than the Flowers" on King Records. A tour was lined up for him to go from Beaumont to Carnegie Hall and play the first western act to appear in Carnegie Hall. Spade Cooley and their band from the West Coast were going to meet us there. So Moon Mullican and the Showboys and Spade Cooley and his fine band were going to be the first two western bands to ever appear in Carnegie Hall. When we got to Alexandria, Louisiana, Moon had hired an agent to book jobs for us all the way up to New York. He ran off with all our money and did not book any jobs. We did not get to Carnegie Hall. Moon had to go back to Beaumont and get pumped up with some more money, then get on a plane, and he went to Carnegie Hall and appeared with Spade Cooley's band and we were still living in a cotton patch in Alexandria, Louisiana, trying to figure out a way to get back home.

Clyde made it back to Texas and worked with two Houston swing bands, the Bar-X Cowboys and the Texas Cowboys, before joining the band of his idol, Cliff Bruner. Cliff was working out of Houston when he called Clyde to come play fiddle and mandolin with his Texas Wanderers.

Clyde remained with Cliff Bruner for about a year, then Bruner returned to Beaumont to manage his club, and Clyde stayed in Houston and worked for Dickie and Laura Lee McBride. "Laura Lee had been the first female vocalist with the Bob Wills band and her husband Dickie was an excellent singer, too. I worked for them for quite a while. We had a real good band. Herb Remington left Bob Wills and joined us playing steel. Mancel Tierney had just left Bob Wills, and he joined us on piano. We had about a nine-piece band."

Other bands that Clyde joined in the 1950s included Andy Schroeder's band out of Odessa and, back in Houston, those of bandleaders Jerry Irby, Bennie Leader, and Johnny Ragsdale. Houston was a recording center in its own right in the 1950s, especially for western swing bands. There were numerous small local companies turning out a decent product that got air play on local radio stations. "George Jones's first record was made in Houston, and the Big Bopper. B. J. Thomas lived here. He made his first records in Houston. There were a lot of songwriters living in Houston. You could get a record played on a radio station easily. Now, of course, that's impossible." Clyde blames poor management and lack of vision for Houston's failure to become a major recording capital like Nashville.

Because he had a family to support and the music business was becoming more uncertain each year, Clyde went to work for the Houston's public works department in 1955. He rose to assistant manager before retiring thirty years later. He continued to play on weekends and sometimes several nights a week, and in 1971 helped to found the River Road Boys, a band that is still performing and recording with some of its original members. The first band included Clyde Brewer and Bob White on twin fiddles; Troy Passmore, guitar; Tommy Houser, drums; and Dick Allen, bass, vocals, and emcee. The current personnel roster of the River Road Boys consists of Clyde Brewer, fiddle, mandolin, keyboard; Jim Johnson, vocals; Tommy Houser, drums; Pee Wee Doyl, bass; Terry Barnet, guitar; Herb Remington, steel guitar; and occasionally one or more horn players. In order to remain popular in the Houston area, the River Road Boys have been forced to divide their time between western swing standards and current top-forty country music; but the purpose of the band remains the same—to get folks to dance. All western swing bands have played current hits; it is their method of playing these and the emphasis on variation through improvisation that categorically places them squarely among jazz artists rather than country or popular musicians.

Clyde's list of influences is lengthy:

We'd get through playing someplace and maybe somebody had an old record player or something and I've got a new Benny Goodman Sextet album—let's go listen to the Benny Goodman Sextet. Piano players wanted to hear Teddy Wilson and Art Tatum; Teddy Wilson with his left hand, and Art Tatum! And bass players wanted to hear the new Slam Stewart record. He was a terrific bass player in the jazz field. Or Chubby Wilson, I think he was a Woody Herman bass player. All the guitar players wanted to hear Django Reinhardt, Les Paul, or George Barnes, and even now they listen to George Benson. Fiddle players like myself, we wanted to hear Grappelli. We wanted to hear him. We wanted to hear Stuff Smith. I've still got some old Stuff Smith records. We all listened to that. We wanted to hear musicians who played better than we did, so we could learn something. If I were to take a solo it would be like maybe I thought Cliff Bruner might have played it, or maybe Johnny Gimble. But I can't copy anybody; I have to give each solo the stamp of my own personality.

Clyde has had some exciting moments as a western swing violinist, and he has experienced some triumphs. The River Road Boys were featured when the Reagan-Bush campaign came to Houston in 1980, and again some years later when Houston was the site of an economic summit during the Bush presidency. They were involved in an award-winning music documentary in 1989 that featured them in conjunction with a Norwegian band that also played western swing. Clyde notes with pride an album entitled *The Twin Fiddles of Bob White and Clyde Brewer and the River Road Boys*, dating from the early 1970s and one of the first jazz albums to be played in communist-bloc European countries. And Clyde has been inducted into both the Texas and Sacramento western swing halls of fame. But Clyde Brewer has no ambition to be a star. "When I started playing, all I wanted to do was to be a good sideman in a good band and be able to do that. Now that's all I want to do right now. I've been fortunate to have worked with the best in our field. That's what I always wanted to do and that's what I still want to do."

BOBBY BOATRIGHT, one of the last fiddle players to be interviewed for this project and also the youngest, was born in 1939 in Denison, Texas. Bobby's father was a bass and guitar player and made certain that his talented children received proper musical instruction. Bobby studied classical violin with a teacher in Denison but was early into the dance scene as well. "I worked with the violin teacher during the week and then would go play a country barn dance on Saturday night." In 1951 Bobby's father formed a band consisting of Bobby and his brother Johnny and other musically gifted neighborhood children; and in 1951 and 1952 this kid band from Denison performed on the Big D Jamboree. "There were six of us, ranging from ten years old to fourteen."

In 1954 the Boatright family moved to Wichita Falls, where Bobby continued his violin study in junior high and high school orchestra programs. Though he was only fourteen and still in school, Bobby was hired by radio personality Bill Mack to play fiddle in his band. Mack was traveling in Texas and Oklahoma playing dances and stage shows several nights a week and doing two weekly television programs, one in Wichita Falls and the other in Lawton, Oklahoma. Bobby remained with Bill Mack for about four years, then joined Jack Frost's western swing band in Wichita Falls. "We were playing dances three or four nights a week for Jack Frost. He had his own nightclub and that kept me pretty well tied down through 1961, trying to play and finish school."

School at this time for Bobby was Midwestern University in Wichita Falls, from which he earned a mathematics degree and teacher's certificate in 1962, the year he also began teaching high school math in Bells, Texas. In 1965 Bobby moved to Cedar Hill and began playing around the Dallas–Fort Worth area. In 1970 Bobby was fiddling for Ray Jennings in the house band at the Stage Coach Inn in Weatherford, Texas. And in 1973 Bobby joined Leon Rausch's Texas Panthers and has remained a steady member of the band ever since. Both Leon Rausch and Bobby Boatright played for Leon McAuliffe and the Original Texas Playboys from 1977 until the group disbanded in 1986, following Al Stricklin's death. Bobby's tie to the Playboys came in the late 1960s when Bob Wills was touring as a solo act and using pickup musicians for his various engagements. Bobby played with Wills for several such concerts at Fort Sill and Sheppard Air Force Base.

During the nearly ten years that Bobby was with the Original Texas Playboys, the band was extremely active performing and recording. Among its recording credits was an archival series for the Smithsonian Institute in Washington, D.C. The Original Texas Playboys appeared three times on the popular PBS television series *Austin City Limits* and were among the featured artists on the sound track of the award-winning movie *Places in the Heart.*

Bobby has also appeared with Playboys II, featuring Johnny Gimble, Herb Remington, Leon Rausch, Eldon Shamblin, Curle Hollingsworth, Tommy Perkins, and Dick Gimble, on the television show *Texas Connection.* There are several spinoffs of the original Playboy bands, and Bobby has performed with most of them. Bobby performs frequently with Dave Alexander and his Legends of Western Swing, a big band committed to keeping western swing alive in the ears and minds of Texans. Their command performances have included the Houston Livestock Show, the Texas State Fair in Dallas, and for President Bush and other dignitaries at the World Economic Summit in Houston. Bobby has played his violin with a star-studded lineup including Hank Thompson, the Light Crust Doughboys, Asleep at the Wheel, Floyd Tillman, George Strait, Willie Nelson, Red Steagall, Mel Tillis, Marty Robbins, Tex Ritter, Janie Fricke, Smiley Burnett, and Sheb Woolley. And he can regularly be heard at various western swing festivals around the country.[20]

As if he were not busy enough, Bobby has kept his own band, the Bar H Cowboys, going and has earned master's degrees in math and physics from East Texas State University. He is currently on the faculty of Weatherford Junior College.

Bobby grew up listening to jazz violin greats like Joe Venuti, Stephane Grappelli, Johnny Gimble, and Keith Coleman.[21] He rates Johnny Gimble the finest western swing improviser and a direct influence on his own playing. "The best player I've ever heard as far as improvising is Johnny Gimble. Whatever he plays, to me, it fits. He can do it and he knows exactly what to do and when to do it. I've never heard anybody improvise like he does." Like most western swing musicians, Bobby has difficulty describing his own personal style and simply concludes that he tries to play smoothly and improvise freshly. But his ears are always attuned to what others around him are doing. He also professes to prefer harmony to melody playing. For Bobby there is great challenge in listening to someone else play melody while he improvises an interesting harmony line. Bobby admits that his classical training did not prepare him to improvise. "I could do a little bit of improvising when I was sixteen or seventeen years old. It took that long before I ventured off into space out here and not be afraid to tackle something. I listened to enough of it and finally decided to start trying it. I'd talk to other fiddle players, and they'd give me hints about what to listen for and what to do, and try to keep me in the right direction."

Bobby's inquisitive mind is still at work, analyzing what others are doing and determining how he can best improvise a perfect harmony part. His own personal styling is not as derivative or dependent as he describes it, for Bobby Boatright possesses his own unique ideas and sound. He does bow smoothly, even in fast numbers, but always with the rhythmic energy and drive that attracted him to western swing in the first place. His liking for harmony is revealed in his frequent use of double stops, creating the sound of twin fiddles even when he is soloing. His improvisations are fresh and original, without a trace of hesitation, and his technical skill is much in evidence. Bobby can be heard at his best in live performances and in a recently released tape album entitled *Among My Souvenirs*, featuring Bobby Boatright and his friends, the Time Warp Tophands.[22]

THREE

Western Swing Guitarists

The guitar is frequently overlooked as an important component of the jazz band because it is so poorly heard on early recordings. Jazz guitar historians Jim Ferguson and Tony Bacon explain, "While the trumpet and saxophone were naturally suited from the outset to the requirements of jazz, guitarists had to struggle for decades to reconcile the characteristics of the music with their instrument's lack of volume and defiant technique."[1] That struggle began in the early days of the music—before it was called jazz. By the late nineteenth and early twentieth centuries, the countryside was dotted with string bands that played for rural dances. Many of the rural blues singers also performed in dance bands, and the typical instrumentation of such a group included violin, banjo, guitar, mandolin, and homemade one-string bass. The repertory of such dance bands was consistent throughout the South and Southwest: country fiddle tunes, folk ballads, hillbilly songs, and blues.[2] In time these rural dance bands began to frequent towns such as New Orleans, Dallas, Houston, and Kansas City, and a new music emerged.

In the towns musicians observed a distinction between bands comprising predominantly winds and those consisting mainly of strings based upon context and function, although the same musicians worked in both types of ensembles. Wind bands played in parades and for civic functions; as in the rural countryside, strings played for dancing. Jazz historian Mark Gridley observes: "It was almost as though musicians walked directly from the street parade into the dance hall, often putting down a brass instrument and picking up a violin. The performing groups accompanying dances were termed 'string bands' or 'orchestras'—violin, guitar, bass viol, and one or two wind instruments, played by the same musicians who had paraded with trumpet and trombone."[3] In short, string instruments, including the guitar, were charter members of early jazz bands, though they had little hope of competing with the louder winds. Guitarists in particular struggled to be heard, which explains the dominance of the banjo, with its more audible, percussive twang, on early recordings.

It was not until structural improvements were made to the guitar in the late 1920s and early 1930s that it began to eclipse the banjo in jazz bands. As early as 1923, the Gibson guitar company built an instrument with an increased volume of sound. Referred to as the L5 model, it had heavier steel strings strung over a strong, thick, arching top with two f-shaped sound holes for projection, an adjustable bridge, and a tailpiece. This was the guitar that Eddie Lang popularized, playing duets with his friend Joe Venuti and performing with the Paul Whiteman Orchestra and as a busy session musician. In 1932 Maria Maccaferri, working for the French instrument company Selmer, devised a guitar with an additional interior sound chamber that produced a clear and rather piercing tone. This was Django Reinhardt's guitar of choice.[4]

But the only way to insure that the guitar would be heard in a large band setting, without placing a microphone directly in front of it and disturbing the band balance, was to amplify it electrically. Some of the earliest experiments in guitar amplification were carried out in the Southwest by Eddie Durham, who played in several Kansas City bands, including that of Count Basie. The Gibson guitar company began producing an electrically amplified model, the ES 150, in 1936, and Durham was the first to record with it, two years later, while working with the Kansas City Five and Kansas City Six, both pickup recording bands from the Basie orchestra. But it took the incomparable genius of another southwestern musician, Charlie Christian, recording with the Benny Goodman band in 1941, to take the electric guitar out of the rhythm section and place it firmly on the front line as a lead soloist.[5]

The manner of playing the guitar changed, as did its construction. Before the 1930s, the guitar was restricted to the rhythm section of the jazz band, usually in the company of a banjo, piano, a bass of some kind, and sometimes drums. Often one rhythm player switched between banjo and guitar; banjo was more likely to be coupled with a wind bass, such as tuba or bass saxophone, while guitar was associated with string bass. Rhythm guitar and banjo were played similarly in early jazz, strummed on all four beats in 4/4 meter. Because of the limited volume of the standard guitar, it was seldom featured as a solo instrument, other than to play simple chord patterns in short breaks.

It was during the Swing Era of the 1930s that the function of the guitar gradually began to change, largely due to the efforts of guitar talents like Eddie Lang, Lonnie Johnson, Charlie Christian, and Django Reinhardt. Using improved guitars with increased sound capacity, these players brought the instrument to the front line as a melodic solo instrument. And they could be heard on records and radio because of improved recording and broadcasting techniques.

It was from recordings and radio that up-and-coming western swing guitarists heard and learned from their heroes, artists who became unknowing mentors. The list of guitar greats is too lengthy to cover in its entirety in this study, but some important individuals who made an impact on the entire jazz scene must be mentioned.

Eddie Lang (Salvatore Massaro, 1904–1933) made an indelible mark on jazz guitar through the seventy recordings made with his longtime friend, violinist Joe Venuti, between 1926 and 1933. He was also the first guitarist to make solo recordings. To Eddie Lang belongs the distinction of being almost "solely responsible for the creation of the jazz guitar, for until he brought intelligence and dexterity to bear, nobody had conceived of the idea of playing guitar in a manner compatible with the demands of jazz solos."[6] Intelligence and dexterity characterized Eddie's guitar playing; his colleagues were constantly mystified by his innate sense of the direction an arrangement would take without his ever consulting the score and were amazed by his genius for innovations without sacrificing the finesse and cleanness of his attack. Eddie's treatment of rhythm and his ear for pitch were incredibly precise, but his presence was so understated that he was often appreciated only by the other musicians with whom he worked. He was occasionally accused of being too precise, of lacking swing, but his view of the guitar as a melody instrument as opposed to strictly rhythmic and his retiring personality gave his playing a more relaxed, less aggressive feel.

Nobody could question Eddie's harmonic originality or his unique gift for making the guitar both a rhythm and a melody instrument simultaneously. Every aspect of his technique was in place along with a genius for innovation: "Here could be found the changing of fingers on the same fret to produce a fresh attack, interval jumps of a tenth to simulate the effects of a jazz piano, parallel ninth chords, flatted fifths, whole-tone scalar figures, smears, unusual glissandi, harmonics, harp-like effects, consecutive augmented chords, and relaxed horn-like phrasing."[7]

It must have been a revelation to guitarists accustomed to their normal role as rhythm players to hear Eddie's rhythm, melody, and chords, like an entire band rolled into one player. Listening to his recordings, one is impressed with the clarity of his tone and the control he exerted on this hard-to-play instrument. His classical training gave him a sound ideal different from blues-oriented guitarists but did not deprive him of rhythmic energy and drive.

One of the highly influential blues-oriented guitarists of the 1930s was New Orleans native Alonzo "Lonnie" Johnson (1889–1970). Johnson was an early example of a crossover artist who fused the characteristic expression and phrasing of the blues with single-string melodic playing, modern chord changes and voicings, and a facile technique. Since Johnson and Lang recorded briefly together, it is possible to compare their individual styles. Lonnie Johnson brought more blues feeling to his playing with such devices as allowing a strummed chord to ring while sliding up or down to another pitch. His tone was thicker than Lang's, which was characterized by clean lines and dampened chords. Both guitarists organized their solos well, but, due to his training, Eddie was almost classical in his sense of form. Whereas Eddie Lang played a standard six-string guitar, Lonnie Johnson doubled two or three of the top strings, like a twelve-string model, so that he could produce a larger, rounder tone.[8]

Johnson's "Swing Out Rhythm" recording, preserved through the Polygram Special Projects, is a driving, bluesy solo number in which Lonnie makes all of his characteristic guitar moves. He colors the melody with blues inflections and slides, unexpected chord changes, and flexible phrasing. "Blue Guitars," courtesy of Fantasy Records, is a standard twelve-bar blues in which Johnson and Lang combine their unique voices. Though the two guitarists possessed entirely different styles, they are never in conflict in this performance. Johnson plays his highly expressive melody part over Lang's subdued, dampened chords and clean fills. The two artists are technically matched, and Lang's one solo chorus shows that "he could hold his own as a blues player."[9]

Another guitarist who influenced a broad spectrum of jazz players was Freddie Green (b. 1911), who joined the Count Basie rhythm section in 1937 and remained an essential element of that band for the next fifty years. Green never aspired to solo status but rather developed the best rhythm guitar style in the business. His unmistakable sound derived from his guitar and the way he played it. The guitar was an acoustic, cello-body model (currently a custom Gretsch) with heavy-gauge strings strung higher than normal from the fingerboard, permitting greater volume. Freddie struck the strings hard, and he held the instrument almost flat so that he was looking down at the neck and could more easily finger large chords on the four lower strings. His ability to play supporting chords and fillers behind one chorus after another without ever missing a beat is jazz legend. Critic Raymond Horricks, in his book *Count Basie and His Orchestra*, writes of Freddie Green:

> He was reliable without being obtrusive, a sound component part of the rhythm, yet with a personal sense of rhythm which is virile and spirited; technically well versed, he has been the ideal rhythm guitarist for the Count. His inherent sense of tempo and his durability when performing a regular beat have set standards well above those of the average band guitarist. With the non-amplified instrument, his touch has been definitive though still delicate, resulting in his supplying each rhythm section he has worked in with a beat that is emphatic without ever becoming ponderous.[10]

Like Freddie Green, George Abel Van Eps (b. 1913) seldom saw the solo spotlight, but he expanded jazz harmony as a rhythm section player in the bands of Benny Goodman, Ray Noble, Peggy Lee, Frank Sinatra, and Jo Stafford. Jazz guitar historian Stan Britt explains,

> George Van Eps remains one of jazz's great chordal exponents. His sound, too, is one of the most distinctive of all players, occasioned as it is by his adding an A string, below the E string, to the normal six-string set-up, and tuning the seventh string a fifth below its normal range. In addition, Van Eps has a great gift for reharmonization, coupled with a superb built-in bass-line that gives his strictly acoustic approach the kind of running excitement of the great extrovert players.[11]

Van Eps was also a composer and arranger whose compositions spotlighted his unique harmonic vocabulary. "Kay's Fantasy" is somewhat obtuse in terms of its structure and melody, but it is a perfect vehicle for the frequent and sometimes unusual chord changes that are Van Eps's stock-and-trade. With the added low string George can actually provide his own bass accompaniment, though he works closely with the bass player for this recording session. He plays some single-string melodic material, but the real interest of this performance rests securely in the chord structures.

The pivotal position in the development of jazz guitar playing belongs to Charlie Christian (1916–1942). In the brief two years Charlie spent with Benny Goodman, he redefined the guitarist's role in the ensemble. He was not the first to play amplified guitar in a jazz band—that distinction belongs to Bob Dunn of Milton Brown's Musical Brownies—but he was the player whose talent popularized that instrument. He was also not the first to use the guitar melodically, but he was the first to attain a level of solo playing that made him the equal of the great horn virtuosi. Some historians include him on the list of best-ever soloists on any instrument. At a critical juncture in the steady march of jazz, Charlie Christian made contributions that helped to redirect jazz's path. Says Stan Britt:

> His unique brand of phrasing is just one aspect of his playing which makes him stand out from jazz guitarists of the Thirties; its horn-like quality parallels the work of tenorist Lester Young—both musicians used unusually long melodic lines, comprising evenly placed notes, phrased in a legato manner. Like Young, Christian concentrated on a freer exposition of the conventional 4/4 time signature, likewise deploying a new approach to the use of basic riffs to produce a kind of rhythmic excitement that was as fresh-sounding as it was exhilarating. And Christian's playing was further enhanced by his subtle use of augmented and diminished chords, plus unusual accents—all of which was to make substantial contributions to the birth and development of bebop.[12]

At a time when jazz—namely swing jazz—had become predictable and commercial, Charlie responded with surprise and originality. When he played a solo, or sometimes a string of uninterrupted solos, he ignored the time signatures and barlines to create free, irregular phrases that suggested a whole new way of thinking about jazz. And like his friend and fellow Lester Young devotee, saxophonist Charlie Parker, Charlie Christian helped to put jazz on a new harmonic track that opened fresh territory for improvisation. Charlie Christian could not be ignored, and jazz guitar could never be the same. His influence extended beyond jazz guitarists to include pianists, violinists, and even horn players.

The only European to command the attention of American guitarists was Django Reinhardt, the gypsy musician born outside of the Belgian village of Liverchies in 1910. Django's course as a jazz guitarist was set by his first hearing of recordings by Eddie Lang and Joe Venuti, Louis Armstrong, and Duke Ellington. His close collaboration with violinist Stephane Grappelli further solidified Django's personal jazz direction. By the time of his death in 1953, Django Reinhardt had become an inspiration for a host of jazz musicians, not all of them guitarists. In fact, trumpeter Dizzy Gillespie claimed Django as one of his principal influences.

Since Charlie Christian and Django Reinhardt were the two most powerful jazz guitar personalities of the 1930s and 1940s, it is instructive to compare their individual approaches. The differences are both external and internal. Christian usually maintained a steady pace in his solos, and Reinhardt could play unevenly and with sporadic splashes of busyness. Christian's melody lines incorporated horn phrasing, while Reinhardt's were more pianistic. Christian's tone was round and full; Reinhardt's was characterized by a sharp bite. Christian's background included the blues, Reinhardt's grew out of gypsy music and the French impressionist school. Christian built upon long patterns of swing eighth notes, Reinhardt created erratic rhythms in which he leaned toward the use of triplets and sixteenth-note figures. Christian used little vibrato, Reinhardt made a large vibrato a key element of his sound. Finally, Christian played an amplified hollow-body guitar, Reinhardt used an acoustic instrument.[13]

The differences between these two great guitarists were also internal and subjective. Christian was the classic master in control of the music and the emotional moment; Reinhardt was the romantic dramatist, controlled by the music and the emotional moment. Django had marvelous technique, but the way he made music was as variable as his own moods. He could play delicately, quietly, then suddenly plunge into loud, aggressive, emotionally charged passages. He could create logically developed solo lines or spin off a sequence of virtuosic flourishes. Django played melody lines, chords, large pianistic leaps, and arpeggios—all with a sizzling drive that was one of his most phenomenal features. Everything Django Reinhardt played was his alone; his sound and techniques were completely unique.

"Naguine" is one of Django's own compositions and one of his few solo guitar recordings. It is a reflective piece that mixes large, orchestrally conceived chords and single-note melodic figures. There is Django's personalized, almost erratic sense of phrasing and rhythm superimposed over his internalized metronomic sense of time. And there are also the characteristic long note bends, flourishes, and noticeable vibrato that make Django's playing so recognizable and also so difficult to imitate.

Other jazz guitarists who have exerted considerable influence on the jazz scene are Johnny Smith (b. 1922), Tal Farlow (b. 1921), Barney Kessel (b. 1923), Joe Pass (b. 1929), and Herb Ellis (b. 1921). John Henry Smith achieved national recognition in 1952, when he played guitar behind tenor saxophonist Stan Getz on the best-selling album, *Moonlight in Vermont*. Smith was crowned top guitarist of the year by *Down Beat* in 1953 and 1954 and won the *Metronome* awards in 1954 and 1955. Smith has been classified as a "cool" jazz player because of his emotional detachment and controlled, intellectual style. Though self-taught, his technique is enviable, allowing him to "accomplish practically any idea, even at the most daunting of tempos." [14] On slow ballads Smith created "lush and lingering guitar chords that had an almost harp-like quality." [15] He accomplished this by developing the unusual technique of holding down single notes while changing chords, thus producing a smoothly flowing sound similar to that of legato piano playing.[16]

Whereas Smith was the cool, intellectual technician, Tal Farlow was the quintessential hard bop exponent; and hard bop is to cool as the color red is to pink. Farlow, the tall, good-looking young man with the large hands and warm, outgoing personality, was just the musician to transplant the hard bop ideas of trumpeter Clifford Brown, drummer Max Roach, tenor saxophonist Sonny Rollins, and pianist Horace Silver to the guitar. He synthesized a variety of approaches into his own personal style: the long, floating, and sometimes irregular melodies of Charlie Christian; the harmonic complexity of Thelonious Monk, Charlie Parker, and Dizzy Gillespie; the controlled sound of Johnny Smith; and the rhythmic drive of Barney Kessel. Yet all of these borrowings become reinterpreted into the unique guitar language of Tal Farlow.

Farlow experimented with the sound-producing mechanism of the guitar. For many years he played with the neck of his guitar shortened by one fret, thus raising its tuning by a half-step, lessening the tension on the strings so that they felt softer and facilitating larger left-hand stretches. He also devised a novel rhythmic technique of turning off his amplifier and strumming the deadened strings to produce a snare drum effect. Farlow designed an amplified octave attachment through which he could modify the sound of his guitar. But all of his experimentation was intended to heighten the emotional punch of his guitar playing.

Barney Kessel probably exerted the greatest influence on several generations of post–World War II guitarists and jazz audiences, because his technique was awesome but at the same time completely accessible. At a time when jazz seemed to be splintering into many different directions, most of them too elusive for audiences to follow, Kessel built musical bridges that welcomed listeners back into the jazz idiom. For Kessel, Charlie Christian was the embodiment of all that was best in jazz guitar playing; and Kessel has been described as "the guitarist who came closest to Charlie Christian in sound and spirit." [17] But it was his experience in 1947, backing bebop pioneer Charlie Parker, that changed Kessel's musical life. Kessel confessed, "I understood what was so fantastic about Parker's playing. From then on, I loved Charlie Parker profoundly. That had a far-reaching influence on the hierarchy of my values. It changed everything." [18]

Kessel has had special meaning for southwestern guitarists because he is rooted in the traditions, like the rural blues, that give southwestern jazz its special flavor. It is his exciting swing that makes his playing accessible and popular, no matter what style of jazz he is playing, and he is capable of great diversity. Mongan dubs Kessel "the most well-versed musically of the first wave of post-Christian guitarists" and explains that he "retained the drive and attack of the Christian approach without sacrificing the wider harmonic possibilities offered by bop." [19]

In Kessel's own view, his strongest asset is his skill in improvisation. "The best thing I can do for the guitar is to improvise, to make up countless variations of songs, and to play anything I hear. I could sit down with a guitar and play for ten hours without repeating myself. While I might travel down some roads I've traveled before it would all be original. It would all be me." [20]

Joe Pass (Joseph Anthony Passalaqua) belongs to the current crop of brilliant modern jazz guitarists with firm roots in the hard bop approach to jazz. Pass is both a listener's guitarist and a guitarist's guitarist. He demands the attention of audiences and colleagues with his great technical facility, the Eddie Lang–like clarity of his melody lines, and his rhythmic drive and swing. Historian John Williams Handy notes that "Pass is nearly incapable of a commonplace musical phrase. His playing is pure musical thought, devoid of cliché, almost devoid of any phrase that could be considered a part of the public domain, and yet strikingly familiar, song-like and interesting." [21]

Herb Ellis makes a perfect partner to Joe Pass in that both are hard-driving hard bop guitarists, they collaborated on several outstanding duet recordings, and both were influenced by Barney Kessel. Mitchell Herbert Ellis was basically a country picker before he went to North Texas State

College as a music major and discovered jazz. The first time he heard a recording by Charlie Christian playing with the Benny Goodman Sextet, his musical direction was completely and resolutely altered—he would be a jazz guitarist. Ellis gave rhythm guitar playing a new lease on life. As a five-year member of the Oscar Peterson Trio (beginning in 1953), Ellis "helped to reintegrate the electric guitar into the rhythm section, evolving a tightly controlled, snappy drive. . . . Ellis's work was light but powerful, blending tightly with Ray Brown's magnificent bass work. . . . The team of Ellis and Brown was probably the hardest swing rhythm pair on the jazz scene during the 1950s." [22]

Herb Ellis is a native Texan who understands the language of Texas blues, which contributes to the fact that he is one of the most identifiable of modern Texas guitarists. "Ellis is unbeatable where swing and drive are concerned; his is a style of classic modern simplicity. The very direct, blues-drenched sound has the same southwestern twang that is found in Charlie Christian's work, and his hard, powerful attack and 'stringy' tonality make constant reference to his Texas origins." [23]

Major western swing guitarists are never mentioned among the influential figures in jazz history because the recordings on which they played were routinely classified as hillbilly. In the Southwest there were highly influential guitar artists who could easily trade places with guitarists in mainstream horn bands. One of the most significant of the western swing guitarists was Eldon Shamblin, longtime sideman for Bob Wills and His Texas Playboys.

When Eldon began playing in the Bob Wills band in 1937, he completely changed the Wills sound, turning it from simplistic Dixieland to modern swing. Eldon developed a unique style, comparable to that of other guitarists of the period but entirely his own; he claims that he was too busy playing to have time to listen to other guitarists. Eldon's playing is defined by a prominent running bass line over which he builds large, ever-changing melodic-chordal patterns in close association with the rest of the rhythm section. Eldon Shamblin brought a new level of musical and technical skill to the Wills band, and the improved level of their musicality and the tightness of their rhythm section owed much to Eldon's long tenure as a Playboy.

Eldon was often felt rather than heard as a primary rhythm section player. His presence was essential to the April 16, 1940, recording session in Dallas that produced "New San Antonio Rose." This was a large band with Bob Wills and Jesse Ashlock on fiddles, Leon McAuliffe playing steel guitar, Louis Tierney switching between fiddle and saxophone, Johnnie Lee Wills on banjo, Son Lansford playing bass, Eldon Shamblin on rhythm guitar, Al Stricklin at the piano, Smoky Dacus behind the drums, and a wind section consisting of Everett Stover (trumpet), Wayne Johnson (clarinet), Tiny Mott (saxophone), Robert McNally (saxophone), Joe Ferguson (saxophone), Don Harlan (saxophone), Tubby Lewis (trumpet), and Tommy Duncan featured as vocalist. This was a big band sound, and the driving rhythmic force that propelled the ensemble forward emanated from the combined efforts of Dacus, Stricklin, and Shamblin.

Eldon never made solo recordings in which he could give free rein to his musical imagination, but his occasional solo choruses with the Texas Playboys provide vivid glimpses into his technical and improvisatory genius. One of those solo moments occurred during a Dallas recording session of November 30, 1938, on the song "That's What I Like about the South," when Wills pointed his fiddle bow at Eldon, and Eldon produced a brief flight of fancy that leaves the listener wishing for more. Comparisons do not come easily when the subject is Eldon Shamblin. He treats the guitar orchestrally, with large barred chords, rather like Van Eps; and he plays with an unrelenting rhythmic drive, similar to that of Freddie Green. But his individual styling and bass-rhythm approach give Eldon's guitar a sound all its own. As a soloist, Eldon came closer to Django Reinhardt than to Eddie Lang or even Charlie Christian. There were technical similarities between Reinhardt and Shamblin—a liking for triplet eighths and sixteenth-note melodic figures, arpeggios, large leaps, a variety of rhythm patterns. But on a deeper level Shamblin and Reinhardt were alike in their thinking about improvisation. Though not as flamboyant as Reinhardt—Eldon tended to play with a laid-back, easy swing—he was every bit as unpredictable, giving the listener the sensation that his solo flight, short though it might be, could take off in any direction at any time and still make good sense. Eldon Shamblin was not the temperamentally volcanic guitarist Django Reinhardt was, but he was equally brilliant and expressive.

Eldon and steel guitarist Leon McAuliffe teamed up at a Dallas recording session, February 24, 1941, for a boogie-woogie number entitled "Twin Guitar Special." After Eldon's introduction, the two guitarists proceeded to play several tightly knit choruses in perfect duet, their parts interchangeable and interconnected, a strong foretaste of the kind of incredible togetherness that bebop pioneers Dizzy Gillespie (trumpet) and Charlie Parker (saxophone) would create on their thrilling up-tempo introductions.

Eldon and Leon merged their talents again two days later for a slow blues, "Honey, What You Gonna Do." They play the first chorus in perfect unison, followed by Tommy Duncan singing a verse and Louis Tierney playing a bluesy third verse on violin. Tommy Duncan's vocal fourth verse is followed by Eldon and Leon's closing tag, again in perfect unison.

Like Freddie Green and Herb Ellis, Eldon Shamblin was the consummate rhythm section guitarist. He provided a driving swing, complemented the bass with his own bass line, brought a modern vocabulary of chords to the Wills band, and created perfect contrapuntal lines to any melody. Eldon Shamblin could have played guitar in any jazz band, but he preferred western swing. He was technically and creatively the equivalent of the other great jazz guitarists who were his contemporaries.

Another guitar great who has been relegated to oblivion because he played only with western swing bands was Junior Barnard. Lester "Junior" Barnard was born in Coweta, Oklahoma, in 1920. His father was a well-known fiddle player around Coweta, and thirteen-year-old Junior got his first professional experience playing guitar behind his dad's fiddle at local barn dances and house parties. At the age of fifteen Junior graduated to dance bands working the Tulsa area and to his own show on radio station KTUL. He also played in the backup bands of various entertainers who came through Tulsa, including Patti Page and Her Musical Pages from Claremore, Oklahoma. About 1935 Junior was hired by Bob Wills to play guitar in a band called the Lonestar Rangers, which was fronted by Bob's father, John Wills. In 1936 Bob created another family band, the Sons of the West, and put his cousin Son Lansford in charge; Junior was transferred to this new band. Junior worked with the Sons of the West out of Amarillo for a year before returning to Tulsa and KTUL. Once back in Tulsa, Junior bought his first electric guitar, a blond Epiphone Emperor arch-top model. In 1937 Eldon Shamblin left the Alabama Boys to join Bob Wills's Texas Playboys, and Junior took Eldon's place on the Alabama Boys band. But Junior soon received another call from Bob Wills, this time to play in brother Johnnie Lee Wills's first band, the Rhythmaires. Some six months later, most of the Rhythmaires were transferred into John Wills's band, now called Uncle Johnny and His Young Five, which recorded on the Decca label. Junior played with the

Young Five until he got his draft notice. He failed the physical because of his overweight condition and moved out to California to work in a defense plant. In 1943 Junior returned to play briefly with Johnnie Lee Wills's band at Cain's Academy and on station KVOO in Tulsa, but he soon took off for Houston to work in the defense industry again.

Meanwhile Bob Wills had enlisted in the army, but after only a brief time was declared physically unfit for military service and discharged. Wills reorganized the Playboys and made California's San Fernando Valley his new base of operations, thus putting him and his band close to Los Angeles recording studios and the Hollywood movie scene. In 1945 Wills moved the Playboys to Fresno and hired Junior to take Jimmy Wyble's place as lead guitarist. He also hired Eldon Shamblin, fresh from military duty and a brief stint with Leon McAuliffe's Cimarron Boys, to be band manager and personnel stabilizer. Besides their regular dance jobs and live radio broadcasts, the Playboys began making the Fresno Roundup series of radio transcriptions, which were aired on station KMJ; in early 1946, they made the famous Tiffany Transcriptions in San Francisco. They were also recording on the Columbia label. Late in 1946 Junior left the Playboys to join Luke Wills's Rhythm Busters, and in 1947 he returned to the Playboys, who had relocated to their new home, Wills Point, near Sacramento.

Tommy Duncan broke away from the Playboys to start his own band in 1948, and Junior alternated working for Duncan and Bob Wills. Junior set out on his own in 1949, forming a band called the Radio Gang, which played at a large dance hall, the Barn, and on radio stations KMJ, KYNO, and KSMA. When the Barn was sold in 1951, the Radio Gang moved over to the Marigold Ballroom, but they were not as successful there as they had been at the Barn. Junior was on a scouting trip, looking for a new dance hall, in April 1951, when he was involved in the automobile accident that ended his life.

Western swing has a substantial following all over the country, but few enthusiasts recognize the name Junior Barnard because he moved so often and spent only brief periods of time with various bands. But western swing guitarists know him well. Eldon Shamblin feels that Junior Barnard was the best guitarist for Bob Wills's brand of western swing. Junior has been compared to Charlie Christian, but his style was really too unique and too far ahead of its time to be equated with that of any of his contemporaries. One can easily imagine how heads turned and dancing feet stopped as people concentrated on his outrageous solo choruses; guitars were not meant to sound that way, yet! Barnard researcher Buddy McPeters writes:

> His hard-hitting electric guitar style, complete with distorted tone, violent bends, and scorching runs—all extremely advanced for the '30s and '40s—heralded the techniques and sounds commonly associated with contemporary rock and roll. Unlike Eldon Shamblin, who to this day plays laid-back country-tinged jazz, Junior was a go-for-broke soloist whose incredible technique featured startling runs, rapid hammer-ons and pull-offs, and even contrapuntal lines. Barnard was such an exciting soloist because he rarely played things safe. But Junior could also play in a subdued manner, especially when backing up a singer.
>
> Although Barnard wasn't as sophisticated an accompanist as Shamblin, he had a strong rhythmic sense and used substitute chords to make progressions flow smoothly.[24]

It was not as an accompanist but as a lead guitarist that Junior contributed to most of the bands with which he worked. And though Bob Wills depended on Junior's rhythmic drive to keep the Playboys up and going, he delighted in featuring Junior as solo lead guitarist, from whom something daring and original could be expected.

Junior Barnard played loudly for his time, producing what McPeters calls an "overdriven tube sound decades before it became widely popular with rock guitarists."[25] He wired the two pickups on his guitar out of phase, thus creating a certain amount of controlled distortion, and pushed each through separate amplifiers, assuring that his guitar would be heard. With guitar conceptions such as these, it is difficult to classify Junior with any single school of guitar playing or to pinpoint other guitarists who may have influenced him. He was an individual, an original, perhaps a school unto himself.

Junior's solo chorus on "Brain Cloudy Blues," recorded by Bob Wills and the Texas Playboys in Hollywood on September 5, 1946, provides an inkling of what he probably played in the freer atmosphere of live performance. After the fiddles play an introduction and Tommy Duncan sings the first two verses, Junior takes off on a chorus that incorporates many of the salient features of his style. The first thing to be noticed is that he is playing louder than anybody else and more aggressively. He mixes large chords and quick-fingered runs, always underlined by interesting rhythm patterns. When Wills calls out "Get low, Junior," Barnard responds with his characteristic amplified distortion, giving this twelve-bar blues a down-and-dirty sound. Tommy Duncan takes the microphone to sing the next two verses in the out-of-meter manner for which the Wills band was famous, and it is Junior's metronomic strumming that bridges the ensemble back around to a steady 4/4 meter.[26]

As a guitarist Junior merged two musics—swing jazz and rock and roll. His techniques and sounds were certainly a foretaste of rock guitar to come, but his steady swing—accenting off the beat rather than on it as rock guitarists do—placed him squarely in the swing jazz tradition. McPeters's conclusion to his article about Barnard places the matter clearly in perspective. "Junior Barnard was one of the first to fuse elements of jazz, country, rockabilly, and rock and roll into an exciting style that was many years ahead of its time. His brother Gene, also an accomplished guitarist, concludes: 'I don't think people realize that Junior was playing today's type of popular music years before anyone else. He was playing rock and roll years before it had a name.'"[27] Had Junior Barnard not died in 1951, before rock and roll was really launched, he might have been one of the first guitar giants in rock history.

Though Eldon Shamblin and Junior Barnard were ignored because of their connections with western swing, Jimmy Wyble became a national figure, probably because he played in both western swing and mainstream jazz bands. Jimmy Wyble is classified in jazz guitar history as an exponent of that controlled, intellectual school of playing labeled "cool." Cool jazz hit its stride in the late 1940s and 1950s as an alternative to both commercialized swing and emotionally and technically charged bebop. While each guitarist who leaned in the cool direction created a unique style, there was a "common denominator in sound; based on [Jimmy] Raney's vibratoless, dulled, pure sound, using a minimum of amplifier volume, and with the same emphasis on linearity."[28]

Linearity is Jimmy Wyble's middle name, as demonstrated by a duet of articles he published in *Guitar Player* in 1979 and 1980. His premise is very basic and logical and, at the same time, difficult to realize in practice: playing two different scales simultaneously in order to "expand chord vocabulary," "develop awareness of harmonic lines," and enhance "left-hand independence."[29] Wyble's intellectualized conception of guitar playing is illustrated in the opening paragraph of his 1979 article.

Scales, what could be more basic? And what could be more limit-less? The infinite possibilities of our basic source—the scale with all its variations—are indeed astounding. To remain growing as a gui-tarist we must deal constantly with two areas: efficiency (achieved through the relentless but patient pursuit of technique) and har-monic awareness (a forever expanding concept which gives us new sounds with which to work). We must investigate, research, experi-ment, seek new paths, try new ideas. But if we try especially to stay in touch with the really basic source—scales—our music will flow, and we will still be able to create in a personal and original way.[30]

A noted guitar teacher as well as a theorist, Wyble provides in each article illustrations that make these intellectual concepts accessible to gui-tarists. Wyble has authored two books on his method of linear playing, *The Art of Two-Line Improvisation* and *Chords to Counterpoint: A Guide to Multi-Line Improvisation* (with Leon White). For at least twenty years, Jimmy Wyble has shared his techniques and theoretical knowledge with private students through clinics; and he has created and published his own guitar method, complete with manuals and demonstration tapes, as well as a series of etudes (technical studies). Through his playing and teaching, Jimmy Wyble has emerged as one of the most influential jazz guitarists of the last thirty years.

Jimmy Wyble was born in Port Arthur, Texas, in January 1922. As a young man, he played guitar in local Houston bands and worked as staff guitarist for a Houston radio station. After he was discharged from the military in 1944, Jimmy went to Los Angeles, where Bob Wills was audi-tioning guitar players. Having grown up in Texas, Jimmy was well versed in western swing and got the job with Wills.[31] Jimmy Wyble was proba-bly the most virtuosic and, at the same time, unobtrusive guitarist Bob Wills ever had. His personal style was subdued, understated, controlled, technically remarkable, and always just right for the moment. For ex-ample, Wyble's linear, nearly vibratoless solo chorus and ensemble work forms a perfect balance to fiddler Joe Holley's extroverted, emotional per-formance on "Roly Poly," recorded in Hollywood by Bob Wills and the Texas Playboys on January 26, 1945.[32] With his interest in expanding harmonies through contrapuntal playing, Jimmy easily formed a musical partnership with steel guitarist Noel Boggs, who was also on the Wills band at this time.

After he left the Playboys, Jimmy worked briefly with the Spade Cooley band and then freelanced in Los Angeles. He recorded with Shorty Rogers in 1952 and Barney Kessel in 1953. In 1957 Jimmy became part of the famed Red Norvo jazz combo. During the eight years he was with Norvo, Jimmy also toured abroad with Benny Goodman (1959, 1960, 1963). Norvo and Wyble both joined the Frank Sinatra tour orchestra in 1964, after which Jimmy settled down to the busy life of a studio musician in Los Angeles. In the mid-1970s Jimmy hit the road again as part of Tony Rizzi's Five Guitarists, playing five-part arrangements of compositions by Charlie Christian.[33] Jimmy spent the 1980s working out the theoretical elements of his linear style and teaching these to others.

Frankie Nemko, writing in 1977, described Jimmy Wyble in these words: "Wyble's two-line contrapuntal approach to soloing makes for one of the most advanced sounds in jazz guitar's recent history."[34] Some of the greatest guitarists in jazz history have come from Texas and Oklahoma—Charlie Christian, Barney Kessel, Herb Ellis, Eldon Shamblin, Junior Barnard, Jimmy Wyble. America's great Southwest surely deserves Nemko's designation: "Guitar Country."[35]

A Few Good Guitarists Talk about Western Swing

ELDON SHAMBLIN was born about 1916 in Weatherford in the southwestern corner of Oklahoma. His family has been part of Oklahoma history since his grandparents participated in the land rush while Oklahoma was still a territory. Eldon does not remember how he got interested in music, except that his mother played the piano. But he knows how his interest in the guitar developed. "An old boy got me interested in guitar. He played with a big band at Southwestern State Teachers College. He was a big band guitar player. I never did like country, still don't. I started in a big band. That's what I always liked." There were no formal music lessons for Eldon; he taught himself not only to play guitar but also to read music, to understand music theory, and to arrange.

In 1933, when he was seventeen, Eldon moved to Oklahoma City to find work as a musician. He played in beer joints and cafes and eventually earned a spot on a local radio station, which paid him two meals a day. "I had a radio show by myself, which is the worst thing I ever did. But I did it anyway. I got a noon meal and an evening meal for doing this thirty-minute show. That was back in 1933 and '34. It was tough." The radio show, while not Eldon's favorite activity, provided him an opportunity to move into the band business. He had heard four musicians perform at a local club and invited them to be on his show. These four—Cotton Thompson, Harley Huggins, Carrel Jones, and Don Ivey—formed the nucleus of the popular Alabama Boys. But in early 1934 they were four musicians looking for work. They decided to try their luck in Tulsa, where they found a spot and scored a success on radio station KVOO. Later in 1934, Eldon was invited to join the newly formed Alabama Boys; after getting his foot in the door with the band, he also joined the KVOO staff band. The leader of the station band was clarinetist Charlie Lawton, who, according to Eldon, wanted to "swing the classics." Lawton and his sister Charlotte, who played harp in the KVOO ensemble, eventually went with the Hollywood Symphony Orchestra. Eldon began to get experience as an arranger during his tenure with the station orchestra because everything was played from notated scores.

Bob Wills happened to hear the radio program one day and offered Eldon a job with the Texas Playboys. Eldon had heard the Wills band and did not rate it favorably at all. "That was the stinkingest band I believe I ever heard." But Wills had an ear for music and an idea of the sound he wanted; he also had a magnetic personality that drew musicians and audiences in. The acquisition of Eldon Shamblin was one of his major steps toward creating one of the finest swing bands in the business.

Eldon joined Bob Wills and His Texas Playboys in 1937, by which time the group had been working out of Tulsa for some three years. Wills had begun improving his band from the moment he settled in Tulsa, adding Jesse Ashlock on second violin, Leon McAuliffe on the new amplified steel guitar, jazz pianist Al Stricklin, Everett Stover on trumpet, Robert "Zeb" McNally playing saxophone and clarinet, and Art Haines on trombone; in 1935 he took the unprecedented step of adding a drummer, William "Smoky" Dacus. But Eldon brought a new harmonic vocabulary into the band and expertise in big band swing arranging that literally turned the Playboys in a new musical direction.

Eldon first recorded as rhythm guitarist with the Playboys on a Columbia session in Dallas in May 1938. The two-day session produced ragtime and blues numbers, but also arrangements of Tin Pan Alley popular tunes like "Moonlight and Roses." Despite the clearly jazz nature of these 1938 releases, Columbia insisted on categorizing Bob Wills and His Texas Playboys as folk musicians.[36]

As a Texas Playboy, Eldon found himself playing a steady routine of dance jobs, and he was continuously amazed at the way Wills handled both the musicians on the bandstand and the large audiences in attendance. Wills seemed to tame the toughest joints and to keep his musicians constantly on their toes.

> He [Bob Wills] had a dynamic personality! Bob himself was such an entertainer! I can truthfully say that as many years as I was on the band, he never failed to entertain me. I enjoyed his antics on stage—super! And the people—I saw old people walk up front and sit or stand there for hours, and never move. Wills could take any kind of a band—that's what I used to tell the guys—I said, "Look, when the old man is sober and here, he doesn't need any of us." That's the way I always felt and I think that's true. He could get up there by himself and entertain the people. Then, if he wasn't there, there was nothing we could do to entertain those people. The guy was something else!

Bob Wills did not view himself as a one-man show, however, and shared the spotlight and the money equally with his musicians. Each member of the band was known by name to the regular customers and to record buyers because Wills identified each when it came solo time. Like most southwestern bands, the Playboys worked on a commonwealth plan whereby, after deducting hotel and transportation expenses, the gate receipts would be divided equally among the band members. According to Eldon, it was nothing unusual for each member to pocket a thousand dollars after a job, and this during the depression.

Wills could attract excellent musicians to the band because he paid well, offered wide exposure before an adoring public, and allowed musical freedom to his sidemen. Each individual had the complete freedom to play anything and everything he or she felt. Eldon explains, "Wills would let me get by with murder on some of those numbers. Anything I wanted to do I could do, as long as it was tasteful, like those chords I put on 'Faded Love.' Wills let me get by with that where most guys wouldn't, if they were country people. That makes a lot of difference. You played what you felt."

As the band grew in size, Eldon assumed more of the arranging chores. Because Wills was unpredictable in a performance situation, calling for solo choruses on the basis of feeling and audience response, Eldon never wrote a complete arrangement. "We would get a skeleton arrangement and let Bob hear it. If he liked it, he would play it again; if he didn't like it, he would never play it again." Wills had a regular scheme for playing numbers that Eldon found somewhat baffling at the beginning. "When I first joined the band, we would play a song through—regular arrangement. Then he'd turn around and play the same thing again. I said, 'Bob, why do you do that?' He said, 'Well, I'll tell you. You never lived on a farm, but I was raised on a farm. When you plow down to the end you have to plow back. I can't play down to the far end and stop. I've got to plow back.' And that was the explanation he always used."

After the "arranged" portion—actually the straight, unimprovised presentation of the melody—Wills would begin pointing his fiddle bow and calling the names of individual musicians to take improvised solo choruses. According to Eldon, "You never knew when he was going to point to you, or on what tune. No routine, he might give you a chorus on something you'd never played before."

By 1940 Wills had amassed an aggregation of first-rate musicians and had built a big swing band comparable to that of Tommy Dorsey, Count Basie, Bob Crosby, or Glenn Miller. He had added enough horns for a complete horn section and kept all of the strings, too. In fact, the front line was shared by violins, steel guitar, occasionally Eldon on lead guitar, trumpets, and reeds.[37] This was the type of band Wills had always wanted to front, and Eldon felt that it was an excellent ensemble. "Bob hired some horn men off of Woody Herman's band. Then he hired a full-time arranger and sax player who wrote a lot of fine, original arrangements. We had a girl singer, a male singer, five reeds, three trumpets, two trombones, plus strings. Even later when he went to California he tried to have that band again, but he never could get the right combination of people again."

This was an extremely versatile big band that could perform all types of music, as their recordings indicate: blues ("Empty Bed Blues"), fiddle tunes ("Beaumont Rag"), cowboy ballads ("Cool Water"), Spanish songs ("La Golondrina"), Hawaiian numbers ("Hawaiian War Chant"), South American novelties ("La Cucaracha"), Jimmie Rodgers hits ("Never No More Blues"), guitar favorites ("Steel Guitar Rag"), jazz arrangements ("I Ain't Got Nobody"), Tin Pan Alley tunes ("Sentimental Journey"), big band swing compositions ("In the Mood"), boogie-woogie ("Bottle Baby Boogie"), Wills's own compositions ("San Antonio Rose"), Ira and George Gershwin songs ("Oh Lady, Be Good"), Hoagy Carmichael's "Stardust," and even classical pieces such as Franz Liszt's "Liebestraum" and Gioacchino Rossini's "William Tell Overture."[38]

By the summer of 1940, Bob Wills and the Texas Playboys had become such an audience draw that Monogram Pictures hired them to appear in a film starring Tex Ritter, entitled *Take Me Back to Oklahoma*. The contract called for Wills and only a small string band, so most of the musicians had to remain in Tulsa; but Eldon made this first picture and the next one.

In July 1941 Wills was back in Hollywood, this time with his entire band, to make *Go West, Young Lady*, starring Glen Ford, Penny Singleton, Ann Miller, and Charles Ruggles. As he was to perform the entire Sammy Cahn score, Wills added more violins, oboes, flutes, and French horns to the band. Late summer of 1941 found the Playboys back in Tulsa and literally on top of the musical world.[39] Eldon remembers the days on the movie set as "the dullest thing that ever was." But the money was good, and playing the premieres somewhat exciting. "We were all on salary, and we made good money. We played the premieres in the towns, in these big theaters. Played six or seven shows a day when they were premiering these movies."

World War II caught the Playboys in the middle of their movie activity, and Wills had to appear in the next series of eight Russell Hayden films with a skeleton crew and without Eldon Shamblin. Wills hired Texas songwriter Cindy Walker to provide a good many songs for these films, thus promoting her career. And Eldon went into the army.[40]

After his discharge, Eldon returned to Tulsa and joined Leon McAuliffe's newly formed Cimarron Boys. With his five horns plus strings and modern arrangements, McAuliffe's Cimarron Boys was a musically outstanding swing band, but it lacked the public appeal of the Texas Playboys. Eldon admits that he was unhappy and ready to leave when Bob Wills called and asked him to rejoin the Texas Playboys. Wills had a hot young lead guitarist in Junior Barnard, who possessed what Eldon described as a "gouging style." But Junior was an unsettled individual, and Wills was hoping that Eldon would restore some stability to the band. "I was handling the business and Junior was playing guitar. Junior would get drunk once in a while, but when he'd get drunk then I'd play guitar. It didn't bother me. I didn't care. The pay was the same. I was interested in making a living. I wasn't looking for fame or glory." Eldon mixed playing guitar and managing through the mid-1950s. He made several national tours and recording sessions with Wills and in 1952 took over the job of running Wills Point.

Eldon Shamblin joined Bob Wills and the Texas Playboys in 1936, and except for his time in military service and a brief stint with Leon McAuliffe, he remained with Wills for some twenty years. His association with Wills and western swing brought Eldon to the attention of Merle Haggard, with whom he performed off and on for eighteen years. To begin with, Eldon worked the casinos in Lake Tahoe and Reno with Haggard, then eventually went on the road with him. According to Eldon, the time spent with Haggard set him up financially for retirement.

> Haggard was a super nice guy to work for; he made money. I always laugh to think about Haggard when he was talking about his office. When he'd get ready to take a tour, he would walk into the office, throw his billfold down on the desk in front of the bookkeeper, and say "Fill it up." We would normally play three days a week. We'd play these places and have twenty or thirty thousand people. We never played any washouts, and the price they were charging for tickets was pretty steep. They sold records, they sold everything. Haggard had a big business. He was getting about fifty thousand dollars a date.

Though the money was good, Eldon never experienced the musical freedom playing for Merle Haggard that he had known with Bob Wills, mainly because Haggard wrote most of his own material and wanted everything performed a certain way. Thus, when Leon McAuliffe called Eldon to become a charter member of the Original Texas Playboys after Bob Wills's death, Eldon was quick to make the move. Eldon was rhythm guitarist for the Original Texas Playboys until the group disbanded in 1987. He can still be heard at occasional western swing festivals and on recordings. He played electric guitar behind fiddlers Johnny Gimble and Mark O'Connor during the Dallas recording session at which "Fiddlin' Around" was produced for O'Connor's 1993 Warner album, *Heroes*.

Eldon has shared his guitar technique and theoretical knowledge with a large number of students. At Rogers State College in Claremore, Oklahoma, he taught guitar, music theory, and piano tuning; and at the Guitar House in Tulsa, he taught guitar classes with twenty-five to thirty students in each class. His method for teaching guitar is to avoid using a method. "Each student was a different ball game for me. I found out what they wanted to do and what they knew already, and I went from there. I didn't have any set pattern. I've always enjoyed teaching that way."

Eldon Shamblin is the quintessential western swing guitarist—strong on rhythm, innovative in his use of chords, and certainly up to an occasional lead solo. When he was first learning guitar, he listened to Eddie

Lang and Joe Venuti; and one of his most prized possessions is a picture taken of Eldon and Joe Venuti at a recording session in the mid-1960s.

Eldon also appreciated Django Reinhardt's playing and listened to young Charlie Christian working clubs in Oklahoma City. But he concludes: "I don't think I copied anybody, really. I don't feel like I did because there wasn't anybody to copy. I was working all the time, so I never had the opportunity to hear anybody else. I didn't have time to copy anyone." Considering the fact that Charlie Christian and Eldon Shamblin were born the same year and were in Oklahoma City at the same time, it is not inconceivable that their influence was reciprocal and that Charlie learned a thing or two from Eldon.

Eldon is certain about the influence of the big bands on his own burgeoning guitar style.

> I liked the big bands. I always liked Glenn Miller's band. I loved those bands. That's what I always listened to. When I joined the Wills band, I was always studying arranging and if you listened to music you always went over to the jukebox and played those big bands. When I started there were very few people you could listen to. You didn't have much variety unless you listened to big bands. That's what was on the radio all the time. That's what I always listened to on late-night broadcasts. I was familiar with all the pop tunes. I wasn't familiar with country music. That wasn't my thing. I figured it like this: you'd take the same music that the big bands played and play it with country instruments. I could play that style with any kind of music.

Eldon bemoans the fact that good rhythm section guitar players are hard to come by and blames it all on the fact that "most of the time when you find a guitar man, he wants to play lead all the time." Like Freddie Green with Count Basie, Eldon Shamblin was for many years the heartbeat of the Texas Playboys rhythm section. Eldon Shamblin is a modest man who dislikes the spotlight. If asked to demonstrate his formidable skill with the guitar, he will shyly protest that he does not play much. But in fact, Eldon plays a great deal, especially in the rhythm section of a western swing band, where he is most at home.

The life of BOB MURRELL illustrates two significant though little appreciated aspects of Texas jazz: first, not all of the great players have pursued careers as professional musicians; second, Texas jazz has been kept alive by hundreds of small bands with only local followings. Central Texas musicians express awe over Bob's talent as a guitarist, but Bob never made a full commitment to commercial music and never regretted that decision. "I've never made a living as a musician, or even tried. Strictly a hobby—for enjoyment, fellowship. I've worked in electronics . . . all through the years as my vocation."

Bob invented, built, and marketed one of the earliest music synthesizers. Called the Guitorgan, it was a "marriage of guitar and organ electronics. When you would play the guitar fingerboard, you would trigger organ sounds." Bob patented his Guitorgan in 1967 and produced it, along with medical technologies that grew out of it, until his company was bought out by a Beaumont firm in 1984. After selling his company, Bob began to work for various instrument retailers around Central Texas, repairing electronic music equipment, mostly amplifiers and synthesizers. Bob had his opportunities to go on the road as a professional guitarist, but the income seemed too uncertain, and life on the road too hazardous to family stability. Bob stayed home in Central Texas and managed to play constantly.

Bob Murrell was born in Waco, Texas, in 1925 and started learning to play steel guitar while attending Waco High School. He received two years of steel guitar instruction, using a Rickenbacker lap steel with one neck, six strings, and no foot pedals or knee levers. In time he found playing standard guitar personally more rewarding, and he switched.

Bob was eighteen before his parents would allow him to work in the honky-tonks around Waco. The main highways leading in and out of Waco were choked with these establishments after the repeal of Prohibition in 1933. In many respects, Waco was similar to New Orleans at the turn of the century—a magnet for musicians because of ample job opportunities in the house bands of numerous local clubs. There was also the busy Texas dance hall scene to keep bands occupied, especially on weekends. Because of its lively musical atmosphere, Waco produced many musicians, some of whom—like Hank Thompson and Willie Nelson—went on to achieve national fame.

Many of the local bands played a repertory of current popular hits and jazz arrangements, with only a smattering of country music. As Bob explained, "I've always leaned toward jazz because of the limitations of country music for the jazz musician." Bob Murrell was a jazz guitarist.

The number and variety of bands with which Bob worked beginning in the early 1940s is amazing. Before and during World War II he worked in a small combo called Marie and Her Buddies—organ, violin, guitar, saxophone, drums—that specialized in current popular standards. At the same time, he was playing in a couple of club bands and a dance hall band or two. For several years he was guitarist in the house band at the Tropical Club, just southeast of Waco. Organist Buddy Woody was leader of the band, which included saxophone, trumpet, drums, and guitar, a standard five-piece jazz combo with organ substituted for piano. Another club band in which Bob played worked at the Terrace Club, just north of Waco. Bob explained that many Waco musicians went on from the Terrace Club to greater opportunities in commercial music. But the Terrace Club was just plain hard work: "a very demanding job, six nights and Sunday afternoon, for forty or fifty dollars a week." With its instrumentation of violin, accordion, steel guitar, standard guitar, bass, and drums, the Terrace Club band played western swing, progressive jazz, and standard popular tunes.

Bob occasionally played steel guitar with the Lone Star Playboys, which had a Saturday morning radio show that broadcast from the Montgomery Ward mezzanine and played numerous dance engagements. This was a string band that not only played some western swing and some honky-tonk music but also staged comedy routines.

A more thoroughly western swing band with which Bob worked was the Texas Swingsters, an eight-piece combo started by drummer Doyle Brink. With Glyn Duncan, brother of Bob Wills's singer Tommy Duncan, on bass and vocals, twin fiddles, a couple of horns, accordion, and guitar, the Texas Swingsters consciously modeled themselves after Bob Wills and the Texas Playboys. Like many local Texas dance bands, the Texas Swingsters did not record; nevertheless, they earned the reputation of being "a good dance band."

After his tour of duty in the navy during World War II, Hank Thompson returned to his hometown of Waco and began his climb to stardom. Bob Murrell was a member of Thompson's first band, the Brazos Valley Boys, and participated on Thompson's first recording session in Dallas. The original band consisted of six pieces—two standard guitars, steel guitar, accordion, fiddle, and bass. Thompson became popular in Central Texas, but there were so many local bands that bookings were scarce, forcing all of the Brazos Valley Boys to work in other groups as well.

Thompson specialized in putting on stage shows, with music and comedy routines, at area schools.

> He would book tours—Penelope, Bynum, these little outlying schools. In those days it was a big thing to have anyone in for entertainment. Those school gymnasiums would be packed, real responsive. We played an occasional dance. But most of his things here were strictly stage shows, just a little variety act. Everybody would be featured on their instrument doing their thing. He had a girl singer. Charlie Adams had joined him on bass instead of Tommy Williams on the record. Charlie stuttered terribly, but like Mel Tillis, he could get up and sing all day. They worked up little comedy routines, Charlie and Hank. Hank was a good emcee. And those comedy skits were a big part of the act.

Playing in Thompson's band gave Bob his longest exposure to country music. Of Thompson Bob says, "Originally he was strictly honky-tonk. It was also classified as hillbilly in that era. He would not tolerate even thinking about drums in the band. That was just not done. And it had to be simple chord changes, as opposed to western swing, which has a heavy, dominating rhythm section and good chord changes. He didn't go into western swing until he moved to Oklahoma—the Wills influence there might have been a factor." Bob had known a measure of freedom in the other club and western swing bands in the area, but not as a member of the Brazos Valley Boys. "Hank's regime was structured, disciplined. You play this passage, that type of thing. We played what he wanted, same way every night."

About 1952 Bob joined a group called the George Nethery Orchestra, which played popular and jazz arrangements for military bases, country club parties, and other society affairs around Central Texas. Bob worked with Nethery until the music scene began to change and Nethery refused to change with it. "The young people coming up wanted the Beatles and Beach Boys, and whatever was going on at that time [early 1960s] in rockabilly and rock 'n' roll. So George faded from the scene."

Waco drummer and music entrepreneur Bill Mounce, formerly of the Texas Playboys, picked up the slack and developed what Bob described as "a stable of local musicians." Mounce became the principal booking agent in Waco, organizing bands to fit every kind of job. Bob was one of the many qualified musicians who enjoyed steady work with Mounce. "That was good experience, playing with different groups all the time and developing styles to be compatible." Before his death in 1995, Bob was the regular guitarist in a favorite local big band fronted by Harold Strand, who programmed the swing music that Bob loved to play.

When asked who had influenced his guitar style, Bob enumerated a great many musicians, including the electric mandolinist for Bob Wills, Billie "Tiny " Moore, jazz guitarists Johnny Smith, Tal Farlow, and Barney Kessel, and popular guitarist Les Paul. Tiny Moore, so nicknamed because he was an extremely large teenage boy, went to work for Bob Wills in 1946, spent two years on the road, then took charge of Wills Point. For six years, from 1956 to 1962, Tiny hosted his own kids' television show, *Ranger Roy and the Anna Banana Show*. Then in 1972 he began a thirteen-year stint with the Merle Haggard band.[41] Bob Murrell explained that Tiny Moore "made the mandolin sound like a guitar" and that he had "learned some of Tiny's licks." The other four guitarists mentioned by Bob encompass the entire field of modern guitar playing. Motivated by his naturally inquisitive and creative mind, Bob Murrell gathered ideas and techniques from varied sources and, combining them with his own musical instincts, brought a wealth of guitar playing to the various Central Texas bands with which he worked. He could have followed many jazz musicians out of Texas and into larger musical arenas, where he would have undoubtedly been acknowledged as one of the top-rated jazz guitarists, but the lure of family and job stability proved too strong.

Pure, nondance jazz has struggled for recognition in Texas, and Bob offers his years of observation as an explanation.

> People don't understand jazz. Jazz has to be listened to. You can't have a jazz band going over here, sit at a table and have intimate conversations with your lovey-dovey or talk about football games. You've got to listen to it to enjoy it. If you don't, it's noise. And that's always been the limitation of jazz. People go to jazz clubs in New York or Chicago and sit there and listen; they don't go there to socialize. You listen for the appreciation of the improvisation or what the arranger was trying to convey.

Bob agreed with his idol, Barney Kessel, that what is said by the improviser or arranger must express the individual: "A jazz chorus is not pure jazz unless they're expressing it from within themselves."

BENNY GARCIA was born in Oklahoma City in 1930. A self-taught guitarist who admired Charlie Christian and wanted to play just like him,

Benny began playing guitar and working while he was still in high school. His first professional job was an early-morning show on radio station WKY. After playing the 6:30 A.M. broadcast each day, Benny would hurry on to school. He also played some nights at the Harbor Lights Club and was bringing in over seventy-five dollars a week, good pay for a high school boy. Eventually the long hours and the schoolwork caught up with Benny. "I finally got fired because I couldn't get to the radio show." Both the radio band and the club band were swing combos that played western swing numbers and popular song arrangements. Benny remembers happily that he acquired his first electric guitar while playing with the Harbor Lights Club band.

About 1946 or 1947, Benny went to work for another radio station in Oklahoma City, and this was how Tex Williams happened to hear him and invite him to join his Western Caravan. "Tex Williams was doing a show at the Warner Theater, when I was working for radio station KOMA. And they came up to the station—Tex and Smokey Rogers and Pedro DePaul, and Deuce Spriggens. They listened to our regular show, and then after we got off the air they asked me if I were interested in going to California. I said, 'Yes, I am.'"

The Western Caravan at this time included Tex Williams (band leader, vocals, guitar), Smokey Rogers (vocals, guitar, banjo), Deuce Spriggens (vocals, bass), Pedro DePaul (accordion, arranger), Cactus Soldi (fiddle), Rex "Curly" Call (fiddle), Max "Gibby" Fidler (fiddle), Johnny Weiss (lead guitar), Ozzie Godson (piano, vibraphone), Spike Featherstone (harp), Muddy Berry (drums), and the incomparable Joaquin Murphy (steel guitar). Williams had a recording contract with Capitol Records, and Benny played on the 1947 session that produced Williams's greatest hit, "Smoke, Smoke, Smoke That Cigarette," which climbed to the top of both country and popular music charts. Benny was also part of the Western Caravan band that recorded the magnificent *Artistry in Western Swing* album, a western swing response to Stan Kenton's monumental *Artistry in Swing*. Benny recalls that they had to hire jazz flutist Ezzie Morales to play the flute parts on the Kenton arrangements.

Williams also played regular engagements at such large dance halls as the Santa Monica Ballroom, Venice Pier, and the Riverside Rancho. Like Spade Cooley, Tex Williams cultivated a band sound that was polished and rhythmically smooth. They played from arrangements and rehearsed endlessly to achieve a tight ensemble. Williams also featured Smokey Rogers and Deuce Spriggens in comedy routines.[42]

Benny worked in California some ten years, three of which he spent with Tex Williams and the Western Caravan. During those years he heard and marveled at the Spade Cooley band, but he could not help but notice that it was Bob Wills who drew the largest crowds. After his three years with Tex Williams, Benny went on tour with T. Texas Tyler and then joined Hank Penny's swing combo, for which he played on the recording session that produced the popular song "Little Red Wagon." Hank Penny and Benny Garcia specialized in playing jazzy twin guitar numbers, and they also enjoyed frequent visitations from such guitar giants as Barney Kessel. "He'd come in and play. Man, you talk about nervous, I was sweating! But I did fine. I'd sit there just having fun. That's the whole idea!"

In 1952 Benny was drafted; the United States was once again embroiled in war, this time in Korea. When he was discharged in 1954, Benny returned to Oklahoma and went to work for Johnnie Lee Wills in Tulsa. Then, about 1958, Benny was invited to join Bob Wills and the Texas Playboys. Wills was spending most of his time in Las Vegas, Lake Tahoe, and on national tours at this time. Johnnie Lee gave up his band and the daily broadcasts on Tulsa's KVOO and joined brother Bob in Las Vegas. It is said that Bob Wills enjoyed neither Las Vegas nor the cross-country tours except for the money; and his need for money to buttress his floundering financial empire kept Wills going.

Benny spent almost two years as a member of the Playboys, thus amassing five years with two of the best western swing bands in the business. When asked to compare the Playboys and the Western Caravan, Benny first points to rhythmic differences. "I don't think the Tex Williams band was quite that heavy on two and four. Williams was smoother. But Bob had that heavy dance beat. You just had to dance to that." Though Williams relied more on intricate arrangements than did Wills, Benny never felt restricted on either band. "I always played the way I felt," he explains. "With Tex Williams, we'd either have a three-part thing to do [Benny, Johnny Weiss, and Joaquin Murphy], or Tex might want Johnny to take sixteen bars, and me take another sixteen, and then the steel guitar, kind of like Bob. It was a way to stretch it out, keep a lot of people dancing." And, of course, with Wills, Benny experienced the famous bow-in-your-direction move that could come at any time and meant to play everything possible.

Tex Williams and Bob Wills, two of the best swing band leaders in the business! What other wonders could befall the guitarist from Oklahoma

City? How about playing in Benny Goodman's orchestra? "Benny Goodman heard me playing at a place called the Keyboard Club, right here in Oklahoma City. The piano player, Dick Shreeve, had worked for Benny Goodman, and Benny was coming to Oklahoma City. Richard insisted I come out and play so that Benny Goodman could hear me, and I did. He took my number, and he said, 'I'm going to be calling you.' And he did call."

Benny's hero Charlie Christian had been a headliner on the Goodman band. Benny worked off and on with Goodman for over two years in the early 1960s, and this work included recording sessions in Los Angeles. A modest man, Benny refuses to brag about the talent that led to his being part of the Goodman organization, but he does not mask his joy over his good fortune. "It was the thrill of a lifetime—almost as much thrill as being with Bob Wills. That was really a thrill for me. But Benny was a different player, you know, different kind of music, which is really what I got into when I first started playing. I learned all those old tunes. We used to do them on the Goodman band, and that was really a thrill. I should have been paying him." Goodman did not play as broad a spectrum of music as did Williams or Wills because he did not incorporate the folk music and rural blues; but all three bandleaders encouraged creative improvisation from their sidemen. "The feeling was there. You had freedom. Goodman wanted you to stretch out; he'd let you really play. As a matter of fact, he'd really make you play three or four choruses, which I'm not used to doing. Bob wouldn't let you do that; it's one chorus is enough. Goodman was different about that; he'd let you go three, and I about died. That was really too much."

But Benny Garcia survived to play more swing music as a member of the Playboys II band, fronted by Johnny Gimble, and as the guitarist in a trio with his lifelong friend and musical colleague, drummer Tommy Perkins. In the trio arrangements Benny must play melody, chords, and rhythm, but he regards himself as a melodist like Charlie Christian. In fact, he still uses a guitar he bought many years ago because of its similarity to the one Christian played. "It's an old L-7 [similar to the ES-150] with a straight bar pickup. Looks like the old Charlie Christian guitar. That's why I wanted it. I found one almost like it. Still got it, and I'll always have it."

KEN FRAZIER is a youngster in comparison with the other guitarists discussed in this chapter; but his inclusion in many western swing pickup bands, especially those assembled by Johnny Gimble, proves that he has thoroughly assimilated and perfected swing guitar styling. Ken was born in Waco, Texas, in 1938. His father, an amateur harmonica player, bought Ken his first guitar, an old Stella model, when the boy was six years old. Though it was a poor-quality instrument, Ken began teaching himself to play it and was soon accompanying his father during family gatherings.

Ken's father worked at a dry goods store in Waco, and it was the owner of the store who presented Ken with his first decent guitar, a Gibson Junior, when Ken was eight years old. With this guitar Ken began competing on local talent shows and performing professionally. His burgeoning career suffered a setback, however, when he contracted rheumatic fever and was forced to spend three months in bed. During this long period of recuperation, Ken's best friends were the radio, his Viewmaster, and his guitar. Listening to such radio programs as Hal Horton's *Hillbilly Hit Parade* out of Dallas, Tex Williams's Western Caravan, the Spade Cooley and Bob Wills bands, Pee Wee King, *Ozark Jubilee*, and Ernest Tubb on Nashville station WSM provided Ken an education in musical repertory and technique.

Ken recovered and celebrated his ninth birthday with the help of a family friend, Hank Thompson, who had just returned from the navy and was rapidly becoming a popular entertainer in Waco. Ken has fond memories of Thompson singing and playing for the birthday party guests and of the friendship that developed between them. In fact, when Thompson married on the Hal Horton radio program, Ken, age eleven, played guitar for the ceremony.

His eleventh year was another bad one for Ken, as he was stricken once again with rheumatic fever and restricted to his bed for another three months. This time he practiced guitar with the aid of a tape recorder, which allowed him to tape songs off the radio.

Ken began playing in bands at the age of thirteen. Besides the usual honky-tonks and taverns, he became part of the show band for *The Waco Jamboree Music Show*, which broadcast every Saturday night from Wright's Arena. This show band gave Ken his first opportunity to play lead guitar. By the time he was fifteen, Ken's course was set. He left school and went on the road with Charlie Adams and the Western All Stars. Adams was a Columbia recording artist who started out as a country singer, in the style of Hank Williams, Johnny Horton, and others. After Hank Thompson's big swing band became popular, Adams decided to convert his hillbilly band to a swing band and play Thompson and Bob

Wills arrangements. To this end he added a second fiddle player and a jazz pianist. As with the Hank Thompson show, when Adams was on stage the music was country, but when he left the stage, his band was transformed into a western swing band. The Charlie Adams band spent three months at Jack Ruby's Roundup Club in Dallas; and it was in Dallas that Ken met outstanding musicians like guitar player Leon Rhodes and jazz violinist Steve Davis, who introduced him to Barney Kessel recordings. Sixteen-year-old Ken Frazier bought his first Barney Kessel album and became a devoted Kessel disciple.

When the Charlie Adams band broke up after traveling a wide circuit of towns in Texas, New Mexico, Oklahoma, and Louisiana, Ken returned to Waco, where Johnny Gimble was scheduled to co-host KWTX television's *Home Folks Show*. Ken was hired to play guitar on the show's first broadcast, after which he took a job at the Peacock Club in San Angelo as lead guitarist for singer Larry Butler. Butler was a country singer and was not drawing nearly as well as a western swing band down the street at the Dixie Club. When Butler took a leave of absence from the job, Ken converted his hillbilly band into a western swing band. Two months later, Butler returned and immediately fired Ken.

The year was 1957, and Ken returned again to Waco, this time to play guitar in Clyde Chesser's band. With a Saturday-evening television show on Channel 6 and frequent engagements at schools and fund-raisers, Clyde Chesser was well known in the Waco area. The band's repertory was a mixture of country and current popular songs.

Having been in the music business since he was a teenager, Ken grew tired of the pressure and dropped out for a brief time. He returned to music in 1958 to play guitar in a local rock and roll band called the Down Beats. This band included Gaylyn Christi on steel guitar, Dale McBride on rhythm guitar and vocals, Jack Fletcher playing saxophone, Big Jim Lawrence on trombone and bass, Mike McClain playing drums, and Ken Frazier on lead guitar. In 1958 Ken was also part of the house band at Waco's famous Terrace Club.

On January 1, 1959, Ken joined the road band of rockabilly recording star Buddy Knox of "Party Doll" fame. After a year with Knox, Ken joined the Jimmy Heap Show out of Taylor, Texas, and remained with Heap for six years, both as lead guitarist and chief arranger. Jimmy Heap was also a nationally known recording artist and much in demand as a show performer in the Southwest. The Jimmy Heap Show was a mixture of comedy routines and assorted popular tunes, show tunes, and original numbers.

When Ken left the Heap band in 1966, it was to further his education. He first earned his GED, then spent a semester at Baylor University in Waco before finishing an associate degree in business and computer programming at McLennan Community College. After college, Ken worked as a salesman and guitar instructor at Thomas Goggan Brothers' music store in Waco. In 1979 he became part of McLennan Community College's commercial music faculty, teaching private guitar and practical theory, arranging, and improvisation courses. He is still a respected member of the McLennan Community College faculty and plays frequently as a freelance guitarist. With his large repertory—country, western swing, popular, and rock—Ken is a versatile and much-in-demand guitarist.[43]

Ken lists as his major influences Barney Kessel, Tal Farlow, Joe Pass, Herb Ellis, Howard Roberts, and Jimmy Wyble. Ken Frazier, like Herb Ellis, is a true Texas guitarist, imbued with the same powerful rhythmic drive and blues colorings. Perhaps for Ken it was less a matter of being influenced by Ellis than of relating to him. Like Roberts, Ken is a complete guitarist who understands every facet of guitar playing. Ken Frazier has experienced much good guitar playing by listening to and emulating his guitar heroes, but his ears have also been keen to other sources—to the techniques of mandolinist Tiny Moore, the big chords of steel guitarist Noel Boggs, and the intricate arrangements used by the Spade Cooley band. Ken assimilated all of this musical data and fused it into his own distinctive style. Like most great guitarists, he can match his style to the context. When he is accompanying a soloist, whether vocal or instrumental, he plays large chords, intentionally sounding like a horn section and providing kicks and coloring to the solo line. And when he is soloing, Ken thinks in terms of the chord structures and their myriad alterations; he plays so as to emphasize chord changes and resolutions. Like Ellis and Kessel, Ken never fails to swing; he cannot help but swing, which sometimes makes playing in country bands a difficult adjustment.

As a jazz guitarist, Ken has mastered the art of improvisation and has this to say about the process.

> Ninety percent of the things that are being played while a person improvises are pre-learned. It's a lick that fits over a chord. The skilled improviser, just like a computer, scans his memory because he anticipates the chord change, and he hears what is going to fit.

At any one time, only ten percent of a solo is truly improvised. The other ninety percent is pre-learned, rearranged and linked together. That's the only spontaneity, really. I've learned from other people. I'll take a phrase or a two-bar motif . . . and all of a sudden I'll catch myself playing it, because there is something reminiscent of that song in the song I am playing. It seems to fit. A lot of times you have to modify a motif to make it fit a certain spot. You'll modify these things, and you'll play sequences like digital patterns. Once you play them three or four times, you're going to modify them until they become yours.[44]

Ken would rather work in a swing band because of the freedom of creativity and the rhythmic drive that identifies the swing style.

Swing is very syncopated, with driving, tight rhythm sections. Even the solos are rhythmically driving. It has its own characteristics: accents placed on the weak part of the beat, coming in with an accented upbeat, staying on the upbeat instead of the downbeat. . . . That lifts the rhythm section. You learn what to do by copying. I think Johnny Gimble was a big influence on me because he never told me how to play, and he never told me what to play; he just set an example. . . . I may not play his exact solos, but all the influences are there. It is hard for me to play unswing, to play a straight-ahead, on-the-beat solo because I want to swing. We haven't talked about chord substitutions, about chord progressions that include the diminished chords that swing players were playing back then that country pickers never touched. But the swing players were looking for those types of chords as vehicles for improvisation. They learned the diminished arpeggio. They learned the octatonic scale. And if you start coloring these chords, like a major I chord —if you start coloring it with anything besides the pentatonic scale—using the major VII, the sharp elevens, the flat thirteens, then you're out of the realm of country music, you're in the realm of jazz.[45]

With his obvious knowledge of the rhythmic, harmonic, melodic, and improvisatory elements of swing jazz, Ken Frazier is one of the best jazz guitarists working today; and only the fact that he, like Eldon Shamblin and Bob Murrell, has worked primarily in western swing has kept him out of the jazz guitar style books.

Cliff Bruner and the Texas Wanderers about 1938. *Left to right, standing:* Rip Ramsey (bass), Morris Gleason (banjo), Cliff Bruner (fiddle), Elmer Goodman (bus driver), J. R. Chatwell (fiddle), Morris Deason (guitar); *seated:* Alton Durden (steel), Max Bennett (piano). Courtesy of Cliff Bruner.

Cliff Bruner and the Texas Wanderers in New York City for a recording session, 1944. *Left to right, rear:* Moon Mullican (piano), Link Davis (saxophone), Logan Conger (guitar), Jimmy Allen (bass), Harris Dodds (steel); *front:* Cliff Bruner (fiddle), Buddy DuHon (guitar/vocals), Curley DeLoache (drums). Courtesy of Cliff Bruner.

Carroll Hubbard in the 1940s.
Courtesy of Carroll Hubbard.

Moon Mullican and the Showboys at the Forest Club, Beaumont, Texas, 1947.
Left to right: Deacon Anderson (steel), Shang Kennedy (bass), Clyde Brewer (fiddle),
Cotton Thompson (fiddle), Merle Powell (drums), Mutt Collins (guitar), Moon
Mullican (piano). Courtesy of Clyde Brewer.

Jerry Irby's band at the Texas Corral, Houston, 1948. *Left to right:* Clyde Brewer (fiddle), Tony Sepolia (fiddle), Colley Sturrock (bass), Sleepy Tompkins (steel), Deacon Evans (fiddle), Jack Kennedy (drums), Jerry Irby (guitar), Pete Burke (piano). Courtesy of Clyde Brewer.

Bob Wills (*kneeling in front*) and the Texas Playboys, late 1940s or early 1950s. Courtesy of Burl Taylor.

Bob Wills and the Texas Playboys, 1953. *Left to right, top:* Bill Cheate, Keith Coleman, Jack Greenback, Billy Bowman, Skeeter Elkins; *bottom:* Eldon Shamblin, Bob Wills, Louise Rowe, Jack Lloyd. Courtesy of Louise Rowe Beasley.

Glenn Rhees (saxophone) and Bob Wills (fiddle) at Cain's Academy, Tulsa, February 8, 1958. Courtesy of Mrs. Glenn Rhees.

Bob Wills and the Texas Playboys at the Division Street Corral, Portland, Oregon, August 29, 1959. *Left to right:* Glenn Rhees (saxophone), Rufus Thibodeaux (fiddle), Casey Dickens (vocals), Leon Rausch (guitar/vocals), Wade Peeler (drums), Bob Wills (fiddle), Luke Wills (bass). Courtesy of Mrs. Glenn Rhees.

Bob Wills and the Texas Playboys at the Showboat in Las Vegas, June 1959. *Left to right:* Laura Lee Owens McBride (vocals), Gene Crownover (steel), Glenn Rhees (saxophone), Rufus Thibodeaux (fiddle), Bobby Lord (from the Grand Ole Opry), Wade Peeler (drums), Dickey McBride (vocals), Bob Wills (fiddle), Luke Wills (bass), Johnnie Lee Wills (banjo), Leon Rausch (guitar/vocals), Darla Darrett (vocals). Courtesy of Mrs. Glenn Rhees.

Bob Wills and the Texas Playboys at the Golden Nugget in Las Vegas, September 4, 1960. *Left to right:* Luke Wills, Glenn Rhees, Judy Kay Fencestermark, Gene Crownover, Bob Wills, Wade Peeler, Leon Rausch, Jack Lloyd. Courtesy of Mrs. Glenn Rhees.

Bob Wills and the McKinney Sisters, Dean (*with microphone*) and Evelyn. Courtesy of Louise Rowe Beasley.

The Seven Rowe Brothers with Al Dexter, 1949. *Left to right:* Lightnin' Rowe, A. D. Rowe, Hank Rowe, Jody Byers, Al Dexter, Jack Rowe, Earl Rowe, Luke Rowe, Buddy Combs. Courtesy of Louise Rowe Beasley. Guy Rowe not shown.

Tommy Allsup and the Southernaires, Hobbs, New Mexico, 1957. *Left to right:* Chuck Caldwell (steel), Louise Rowe Allsup (bass), Tommy Allsup (guitar), Danny Lucas (drums), Mancel Tierney (piano), Louis Tierney (saxophone/fiddle). Courtesy of Louise Rowe Beasley.

The Western Allstars at the Aragon Ballroom, Dallas, 1958. *Left to right, top:* Jimmy Belkin, Jesse Harris, Louise Rowe, Lyle Wommack, Reuben Arnold; *bottom:* Jerry (last name unknown), Johnny Manson, Eddy Willis, Leon Chambers. Courtesy of Louise Rowe Beasley.

Dewey Grooms and His Texas Longhorns, 1950s. Curle Hollingsworth is standing on the right end. Courtesy of Curle Hollingsworth.

The Miller Brothers Band, 1950s. Curle Hollingsworth is standing second from the end on the right. Photograph courtesy of Curle Hollingsworth.

The McKinney Sisters, Dean (*left*) and Evelyn. Courtesy of Louise Rowe Beasley.

Bobby Bruce. Courtesy of
Bobby Bruce.

Tommy Morrell. Courtesy of
Tommy Morrell.

Johnny Cuviello at a western
swing awards night in
Sacramento, California, 1994.
Courtesy of Johnny Cuviello.

Truitt Cunningham. Courtesy of
Truitt Cunningham.

Truitt Cunningham and the San Antonio Rose Band. *Left to right:* Skeeter Elkins (piano), Tommy Wheat (lead guitar), Bobby Boatright (fiddle), Truitt Cunningham (bass/vocals), Glenn Rhees (saxophone), Casey Dickens (drums), Bobby Koefer (steel), Duke Brown (rhythm guitar), Curley Lewis (fiddle). Courtesy of Truitt Cunningham.

The Original River Road Boys. *Left to right:* Herb Remington (steel guitar), Jim Johnson (vocals), Pee Wee Doyle (bass), Bill Dessens (guitar/fiddle), Tommy Houser (drums), Clyde Brewer (piano/fiddle). Courtesy of Clyde Brewer.

FOUR

The Steel Guitar in Western Swing

he steel guitar, a little-explored string instrument, is practically a requirement in western swing bands. It is easily identified by its characteristic note-bending and glissandi, and in the hands of a gifted player, it is capable of an incredible variety of effects. Those who have seen western swing bands in live performance realize that the steel guitar looks different from standard guitars and is played by a combination of finger-picking and sliding a metal bar along the strings. But few observers grasp the enormity of the task involved in mastering the instrument, both technically and in terms of its potential for effects.

The steel guitar originated in Hawaii as a variant of the Spanish guitar, which was introduced by Mexican cattle herders around 1830. The Hawaiians converted the Spanish guitar to their own musical tastes. First, the tuning was adjusted to an open, or "slack key," tuning so that the strings correlated with the notes of a major triad. Then Hawaiian guitarists laid the standard instrument flat across their knees and used objects such as combs or knives to slide along the fret board and produce the glissandi common to Hawaiian music. Thus was the Hawaiian guitar born.[1]

The Hawaiian-guitar style of playing was popularized in the United States by touring Hawaiian groups around the time of World War I.[2] American folk musicians, primarily rural blues men, had developed a related method of sliding knives or bottlenecks along the fingerboards of their standard guitars in order to obtain a wailing sound. Thus, the gliding and bending style of Hawaiian guitarists was familiar to southern listeners, but the positioning of the guitar flat in the player's lap was a new approach. The Hawaiian guitar was quickly absorbed into country music, becoming a fixture in the South-west by the late 1930s and gaining popularity in the Southeast as well. Author Charles T. Brown, in characterizing the country and western tra-dition, states: "The steel guitar is one of the most important instruments in country music; often the character of the country sound is defined by the steel guitar." [3]

Quick to capitalize on the growing popularity of the Hawaiian gui-tar, U.S. companies began to produce and market an instrument with a raised nut to hold the strings higher above the fingerboard and a steel bar for slide playing, thereby giving rise to the label "steel guitar." [4] The steel guitar suffered from the same problem of insufficient volume that affected the standard guitar in a band context; and like the standard guitar, only electrical amplification could enable the steel guitar to compete with horns.

The earliest experiments with electrical amplification of the guitar occurred in the United States in the 1920s and 1930s. There is much dis-agreement regarding who first devised a workable guitar pickup, thus solving the primary problem of guitar amplification, and names such as Lloyd Loar and Lewis A. Williams, Rowe and DeArmond, Beauchamp, Barth, and Rickenbacker are bantered about. But there is general agree-ment that electrical amplification was applied to the steel guitar before the standard guitar and that the Adolph Rickenbacker company (Electro String Instruments) out of California was the first to commercially pro-duce and market amplified steel guitars, beginning in 1931. [5] Guitar his-torian Tony Bacon gives this account of Adolph Rickenbacker (1887–1976), the California tool and die maker of Swiss extraction who is cred-ited with the amplification of steel guitars:

> [Rickenbacker] first had dealings with the guitar industry in the late 1920s when he made bodies and other parts for the National String Instrument Corporation, makers of the Dobro. The designer George Beauchamp left National in about 1930 and formed with Rickenbacker the Electro String Instrument Company. In 1931 Electro introduced two models of electric steel guitar, the A22 and A25, designed to be played across the knees; they were nick-named "Frying Pans" because of their round bodies and long necks. Probably designed by Beauchamp in collaboration with another former National employee, Paul Barth, these guitars are generally referred to as the world's first commercially produced electric gui-tars, though there are other contenders for the title. During the

1930s and 1940s they made mainly lap electric steel guitars (including instruments with a double neck) and free-standing electric Hawaiian guitars.[6]

In his photographic book *American Guitars: An Illustrated History*, Tom Wheeler insists that the first "Frying Pan" was built by another former National employee, Harry Watson, out of maple and that its body dimensions were 31¾ inches long, 7 inches wide, and 1⅝ thick, with twenty-five frets, celluloid binding, and a molded synthetic plate encasing its heavy tungsten horseshoe magnet. The commercially marketed A22 and A25 models were made of cast aluminum. The A22 was the smaller of the two instruments, 22½ inches long, compared with the A25's 25-inch scale. Both had volume knobs but no tone controls. By the early 1940s, Rickenbacker's Electro Strings was producing the Model B, a black guitar-shaped lap steel with both tone and volume controls and white fret markers. Rickenbacker also manufactured some early double-neck lap steel guitars.[7]

By the late 1930s, other U.S. guitar manufacturers had added lap steel guitars to their product lines. Gibson advertised its first electric Hawaiian guitar, the EH-150, in January 1936. This was a six-string, 13½-inch-long maple body lap model with twenty-nine fret markers, one cobalt-magnet straight-bar pickup, a rosewood fingerboard, and both tone and volume controls. In 1940 the Gibson guitar company added six pedals to the freestanding steel guitar, creating the first pedal steel. Dubbed the Electroharp, it was the brainchild of machinist John Moore.[8]

The steel guitar evolved rapidly from the time it was first introduced by Hawaiian groups around 1917. By the 1950s some models had as many as four necks, and others included knee-levers and several pedals to accomplish rapid tuning changes. When an instrument had multiple necks, one was usually set aside for special effects, like bird calls and train whistles.[9]

The steel guitar has been part of the western swing ensemble since Milton Brown "crystallized the basic instrumentation, style and repertoire" of the music.[10] It was a bold move that Brown made in 1934 when he hired Bob Dunn, a former jazz trombonist and guitarist, to play steel guitar in the Musical Brownies. Brown's musical concept for his band included re-creating the sound of a horn section on the steel guitar. Like a section of saxophones, Bob Dunn produced harmony and hornlike riffs behind soloists and played horn-inspired solos when called upon to take a chorus. As a front-line player, Dunn participated in melodic duets and trios with fiddles and, occasionally, guitars. Bob Dunn made the steel guitar an essential member of the western swing band.

Dunn increased the volume on his steel guitar by attaching a crude pickup that allowed the sound to be sent through an amplifier. Though the Rickenbacker A22 and A25 "Frying Pans" had been available since 1931, Dunn worked his electronic magic on a standard guitar played across his knees in Hawaiian style. A picture of the Musical Brownies taken at one of their WBAP radio broadcasts in 1935 shows Dunn seated on the front row with what appears to be a Dobro, probably a single-resonator Duolian built and marketed by National Guitar Company in the early 1930s.[11] The bodies of these guitars were made of a brass alloy that could be given a walnut coloring. The typical Duolian had a twelve-fret mahogany neck, slotted peghead, and f-holes cut into the upper body. A metal plate with four ribs running from center to rim covered the single ten-inch resonator. The Duolian was built in both the round-neck Spanish and flat-neck Hawaiian styles.[12] It was to a guitar such as this that Bob Dunn connected a pickup and amplifier; using this homemade amplified steel guitar, he recorded with the Musical Brownies in 1935. Jazz historians have credited guitarist George Barnes of Chicago with being the first to record with an electric guitar, backing blues artists in Chicago in 1935.[13] But Bob Dunn was also recording with an electric guitar—an electric steel guitar—in Chicago in January of 1935, and quite possibly he preceded Barnes. The fact is that steel guitar has been afforded no place in jazz guitar history.

But the steel guitar and Bob Dunn have major places in western swing jazz history, for Dunn was the progenitor of western swing steel guitar style. Since the steel guitar was new to jazz, other guitarists attempted to analyze Dunn's techniques, which was difficult because Dunn was imitating horns. One thing was certain: Bob Dunn did not produce whiny country steel sounds or ethereal Hawaiian effects. On "Taking Off," recorded in Chicago in January 1935 by the Musical Brownies on the Decca label, Dunn played jazz hot licks and riffs that sounded remarkably like a very good trombone player on two outstanding solo choruses. With his lead-off chorus, Dunn set the pace for the performance and challenged the other musicians to improvise at his level. Behind the subsequent solos Dunn barred large chords that sounded like a horn section providing background fills.[14]

Bob Dunn brought jazz to the steel guitar and the steel guitar to jazz. He established the steel guitar as a charter member of the western swing band and outlined its harmonic and melodic functions. But it was another steel guitar player, Leon McAuliffe, who popularized the instrument.

Leon McAuliffe was born near Houston around 1919. A musically precocious youth, he was working as staff steel guitarist for Houston radio station KPRC by the age of fourteen. Because the steel guitar was relatively new, Leon had no steel guitar heroes upon whom to model a style. As he told David Stricklin in a 1985 interview,

> I learned to play Hawaiian music because that's what the steel guitar was primarily used for. And the pop music of the day, the big bands didn't use it because the volume wasn't there. You couldn't compete with horns, and so about the only other outlet was a little trio, and the normal trio was a steel guitar, a standard guitar, and a ukulele. We learned Hawaiian music, and then, of course, I was listening to the popular records of the day. I saw my first musical with Bing Crosby, *The Big Broadcast*, and things like this. And I wanted to learn things other than Hawaiian music.[15]

Leon got his chance to play something other than Hawaiian music in 1933, when at the age of fourteen he was hired by the Light Crust Doughboys.

> W. Lee O'Daniel wanted a steel guitar in the band and he just didn't happen to find one in Fort Worth. So he called his sales manager in Houston and said, "See if you can find me a steel guitar player." Well, the first place he went was to KPRC there, which was part of the Texas Quality Network. I happened to be the only steel player on KPRC. So he got hold of me and I auditioned for him a little bit. He said, "Sounds all right to me. But I'll send you up to Fort Worth and pay your expenses up there and you can audition for the folks that know." I went to Fort Worth and auditioned on Monday morning, and they put me on the radio program that day. There wasn't much competition, I'll put it that way.

At this point the Light Crust Doughboys was simply a Texas fiddle band that played a fairly traditional repertory. The only leads were provided by Bob Wills on fiddle and Milton Brown singing, and everyone else fulfilled harmony and rhythm functions. Leon recalled that in the beginning he did not have much to do: "I had to find a slot to get in and stay out of people's way. The tunes—well, what do you do on a break-down with a steel guitar? I experimented. I found that I could use har-monics, and it made a nice background for the fiddle and/or voice. I could play some chords so I would get in another register. I'd either get above or below the other parts in order to stay out of the way. They didn't give me choruses. I just played background."

At the time Leon went to work for the Doughboys, he was playing a Dobro resonator guitar, probably a National Duolian. His first amplified steel guitar was purchased for him by Bob Wills, who had left the Dough-boys to form the Texas Playboys and called sixteen-year-old Leon to join him in Tulsa in 1935. Wills had heard a recording of Bob Dunn playing electric steel guitar with Milton Brown and His Musical Brownies and wanted his steel player to be similarly equipped. The electric steel im-proved Leon's life considerably because it gave him the volume to be heard among the other instruments in the Wills band.

Bob Wills made another significant change in Leon's musical life by calling on him frequently to take solo choruses and encouraging him to explore the full potential of electric steel guitar. "Steel Guitar Rag," Leon's signature piece, was born out of this atmosphere of freedom and experimentation. Leon recalled,

> I had messed around and made up a little tune. It was the first tune
> I played on the Doughboys program, and the first tune I played on
> Bob's program [on KVOO]. Now whenever you make up a song
> and it sounds good to you, you don't know whether it's going to
> sound good to anybody else or not. I played it, and all the musi-
> cians liked it and then I played it with Bob, and that night we went
> and played a dance and Bob liked it. He called it "Steel Guitar Rag."
> Well, Bob could see the reaction from the people, and he knew that
> we had a good song on our hands, so I played it every night.

Nearly every steel guitar player since has played "Steel Guitar Rag," which Leon first recorded at a Playboys session in Chicago in September 1936. This 1936 recording session also produced the phrase "Take it away, Leon," with which McAuliffe was identified for the rest of his pro-fessional life.

> Before we started recording "Steel Guitar Rag," Bob told me, "I'm
> going to do something different on this one. You hit a chord, and

I'm going to say something and then you start playing." So, I just did a slide into an E chord, and Bob said, "Look out, friends. Here's Leon. Take it away, my boy, take it away." I started playing. When the record came out, not only was that song a hit, but people were going around handing each other things and saying, "Hey, take it away, Leon." It stuck for a long time.

The Playboys band that Leon joined in 1935 was musically unpolished and rather limited in its repertory. Many of the musicians who left the Light Crust Doughboys to go with Wills were adequate players of traditional music, but they lacked the skill and interest to expand into the jazz and popular fields where Wills wanted to go. Wills was constantly in search of players who could help him realize his musical dream, and hiring young Leon McAuliffe was a step in the right direction. Acquiring Eldon Shamblin two years later was, in Leon's words, "the crowning block on the thing."

Herman Arnspiger was a fine guitar player for certain things. But Bob wanted to do more. He had me learn the pop songs of the day. We all listened to *The Lucky Strike Hit Parade*, and we were listening to the good songs and the good records that we liked: Bing Crosby and Gene Austin and a lot of those guys. Bob liked the blues songs. He liked a little bit of everything. A lot of those things we learned from sheet music. You could get the sheet music quickly when a new song came out, and you couldn't buy the record as fast as the sheet music. Herman never learned progressions, and he only got as far as the breakdown-type, country, three-chord things. He was real good at what he did, but he wasn't interested, and he'd mark out songs that had chords he didn't know. Here came Eldon who knew more chords than anybody. I had studied chords. I kept studying chords, but I didn't know them anything like Eldon did. Eldon was instrumental on my steel guitar in helping me come up with the tunings as I began to get multiple-neck guitars with eight strings on them.

Leon McAuliffe and Eldon Shamblin formed a guitar partnership that resulted in many creative musical moments, one of which produced another signature song, "Twin Guitar Special."

Bob played a fiddle tune called the "Joe Turner Blues" and I was always hunting for background to put in it. I started playing a basic boogie bass-type fill to it. I played it a couple of times with Eldon sitting there on the other side, and he started playing harmony to it. Whenever anything pleased Bob, his eyes would light up and he'd really get with it. He turned and let us know. Eldon and I said, "Well, that pleased the old man; let's do something else." After the rest of the band would go, Eldon and I would sit there, and we decided to write a blues chorus, with two guitars. We had quit playing "Joe Turner Blues," but were playing "Milk Cow Blues," which is about the same tempo and chord progressions, and we used our twin guitar chorus in "Milk Cow Blues." The reception on it was good. Everybody liked it. So we decided to make a whole tune. We wound up with an introduction to the chorus and an ending, and it was up-tempo. "Twin Guitar Special" is what it was called, and we recorded it. Amazingly it really wasn't a number that had a melody you could sing or hum; it was mostly hot licks, but we would get requests for it.

Playing for Bob Wills was a learning experience for Leon because Wills kept adding musicians to the band and building a musical unit that could play any kind of music with authority. Wills's musicians could not afford to rest on their past achievements but had to continually stretch and grow musically.

When the United States entered World War II, Leon, like many of the Playboys, enlisted in the army. After the war he returned to Tulsa and established his own band, the Cimarron Boys, named after their headquarters, the Cimarron Ballroom. For the next twenty years Leon fronted this band, which was recognized by other musicians as one of the best western swing bands in the business, though at times the Cimarron Boys played beyond the musical understanding of their audiences. Leon was a perfectionist who demanded countless hours of rehearsal from his sidemen. They played involved arrangements that incorporated progressive harmonic and structural thinking; but they maintained the prominent dance beat and improvisational spontaneity that kept people coming back for more. The Cimarron Boys recorded over 200 sides and achieved almost as much fame as the Texas Playboys.

In December 1973, after suffering a crippling stroke, Bob Wills gathered a few of the original Texas Playboys and some friends around him to make one final album, *For the Last Time*. Included on the session were

Leon McAuliffe, Smoky Dacus (drums), Al Stricklin (piano), Johnny Gimble (fiddle), Hoyle Nix (fiddle), Leon Rausch (guitar, vocals), Eldon Shamblin (guitar), Keith Coleman (fiddle), and Merle Haggard (guitar, vocals).[16] Leon remembered: "Bob wanted to do a final album before he died. He called us together, and of course, we couldn't have turned him down for anything. Everybody wanted to do it. We got ten songs recorded in the first hour. Of course, they were songs that we knew; that's the ones Bob picked. And we had recorded them before, and we used them all the time. But the recall was instantaneous. We had no trouble. It was pretty much ingrained in us. It just all came back."

After this recording experience, Leon was not surprised that the old Playboys could click instantly, as though no time had elapsed, when the Original Texas Playboys, under Leon's direction, made their debut on *Austin City Limits* in September 1975. They had no thought of staying together as a working band, having reunited only to perform on this first-ever show of the series. The Playboys shared the stage that night with an up-and-coming western swing revival band, Asleep at the Wheel, and Leon was concerned that the band would not be able to reach the audience.

Fifty years is a long time, and all the folks out there are new folks. We figured we'd do *Austin City Limits*, and if somebody wanted us, then under certain circumstances we'd go play. I guess the first surprise was the first *Austin City Limits*, because here's a studio with about eight hundred college kids in it. Asleep at the Wheel went on. They did their segment before we did ours, and they were doing our music. They got a tremendous reception. Smoky Dacus and I were sitting and watching them at the back. He said, "Man, I hate to get up there after that." I said, "Well, the only thing that we have going for us is that they're doing our music." So we got up and did a lot of the same songs, and the reception was unbelievable. They wouldn't let us quit. We were going to do forty-five minutes. Each group would play forty-five minutes and they'd edit down to thirty. We went an hour and twenty minutes. They had to reload the cameras and everything else because they stomped their feet and stood up and wouldn't let us out.

The surprise continued the following night when the Original Texas Playboys played to an equally enthusiastic, sold-out dance crowd at the Broken Spoke in Austin. For the next ten years the Original Texas Playboys kept western swing alive and well through concerts and recordings. They disbanded in 1986 following the death of pianist Al Stricklin.

Leon was not ready to retire from music-making, however, and in 1987 he accepted an offer to teach in the commercial music department of Rogers State College in Claremore, Oklahoma. The course Leon taught, "The Music Industry," was a practical seminar on human relations and legal issues in the music business. He poured much of his own money into equipment for the department's sound studio, where he spent time recording and producing his own music and that of his students and fellow local musicians. He also established and directed a student western swing ensemble, the New Cimarron Boys, which played locally and on two weekly broadcasts from the college's radio station, KXON.[17]

Attempts to describe Leon's style usually include comparison with that of Bob Dunn. Whereas Dunn's background was jazz horn and guitar, Leon's was Hawaiian steel and Texas string band, with a heavy infusion of South Texas blues. Leon's melodic figures were less hornlike than Dunn's and more idiomatically steel guitar. The 1936 recording of "Steel Guitar Rag" by the sixteen-year-old McAuliffe was certainly not a technical masterpiece. In fact, Leon's role in this performance was to state the theme, which other Playboys then used as a vehicle for solo improvisation. Al Stricklin's piano chorus and Ray DeGeer's takeoff saxophone are more thoroughly jazz than Leon's several slightly varied repetitions of the theme. But Leon's characteristic style is firmly in place—blues-influenced bends, big clear chords, and Hawaiian glissandi.

For "Silver Bells," recorded by the Playboys in Dallas on November 28, 1938, Leon used harmonics and glissandi in the upper register of his steel guitar to tone-paint delicate bell-like effects against the more strident fiddles and the driving rhythm. Leon's tone was clear as crystal.

When the Playboys recorded their arrangement of the popular ballad "I'll See You in My Dreams" in Dallas on May 16, 1938, Leon's steel guitar took on multiple personalities. In the first ensemble chorus it was a member of the three-piece horn section (trumpet, saxophone, clarinet); behind the clarinet solo it was a bell-like and then muted trumpet-sounding harmonic background; and for the ensemble-out chorus it played an essentially saxophone-like lead line.[18]

Other western swing guitarists developed more technically flashy and rhythmically driving modes of playing. One of these, Noel Boggs, exerted considerable influence on other players. Noel Edwin Boggs was born in Osage County, Oklahoma, in 1917 and began learning steel guitar at the age of twelve. By the age of sixteen he was playing on local radio shows and giving steel guitar lessons. When he was nineteen, Noel began touring with dance bands.[19]

In the summer of 1944, Noel was hired by Bob Wills as part of a nationwide touring band. This had already been an eventful year for Wills. Earlier in the year he had assembled his largest band ever, twenty-two pieces, comprised of four fiddles, three guitars, bass, piano, drums, four saxophones, four trumpets, four trombones, and two vocalists. Some of the horn players had come from the Jimmy Dorsey and Glenn Miller orchestras, and Wills had finally amassed his ideal band. Unfortunately, this band never recorded, and it was rather short-lived, lasting only six or seven months. There were problems with the band, most of them generated by horn players who were accustomed to working according to union rules and did not want to tour. Another problem was Wills's conception of the music and audience expectations—after he had assembled just the band he had always wanted, his band sound lost its distinctiveness and became just like every other big swing band in California. Bob's followers wanted strings, and they wanted to hear tunes that sounded best when played by strings. So Wills fired most of the horn players and concentrated on the front line of fiddles and guitars. The string players continued to play hot jazz chouses and to provide background fills, essentially taking the place of the horns. Hot fiddles playing jazz choruses became a Wills trademark, as did guitarists improvising solos like trumpet, trombone, and saxophone players and combining to sound like a brass section. This was the band that Noel Boggs joined in July 1944.

Wills was going on tour with a show that he called Bob Wills and His Great Vaudeville Show. It played dances in various cities across the country and appeared in concert engagements at the Saint Charles Theater in New Orleans, the municipal auditorium in Birmingham, the Kentucky Theater in Louisville, and the Oriental Theater in Chicago. Wills's tour band consisted of Jesse Ashlock and Joe Holley playing fiddles; Alex Brashear, formerly of Norma Teagarden's jazz orchestra, on trumpet; Rip Ramsey playing bass; Noel Boggs on steel, forming a guitar trio with Jimmy Wyble and Cameron Hill; Monte Mountjoy, formerly of the Red Nichols band, behind the drums; Millard Kelso at the piano; and Tommy Duncan and Laura Lee Owens providing vocals.[20] This was an outstanding western swing band, probably one of the best ever assembled, and Noel found soulmates in jazz guitarists Cameron Hill and Jimmy Wyble, with whom he formed a hot guitar trio within the larger band.

After six months on the road, Wills and the band returned to Hollywood and almost immediately scheduled a recording session for Columbia. They recorded again for Columbia in April and October of 1945 and kept up a steady routine of dance jobs and radio and television appearances. Thousands attended their dances, and it was generally agreed that the Playboys drew larger audiences than Dorsey or Goodman and that Bob Wills was the highest-paid band leader in the country.[21] Noel Boggs was getting a great deal of exposure on this Bob Wills band.

In the summer of 1946 Noel left Wills to join the reorganized Spade Cooley band, which was fast becoming popular on the West Coast, partly because of Cooley's innovative, updated arrangements.[22] Tex Williams and other members of Cooley's band had broken away to form the Western Caravan in May 1946, and Cooley had responded by recruiting a larger horn section around the nuclear strings. This Spade Cooley band provided a perfect atmosphere for Noel, and, as Bea Poling Perry says in a profile of Boggs, "He truly came into his own musically and developed a style that put him in demand for recording and personal appearances, making him one of the most recognized faces in the Los Angeles area."[23] Noel's guitar partner, Jimmy Wyble, was also a member of the Cooley band at this time. The Spade Cooley band of which Noel was a part was a tremendous success, playing to huge crowds at the Riverside Rancho, Santa Monica Ballroom, Venice Pier, and other large California dance halls. By 1947 Cooley had a weekly television show on KTLA that was for six years the top-rated program on California television.[24]

When Spade Cooley abandoned his television show in the mid-1950s, Noel formed his own bands, with which he worked the Nevada casino circuit and USO tours to Alaska and the Orient. He recorded with various artists, including the Sons of the Pioneers, Roy Rogers, Gene Autry, Doye O'Dell, and Hank Penny, and he played on the movie soundtracks of *War of the Worlds* and *The Lieutenant Wore Skirts*. Noel Boggs died of a heart attack on July 31, 1974.[25]

For at least part of his career Noel Boggs used a four-neck, standup steel guitar, with his name prominently displayed on the front. The Playboys' January 1945 recording session in Hollywood, right after they got off the road, produced a number of hits, including a perennial favorite with western swing audiences, "Roly Poly." This is a swinging number that features Joe Holley playing hot licks on fiddle and Alex Brashear tearing loose on muted trumpet solos. But the true center of this performance is the heady, absolutely synchronized work of the three guitarists—Hill,

Wyble, and Boggs. These three begin the song with a perfectly coordinated, harmonized introduction, after which pianist Millard Kelso, trumpeter Alex Brashear, and fiddler Joe Holley alternate solos on the thirty-two-bar a a b a' first verse of the song. While these three take turns, Noel provides a background replete with rich, full chords. Noel continues to chord behind singer Tommy Duncan, while Wyble, Brashear, and Holley provide intricate countermelodies. The next chorus belongs to Wyble and Boggs. Wyble fills out sixteen measures with his typically complicated, rhythmically exciting, harmonically progressive single-string melody playing, and Boggs responds with sixteen measures of the big modern chords for which he was famous. Duncan sings the second verse, as before, with Boggs chording in the background, and Brashear and Holley creating countermelodies. Boggs is featured playing his harmonically rich and progressive chords on the final ensemble-out chorus.[26]

Shortly after Noel joined Spade Cooley's band, he participated in a recording session for Columbia in Hollywood on June 6, 1946. This session produced an amazing arrangement of an old fiddle tune that the band renamed "Swinging the Devil's Dream." Three fiddlers (Cooley, Andrew "Cactus" Soldi, and an unidentified musician) start with a rollicking rendition of the tune, played in unison, then in three-part harmony, at the end of which accordionist Pedro DePaul and drummer Muddy Berry moderate the fast two-beat pace to a slower swing-four, and the fiddles present the tune again in the new meter and tempo. Noel Boggs plays a sophisticated melodic-harmonic solo improvisation on the chord structures of the B section, and DePaul takes the turnaround into a minor key with his accordion. Lead guitarist John Weiss carries the music back to the B section and major mode before fiddles and accordion finish out the verse. Drummer Berry alters the pace again with a short drum solo, and the fiddles return to their fast-paced jazz two-meter. The number ends as it began—with a sweep of Featherstone's hands across the harp.[27]

What can be said of Noel Boggs on the basis of these two cuts is that he was primarily interested in the harmonic resources of the steel guitar. With the huge chords he played, he could take the place of a section of guitars or of horns; his advanced tonal thinking put him on the harmonic cutting edge and kept his sound fresh and modern. With his expanded harmonic vocabulary, it is easy to understand why he was a favorite sideman around Los Angeles.

The consensus pick for all-time best steel guitar player, Joaquin Murphy, is also the most elusive personality in the business. Murphy lives somewhere in Southern California and rarely appears in public. But during his days with Spade Cooley and Tex Williams he was the living legend that other steel guitarists aspired to emulate. Tommy Morrell, himself an outstanding steel guitarist, says of Murphy:

> He was the first real sophisticated jazz steel guitar player. That's the best way I can describe it, and he was a lot better than anybody else—he was fast. He and Noel Boggs paralleled each other. Noel Boggs played a lot of chords. Joaquin Murphy played a lot of single-string. Before that, it was Leon McAuliffe and Bob Dunn. They were a little bit more old-timey, and Murphy, he was kind of like Charlie Parker was to the saxophone players. He was playing things that nobody had ever heard and playing them really well. And he was with a band that was being recorded, so, he was not only good, he was being heard. Murphy could do things that nobody else could.

The comparison between Joaquin Murphy and bebop saxophonist Charlie Parker is especially appropriate because Murphy, like Parker, expanded not only the technical dimensions of steel guitar playing—he played more notes at faster tempos—but also the conceptualization of the music, spinning out his short, unpredictable, agile melodies over a larger vocabulary of chords.

Joaquin Murphy was hired by Spade Cooley in late 1943 and played on Cooley's first recording session on December 4, 1944, out of which came the hit "Shame On You." Murphy was given a prominent place on the recording, taking the first solo chorus after the vocal lead and carrying the melody and chord progressions well beyond the simplistic I-IV-V7-I of the original tune; he also added to the rhythmic drive and interest of this otherwise predictable number.

Less than a year later, on July 24, 1945, the Cooley band was once again in a Hollywood studio recording for Columbia. Among the cuts that were not released at that time, but which clearly demonstrate the improved arranging skills of Cooley and accordionist Pedro DePaul, is the popular ballad "Troubled Over You," which featured Tex Williams on the vocals and once again highlighted Murphy on a takeoff solo. Murphy's solo is more rhythmically aggressive than that of "Shame on You" and consists of more single-string melody work and fewer chords; his conception of his melodic solo is far-reaching in its harmonic scope.

The year 1946 saw a plethora of recordings by the Cooley band and, late in the year, significant personnel changes as well. A January 3 recording session for Columbia produced several major successes—"Hide Your Face," "Detour," "You Can't Break My Heart," and "Crazy 'Cause I Love You." "Hide Your Face," with its prominent chromatic modulation and involved ensemble work behind vocalist Tex Williams, features Murphy, guitarist John Weiss, and accordionist DePaul on a takeoff chorus in which all three play rhythmically and harmonically intricate melody lines and large, altered chords. Murphy's solo on "Detour" derives from modern chords and hot licks, while on "You Can't Break My Heart" he plays a bridge comprised of unusually bent chords. An up-tempo arrangement of "Crazy 'Cause I Love You" features Murphy on a driving solo in which he explores the outward reaches of the song's melody and harmony.

The Cooley band was back in the studio on May 3, 1946, with new, interesting arrangements and several new sidemen. Muddy Berry had replaced Warren Penniman on drums and was given a prominent place in some of the numbers; Paul "Spike" Featherstone had been added to give the band a new sound with his big harp, which is heard to good advantage at the beginnings and endings of songs. "Oklahoma Stomp" features Murphy and Weiss all the way through, alternating on solo choruses between themselves and sometimes with DePaul. Murphy plays an incredible number and variety of notes, hot licks, and rhythm patterns at an amazingly fast tempo. His rendition of McAuliffe's "Steel Guitar Rag" is played at a faster tempo and with tunings different from the original.

When Tex Williams broke off from Spade Cooley in May 1946, Joaquin Murphy left with him.[28] Williams recognized the genius of Murphy and used him as frequently on solo choruses as Cooley had. "Joaquin Special," first recorded on the Capitol label about 1948, highlighted Murphy's technical prowess as a single-string lead player, and the amazing theme and variations on "Tennessee Wagoner" utilized Murphy's advanced harmonic thinking. On "Red Ball Whistle" Murphy created the sounds of a train whistle and provided large chords behind Williams's vocals. There was a great deal of sophisticated arranged ensemble work on the Williams band, and Murphy always found the perfect niche from which to contribute chords and countermelodies. But he was always ready with a hot, driving solo, as on the jazz favorites "South" and "Deuces Wild."

These four pioneers—Bob Dunn, Leon McAuliffe, Noel Boggs, and Joaquin Murphy—laid the groundwork for jazz steel guitar. Jazz horn player and guitarist Bob Dunn experimented with amplifying the steel guitar and brought the instrument into the jazz ensemble. Leon McAuliffe popularized the steel guitar and composed one of the instrument's most frequently played pieces, "Steel Guitar Rag." Noel Boggs was like the George Van Eps of the steel guitar, broadening its harmonic vocabulary. And Joaquin Murphy, the true virtuoso, combined the attributes of Charlie Christian and Charlie Parker in bringing the steel guitar into prominence as a solo melody instrument.

A Few Good Steel Guitarists Talk about Western Swing

HERB REMINGTON was born in Indiana in 1926. Because his father was a traveling salesman, the family moved frequently. Herb remembers attending some fifty elementary schools and five high schools in various states. He and his mother were living back in Indiana when Herb graduated from high school, and he admits, "It's a wonder I got through school. My interests were elsewhere. I had a bad case of steel guitar."

Herb gives credit for his early interest in music to his mother, who was a pianist and his first music teacher.

> I can remember my legs not even touching the floor; you know how that is with the piano bench. She subscribed to *Etude* magazine after I learned how to read, with her help. And *Etude* magazine, back then, was published monthly and you would get piano duets, where one would play the high part, and one the low part, on the same piano, and we did that. That was my beginning in music. I didn't like piano. I did it for Momma. I played piano through age six or seven, then baseball took over. I forgot about the piano. No more piano until I was about nine.

Herb's return to the piano was short-lived, however, due to the visitation of a door-to-door salesman who hooked young Herb and his mother on weekly guitar lessons at one dollar per lesson. Though the depression was on, Mrs. Remington scraped together the money for the lessons because Herb had found his musical interest. At the end of the year of lessons Herb had earned a free guitar, with which he began to appear in amateur shows. Then came another door-to-door salesman, this time selling Hawaiian lap steel guitars.

> They came to the door with this thing, this guitar that they put on your lap. You had a metal bar in your hand and you would slide that thing up and down, and some of the noises on that just really

excited me. I had to do that. So here we go again, lessons for that. Then Hawaiian music got my attention. Back then there were Hawaiian movies like *Song of the Island*, Betty Grable and Bing Crosby. And so the music was in the air, and movies, and I was familiar with that and how that steel guitar sounded. I really loved it. After a while, I got proficient enough that I got an electric steel guitar and then formed my own little Hawaiian group. Now, here we are back in Indiana, about as far from Hawaii as you can get.

Calling themselves the Honolulu Serenaders, Herb's schoolboy Hawaiian band played ice cream socials, wedding receptions, bar mitzvahs, and whatever else came along. Herb also played steel guitar in lounges during his junior and senior years in high school.

Immediately after graduation in 1944, Herb headed for California, where everything seemed to be happening and where he hoped to hook up with a Hawaiian music group. But Herb found no Hawaiian music in Los Angeles; instead he auditioned at the Riverside Rancho for singing cowboy movie star Ray Whitley, who was piecing together a western swing band. Herb recalls, "Two other guys auditioned; it was the first time I ever saw a double-neck steel guitar. A guy named Joaquin Murphy played. I thought sure he would get the job because he had that double-neck steel, but I got the job. Well, that was wonderful. I think I started at ninety-seven dollars a week. Back then, that was pretty good money." Herb enjoyed being in Whitley's band for three weeks, and then his draft notice arrived.

Like so many professional musicians during World War II, Herb was able to devote part of his military service to his music. "I carried that little single-neck Hawaiian lap steel with me throughout my whole tenure in the service and played at local NCO clubs and officers' clubs on weekends. Made a little money there, and met some great people." After he was discharged from the army in 1946, Herb headed straight back to California, where he heard that Bob Wills was auditioning steel players for his brother Luke's band. "I went over and played for Bob and all his boys in a motel room in Hollywood. I played 'Steel Guitar Rag' and a tune called 'Dream Train.' Bob said, 'Well, let's take the kid here, and give Roy to Luke.' So I got the job with Bob, and they put a cowboy hat on me that came down over my ears, and boots. I was there for five years."

One of the first jobs Herb played as a Playboy was a battle dance with Spade Cooley's band. He was certain that he had lost his new job when, on "San Antonio Rose," the unimaginable happened and his steel bar slipped out of his hand and went scooting across the dance floor. Noel Boggs was playing steel for Cooley, and quickly came to Herb's rescue, playing the steel guitar chorus as he had done when he was a Playboy.[29] Working on the Wills band had a significant impact on the rest of Herb's career: "It was a foundation for everything I've done since," he says.

> It was like working with the Beatles in the 1960s. Bob was top dog. He was the man of the moment. Every place we played there were thousands of people just worshipping at Bob's shrine, and anybody that played with Bob also had to be just as humongous. We were treated like kings everywhere, and it was really a great time. I loved every minute of it. Bob overpaid everybody. A very big-hearted man—he knew what he wanted and he was a taskmaster. But if you toed the line and did what he wanted in the band, which wasn't all that much: stay straight, be clean, play well, do your best at all times, and get along with everybody—that's all he required. He was a great guy to work for, and everything that I've done since has referred back to him.

A plaque hanging on the wall of Herb's steel guitar shop describes him as a western swing steel guitar pioneer who blended the Hawaiian sound with western music. Herb's unique style coalesced during his years as a Playboy, when he combined his "Hawaiian touch" with the driving rhythm and freewheeling improvisation of western swing. For Herb, Hawaiian music and western swing entail different methods for playing steel guitar; he merged the two: "The Hawaiian sound is a more lyrical singing sound than is western swing. It sings without saying words. The sliding sound of the steel is like a voice. It rolls from note to note. A person who learns Hawaiian steel just plays more slides. You hear that glissing all the time, whereas in western swing, there's a little more staccato and a little more pushing and driving. If you mix the two together, you've got me."

While on the Wills band, Herb began to explore his creative ability as a composer-arranger. He wrote a large number of tunes, two of which, "Boot Heel Drag" and "Remington's Ride," remain in the steel guitar repertory. Herb tells a slightly different version of the story concerning improvisatory freedom in the Wills band—not that he felt restricted, but that he sensed that there were certain traditions to be maintained. "You tried to copy those who had come before you, and I followed after Leon

McAuliffe. If you played 'Steel Guitar Rag' with Bob, you'd try to play it like the original. It wouldn't be the way I would play it necessarily, but it would be what Bob wanted because that's what the people wanted. Others, like Spade Cooley, made renditions of that tune with the up-up tempo, and the steel player using different tunings and putting his little tricks in that weren't there originally."

After his time with Bob Wills, Herb toured and recorded with T. Texas Tyler, who had an outstanding western swing band. He was also highly sought after for recording sessions and worked with Floyd Tillman, Spade Cooley, Merle Travis, Lefty Frizzell, Hank Penny, and many others.

With the rise to popularity of rock and roll in the mid-1950s and the near demise of big band swing, including western swing, and traditional country music, Nashville record producers concocted the slick "Nashville sound" designed to rescue country music from impending doom. Especially hard hit by the Nashville sound were fiddle and steel guitar players. Herb knew he was proficient enough to make a place for himself in Nashville, but the prospect of what and how he would have to play steered him in a different direction.

Nashville was not associated with western swing so they had their own way of doing things, and the steel guitar was a backup instrument. Occasionally they let it have a lead line, but usually it was on a tuning that was developed for the backup qualities of what they required. It was really a country Nashville sound. You can hear that particular tuning—the Nashville E 9th tuning—and recognize it as being a Nashville sound, even today. It seems like everyone plays that setup, they let the pedal guitar dominate the sounds and they all start sounding alike. That's a shame, because I think that the personalities of the earlier musicians, where you could recognize each person by the way he played, was wonderful. When it comes to Nashville country it's just three-chord tunes. The music is simplistic. They can make a G chord and mash a pedal and make it a C chord, and they play simplistic things like that behind a vocalist and say they're playing steel guitar. They aren't interested in a tuning setup that gives you lots of different chords. If I went to Nashville and played my way behind some country artist, they'd say, "You're western swing." I would try to emulate what they're doing, but the tunings that I use and the technique I've played is nothing like what they want. So I knew not to go to Nashville.

Instead of going to Nashville, Herb relocated to Houston, where he and his talented wife, Mel, formed a Hawaiian music ensemble, the Beachcombers, with which they toured nationally for fifteen years. Herb shed his cowboy hat and boots, donned an aloha shirt, white pants, and a lei, and rode out the rock and roll storm playing luau parties for the country club set. They played a variety of music. Herb maintained the Hawaiian flavor through the first hour and the floor show, and then took requests, which often included western swing standards like "Steel Guitar Rag."

In 1958 Herb got his own solo recording contract with Okeh Records, which released six 45 rpms, all original material that Herb composed. While none of these songs became national hits, they received substantial air play in the Houston area. Herb states that he was the first steel guitar player to overdub, or make multitrack recordings; he used this technique on his "Steel Guitar Waltz."

After coming off the road, Herb began to find playing opportunities in western swing bands that were reemerging on the music scene, as the seventies brought a resurgence of interest in older styles of music. Austin was a particularly fertile ground for revival bands, and Herb began commuting from Houston to Austin three or four times a week to play in Al Dressen's twelve-piece western swing band, which booked at the Broken Spoke Club. Herb's exposure with this band led to his playing for a number of television beer commercials and ultimately, in 1982, to his being hired to perform in Clint Eastwood's movie *Honkytonk Man*. The job had first been offered to Leon McAuliffe, but McAuliffe wanted too much money and would not negotiate. So the producers went to Johnny Gimble, who directed them to Herb. Herb takes great pride in the part he played for that movie. He not only played an old Fender lap steel throughout the picture—they wanted authenticity—but also wrote two numbers that were used in the score, "Ricochet Rag" and the sentimental "Texas Moonbeam Waltz."

Herb has spent the 1980s and first half of the 1990s concertizing, recording, and playing festivals with the Playboys II band and with a local Houston western swing band, the Cosmopolitan Cowboys. He also produces records and builds his own brand of steel guitar, the Remington Steel, of which he is justifiably proud. He has made subtle changes in the instrument that are readily appreciated by players: rounding off the sharp edges of the knee levers for additional comfort and creating a steel guitar that is lighter, more portable, and easier to set up and tear down. He builds instruments known for their clarity of tone and sustaining power.

Some of his regular customers are not even players; they're just infatuated with the steel guitar. "I've got people who can't play, and they buy a new guitar every year just to sit and look at it like a piece of furniture, like a piano or an organ. You're in another world, this steel guitar world." At present Herb Remington, "the Kid," as Bob Wills dubbed him nearly fifty years ago, is a highly respected member of that special world. Though past retirement age, he has no intention of quitting. In fact, just two months before this interview, Playboys II and Asleep at the Wheel played for a Texas Festival at the Kennedy Center in Washington, D.C.

Herb Remington possesses a recognizable identity as a steel guitar player, a "signature" uniquely his own, which he attributes to "the way he holds the bar," "how he puts the picks on his fingers," and "how he attacks that monster." He also holds a broad view of the function of the steel guitar in a western swing band.

> What is the purpose of the steel guitar in western swing? A harmonic singing, harmonics on top of the fiddles. Then the other part is lower-toned, sustained notes behind solos, or a chord played by itself, or a melody line in duet with a standard guitar. The steel guitarist will phrase his lines to sound like those of a standard guitar. The steel can sound like two standard guitars playing harmony. It has a full range of tones and things it can do. And you never get tired of playing it, because there's always something new to discover.

Herb did not get a solo chorus on "Brain Cloudy Blues," recorded by the Playboys on the Columbia label in Hollywood in September 1946, but he played his recognizable high harmonics, complementing the opening fiddles, and his characteristic low, sustained chords behind singer Tommy Duncan and the wildman electric guitar solo of Junior Barnard.[30]

More can be ascertained about Herb's style from his solo albums, such as *Pure Remington Steel*, released by Stoneway Records in 1990. Of particular interest are the cuts of Herb's own compositions, "Remington's Ride" and "Boot Heel Drag." "Remington's Ride" is a virtuoso piece in which Herb demonstrates the full capacity of his technical skill and his guitar's wide range of special effects. His tone is large and rich with overtones, both at the low and high ends of his double-neck steel guitar. He combines rapid finger-picked phrases with the big, colorful chords, modulations, and Hawaiian glissandi that characterize his playing. "Boot Heel Drag" is an up-tempo boogie-woogie number, in which Herb effectively demonstrates the steel guitar's potential for single-string melody playing and harmonic background work. Again he explores the entire range of the instrument and transforms typical Hawaiian glissandi into riff patterns. Always rhythmically driving and creative in his improvisations, Herb Remington has truly achieved a complete synthesis of Hawaiian guitar and western swing.[31]

TOMMY MORRELL is busy these days keeping western swing recharged with his Time Warp Tophands band and their historic record series, which includes informative liner notes about the pioneers behind the music they play. Born in 1938 in Oak Cliff, a suburb of Dallas, Tommy grew up in a family of serious swing jazz fans with a huge collection of recordings by Benny Goodman, Count Basie, Stan Kenton, and more. When he was an eleven-year-old student at Oak Cliff Saint James Elementary School, Tommy was bitten by the steel guitar bug.

> A representative of the Trick Brothers Institute of Accordion and Guitar came to my school, offering us lessons and selling guitars. I took a few lessons, and, of course, what you'd do is you'd go take these lessons, and then they'd sell you a guitar. That's how they made their money. I went down and bought my own steel guitar; and it was five times better than what they were selling, and cost twenty dollars less. I showed up for class the next week, and they kicked me out. If I'd walked in with all those kids, with a better guitar that cost less, well, that would have been bad advertising for Trick Brothers.

Being dismissed from guitar class actually improved Tommy's playing because he took the basics he had learned and experimented to create his own unique style. He was blessed with a group of musically gifted young friends, and by the time they were in their mid-teens, Tommy and his friends had spent countless hours practicing together. They formed a little band that worked around the Dallas area and occasionally sat in with older, more experienced players.

A turning point for Tommy came when he and his friends visited the Longhorn Ballroom where Dewey Grooms, the club's owner, fronted a fifteen-piece western swing band that included Johnny Gimble, Baldy Rambo, and Paul Woodard playing fiddles, Curle Hollingsworth pounding the piano, Wayne Foster on drums, Torchy McCluney on guitar, and a young Maurice Anderson at the steel guitar. This was Tommy's first exposure to western swing and he was hooked: "I said, 'Shoo! Whatever this is, I love it.'" He has been loving it ever since and has almost refused to play anything else.

As soon as he finished high school, Tommy and a friend headed for California. "I didn't even wait for my diploma," he says. "We drove a car—delivered a '56 Olds—out to California." Western swing in California was approaching the end of its glory days, but there was still a great deal of activity. The Spade Cooley and Tex Williams bands were drawing crowds, and Tommy became friends with a trombone player named Phil Gray, who worked for Cooley. "Phil Gray had a Sunday-night job at Wade Ray's club, called Cow Town, and I worked with him. I stayed out there for a while, and I got to meet Joaquin Murphy, and I actually subbed some for Noel Boggs." But the uncertainty of employment in Los Angeles drove Tommy back to Dallas after just a few months.

Upon returning to Dallas, Tommy went to work for Billy Gray, who in Tommy's opinion had "the best western swing band going." Gray had played rhythm guitar for Hank Thompson before going out on his own. "I was just out of high school. It was like going to work for Stan Kenton if you were a horn player. He had access to good musicians and material, and he was a pretty good singer. He was at the right place at the right time and had the right musicians. I worked with Bobby Koefer—we did two steels for about a month while I learned the arrangements."

When Billy Gray released Tommy because he wanted to hire a steel player who could sing, Tommy moved south to Waco and went to work for Jerry Dykes. Waco was a thriving little musical city with a plethora of bands. Tommy made the acquaintance of one Waco saxophonist, Billy Ray, younger brother of jazz violinist Buddy Ray, whose fantastic collection of jazz recordings included several by guitarist Barney Kessel. Kessel's playing exerted a profound influence on Tommy.

From Waco, Tommy moved west to New Mexico, where Carlsbad and Hobbs were centers of nightclub life and western swing activity due to the busy oilfield operations nearby.

I worked a little jazz club in downtown Hobbs with Mancel Tierney, who was one of Bob's big piano players. Carlsbad and Hobbs were all tied in with Odessa, and Midland, Lubbock, Amarillo, and all that stuff. All the bands interchanged. All the bands would come through Hobbs. Bob Wills would come in and Johnnie Lee Wills. It was a social point, so to speak. Everybody coming east and west would stop in Hobbs and play. I've never been any place like that in my life. Those people, all they wanted to do was party and drink and fight. They'd go to work at four or five in the morning, and we're talking about heavy-duty roughnecking. And they'd get off at seven—go home and take a shower, and stay up until time to go to work; they'd do this all the time. I was out there for six, seven, eight years, and it seemed like nobody ever got any sleep out there. It was incredible. They had duels outside. They had bouncers who'd run guys up and down barbed wire fences, and some of them would go out behind the liquor tank and fight for the fun of it. It was the wildest place I've ever seen. All the clubs were going. That's why it was important because the clubs would support the musician life.

Returning to Dallas in the early 1960s, Tommy went to work with the Starlighters band, which he describes as "a real legitimate offshoot of the Bob Wills–type band. They were a western swing band that worked all the time. We played mostly air force bases, NCO clubs, naval bases, things like that, and we didn't play anything commercial. We just played western swing." Though a relatively localized band, the Starlighters was a top-flight western swing group. When Tex Williams decided to tour the Southwest, he left his big band in California and hired the Starlighters, which, as Tommy explains, "had as good a band as they did out there." The Starlighters also toured with the Grand Ole Opry. In fact, it did a tour with Tex Williams on the Grand Ole Opry, which Tommy found amusing because most of the Opry people had no idea who Tex Williams was, their musical worlds being so separate. As a Starlighter, Tommy had the experience of jamming with Glen Campbell in a club in Albuquerque, New Mexico. "We'd pull in and go into the club, and he'd tell his band to go home. They'd go home. We'd sit in and play with him the rest of the night. This was before he got famous. We had a real good band."

Because he had worked with Bob Wills on occasion when Wills would come through Hobbs, Tommy qualified as a former Texas Playboy, and when the Original Texas Playboys was formed under the direction of Leon McAuliffe, Tommy got the job as steel guitarist for several road trips and recording sessions. Back in his earlier days in Waco, Tommy had met Leon Rausch, who was playing guitar and singing with another Waco-based band. Leon has hired Tommy frequently to play dances and recording sessions with his Panther band. Then, of course, Tommy has his own performing and recording western swing band, the Time Warp Tophands.

"All I've been doing the last ten or fifteen years is playing western swing. I'll job out if somebody's got a job doing something else. I play some guitar on some big band jobs sometimes, and every once in a while, somebody will get me to sub on a Top Forties deal, but I tell them that I don't know any of the songs. If they know them, good, I'll follow. But if they don't, I'm not going to learn them."

Tommy has also built and marketed steel guitars as a partner in the MSA Corporation. His business started accidentally while he was living in Hobbs and was asked by a fellow musician to build a steel guitar like the one he played. Tommy made no profit from his first guitar because he underestimated labor time and cost of supplies. But he learned quickly and took on a partner, Danny Shields from Wichita, Kansas, with whom he built Morrell-Shields guitars. When Tommy returned to Dallas after some seven years in Hobbs, he became associated with another steel guitarist, Maurice Anderson, and Morrell-Shields was expanded to Morrell-Shields-Anderson, or MSA Steel Guitar Company, which produced some of the finest instruments in the business. In 1971 Tommy Morrell and Maurice Anderson dissolved their partnership, with Tommy dropping out of the business and Maurice continuing for a number of years.

Tommy Morrell's style has evolved along with his understanding and appreciation of western swing. As a boy, he learned to play a simple instrument without pedals; but as he progressed into early adulthood and discovered jazz and especially bebop, he opted for the convenience and versatility of pedal steel guitar. Tommy has matured both in years and understanding and has come to recognize the beauty in simplicity. He now plays a nonpedal, multiple-neck Bigsby steel guitar built in 1954. Giving up the pedals has not decreased Tommy's efficiency as a player.

Among those who have influenced him, Tommy lists Joaquin Murphy, Noel Boggs, Herb Remington, Leon McAuliffe, Bobby Koefer, Bob White, Pee Wee Whitewing, Jerry Byrd, Alvino Ray, and relative unknowns like Rico Turchetti, Johnny Bonvillian, and Pete Martinez.

> There was a guy who lived in New York, named Rico Turchetti, that nobody's ever heard of. I had some stuff by him. There was a guy in New Orleans named Johnny Bonvillian, who played just about as good as Joaquin Murphy, and nobody ever heard of him. He never left New Orleans. When I was still in school, I found him on the radio. I would wake up in the morning and put my tape recorder on WWL New Orleans. He was really low-key. He's still

around. I was in New Orleans a few years back and called him, and he came and got me and took me over to his music store. He went back in the back and found a letter that I had written him when I was a kid, asking him what tunings he used. Another player, Pete Martinez, wasn't nearly as famous as Joaquin Murphy, but he was out there, like 1946 through 1951. He played with Jimmy Wakely, played some with Tex Williams. There were only three or four real steel players in L.A. and he was one of them.

Tommy Morrell is, like his idol Joaquin Murphy, a fast, aggressive, single-string melody player. For his Time Warp Tophands recordings, Tommy has assembled an outstanding band including Johnny Case playing piano and vibraphone, Clint Strong on lead guitar, Benny Garcia on rhythm guitar, Mac MacRae at bass, Tommy Perkins behind the drums, and Bobby Boatright on fiddle. Though Tommy's liner notes and even the new titles assigned old favorites are humorous, the playing on these albums is jazz serious. This is western swing at its best—tight, forceful rhythm and free solo improvisation—on tunes such as "Rosetta," "Room Full of Roses," Duke Ellington's "Mood Indigo," Benny Moten's "Moten Swing," "It Had To Be You," Stan Kenton's "Painted Rhythm," "I Can't Give You Anything But Love," and "Bluesette." There are also some Tommy Morrell originals, like "Dinosaur Droppings" and a Morrell rearrangement of Chuck Berry's "Deep Feeling," now entitled "Pterodactyl Ptales."[32] In his *How the West Was Swung* albums, Tommy and friends do more than preserve western swing; they modernize it with updated approaches to rhythm, melody, harmony, and texture. But while their arrangements will engage the intellects of jazz experts, they will also delight the uninformed majority who seek only great dance music.

MAURICE ANDERSON, a contemporary of Tommy Morrell's, was also born in Dallas in 1940. Like Herb Remington, Maurice's introduction to music took the form of piano lessons, which he thoroughly disliked. But one day he heard the steel guitar on the radio and, though he had no idea what the instrument was, told his mother that he wanted to play it. The next Christmas, Maurice received his first steel guitar, and from then on, he says, it was "love at first sound, and it never stopped." He took a few lessons, but learned mostly by listening and trial-and-error experimentation. Maurice claims that he could teach himself because the steel guitar was a much less complicated instrument when he first began studying it.

The music that Maurice listened to and was influenced by for years to come was swing, and especially western swing coming out of California—Spade Cooley and Tex Williams. "I liked the big band sounds. I liked the Glenn Miller blends, and I liked the Stan Kenton orchestra, and I would listen to that kind of music and western swing. Those two things built my musical base. I got my chord voicings from the big band era. I used to listen to the way a sax section or a trumpet section and trombone would form a chord, and those are the chords I tried to play."

Maurice was playing professionally before he got out of high school; on the night he graduated, he accepted steady employment with the resident band at the Silver Spur Club in Dallas.[33] When he was only twenty years old, Maurice got a call from Red Foley to come to Springfield, Missouri, and join the band of *Ozark Jubilee*, one of the first nationally televised country music shows. The Foley band played a weekly show and toured the area playing concerts and dances. Though Maurice did not especially enjoy playing country music, *Ozark Jubilee* was a good training ground in that it allowed him to broaden his ability to play in a variety of styles. Maurice is convinced that the key to success in the music business is versatility. "If you are going to be a professional, you've got to play the game. I always tried to fit into any musical scenario, be it jazz, or big band, or country music, or western swing, or Hawaiian music. You had better do everything in the music business or you will do nothing in the music business."

Though Maurice can play any style of music, his preference remains swing. His dream came true in 1962, when he was invited to join Bob Wills's Texas Playboys. He was just out of military service when he heard that Wills was auditioning steel players.

> I went down to the Longhorn Ballroom in Dallas in the afternoon while they were rehearsing and sat in, and Bob offered me a job. I was awestruck. When Bob asked me if I wanted the job and I told him yes, then I asked him, "Well, do you want me to know your records and copy the licks and all that kind of stuff?" And he said no. Bob said, "I want you to play exactly the way you want to play. All you've got to remember is that when I point my bow at you, I want you to play everything you know." He never stifled my creativity, and he didn't expect me to learn to play exactly the way his records were. He said, "Now you play it your way and you play the best you can every time I tell you to play."

Maurice worked for Bob Wills for nearly two years and never felt ill at ease, though he had been preceded by several legendary steel guitarists. "Those things follow you onto the bandstand, because you think of the guys who were there before you. But Bob made me feel so good because when someone would ask him to name his favorite steel player, he would say, 'Oh, the one I've got with me now.'"

When Maurice left Wills in 1964 and returned to Dallas, he remained busy playing, teaching, and building steel guitars. He survived the rock era by forming a jazz trio, on which he alternated playing steel guitar and bass and sometimes sang. The trio played lounges and country club parties.

Maurice also became involved with Tommy Morrell and Danny Shields in building and marketing steel guitars. The MSA steel guitar became one of the most popular instruments on the market, with sales not only in the United States but also in Europe. Maurice made business trips to Europe and was amazed by the devotion that Europeans demonstrated for the steel guitar. Though his partners pulled out of the business in 1971, Maurice kept MSA going until 1983, when the severe recession put the $3,000 steel guitar out of reach for all but the most commercially successful musicians. During his nineteen years as a steel guitar manufacturer, Maurice promoted not only MSA guitars but also the viability of the steel guitar as a jazz instrument; during this time he proved his point by playing engagements with such jazz giants as Johnny Smith, Louie Belson, Howard Roberts, and Barney Kessel.[34]

Because of his versatility as a player, Maurice has worked many jobs—recording sessions, concerts, television programs, and movies. He has backed a host of famous performers, including Willie Nelson, Lefty Frizzell, Tom Jones, George Strait, and Gene Autry. Maurice made several appearances with his wife's band on the popular television series *Dallas* and was one of a group of musicians gathered to play the soundtrack and appear in Willie Nelson's movie *Honeysuckle Rose*. Since 1980, Maurice has played in the show band of Johnny High's Country Music Review, a regular Saturday-night performance staged at the Will Rogers Auditorium in Fort Worth. The soloists backed by the band are often amateurs, some of whom have used the show as a springboard to professional careers. Maurice writes most of the arrangements for the show.

Maurice has also been teaching for a number of years—private students and clinics—and has devised and published a steel guitar method based upon a mathematical division of the instrument. With this mathematical method, Maurice hopes to make an extremely complex instrument more readily accessible to a larger number of people. The steel guitar has evolved, and Maurice revels in its new technology.

> When I first started playing, everybody had a triple-neck guitar. There was no way to change the tunings on any string. You had three fixed tunings. So you had a different sound on each tuning. Then in 1956 a good friend of mine, Bud Isaacs, came out with a song with Webb Pierce called "Slowly I'm Falling." He played the pedal steel, and that set the world on its ear. The instrument evolved from a triple-neck to a double-neck where there were pedals on the two necks with two different tunings. The mechanics of the pedals and knee-levers to alter the tuning of the strings made the steel guitar a different instrument from the flat steel and three-neck steel. Now, with each string I can twist another sound out of it. I can pull that tone string to seven different notes. The technology is so good now that it will exceed the limitations of the string. It will raise three times and lower three times while staying on the note it is tuned to, for a total of seven notes. And now with the synthesizer, the MIDI (musical instrument digital interface), for which I have a special pickup on my guitar, my steel guitar can become a trigger mechanism to any instrument I want to play. If I want to sound like a piano, or a harmonica, or a symphony of strings, I can.

Not everyone in the business approves of the technological changes in the steel guitar, and Maurice has been criticized. "When pedals came out everybody said yeah, but that's just not the way it ought to be; that's not even the steel guitar anymore. But those guys are sitting home. As far as trying to stay active with whatever technology offers, I'm going to try it."

Maurice Anderson is a gifted and versatile steel guitarist who credits his success to a positive attitude, a good sense of humor, and a desire in remaining up-to-date in his playing style and equipment. All of these attributes surely contributed to his being hired by Mark O'Connor to play steel guitar on "Fiddlin' Around" from the album *Heroes*.[35] Maurice provides fills and a solo chorus in which he demonstrates the efficiency of the pedals to alter the sounds and pitches on the steel guitar. Everything he plays, chords and melodic passages, is perfectly melded with the other instrumentalists' lines and harmonies. Maurice has a distinctively mellow, cool sound and a tasteful way of infusing his presence into an ensemble. But this does not imply that Maurice is a timid guitarist. Perry Jones's profile of Maurice Anderson outlines not a timid guitarist but a brilliant artist; his comments also seem an appropriate conclusion to this chapter: "I attended a clinic of his in Reno, Nevada, during the mid-70s and found his music to be a masterful combination of mainstream jazz, pop, country, blues, and swing. He was surrounded by some brilliant musicians and together they played with force, power, style and delicate intimacy. Maurice played some mind-boggling jazz riffs and proved to everyone that the steel guitar was indeed a jazz instrument. But more than that, he performed like a sculptor as he molded that mass of metal, strings, and wood into Art and Beauty for others to behold. He captured the collective imaginations of the entire audience from traditionalists to New Agers." [36]

FIVE

The Western Swing Rhythm Section: Banjo and Bass

S wing is a rhythmic concept, and swing jazz is defined by its rhythm section. There are, of course, other typical characteristics of swing jazz: preference for large ensembles of ten or more musicians, greater dependence upon written arrangements, decreasing occurrence of collective improvisation, regular appearance of saxophones and string bass in ensembles, the use of the high-hat cymbal among drummers, and a higher level of technical proficiency in terms of speed, agility, tone color, and intonation.[1] Swing jazz can exist without one or more of these components, but it is not swing without its definitive swing rhythm.

Swing rhythm sections maintain a steady quadruple meter (4/4) in which the bass instrument, the bass drum and cymbals from the drum set, the piano, and the rhythm guitar or banjo strike every beat with equal intensity. Against this continuous background of four equal pulses, the drummer superimposes a pattern of subdivided beats on the ride cymbal. The resulting juxtaposition of evenly accented and unevenly subdivided beats results in the characteristic swing rhythm by which the music is recognized.[2] Two-beat patterns do occur in swing rhythm sections, but it is normal procedure for the rhythm players to revert to the smoother, more fluid swing-four meter during solo choruses.

The rhythmic nature of jazz began to change in the late 1920s, when individual musicians and some bands paved the way for the newer swing rhythm approach that had assumed dominance by the mid-1930s. Early jazz, sometimes labeled "Dixieland," "traditional," "New Orleans," or "Chicago" jazz, was built upon a basic two-beat feel supplied by rhythm sections consisting of a variety of instruments—banjo, guitar, tuba, bass saxophone, string bass, piano, and drums.

Certain musicians and bands working in the Southwest were pivotal in moving jazz rhythm sections from syncopated two-four to the smoother swing-four. The main jazz attraction in Dallas in the late 1920s and early 1930s was Alphonso Trent and His Orchestra, which was firmly ensconced at the Adolphus Hotel Ballroom and recorded on the Gennett label. Other southwestern jazz musicians raved about the Trent ensemble. After listening to Trent recordings and allowing for their poor recording quality, Ross Russell, author of *Jazz Styles in Kansas City and the Southwest*, concludes:

> The Alphonso Trent Orchestra, on the strength of its astonishingly advanced arrangements and smooth, precise performances, can be compared favorably with Fletcher Henderson and McKinney's Cotton Pickers. The musicianship is beyond reproach. Difficult unison and voiced passages, often in difficult keys . . . are taken with consummate ease. The band never fails to swing. The writing, with bold juxtapositions of brass and reed passages, the use of antiphony, and the voicing within the sections were years ahead of anything in Texas. For that matter, it was more sophisticated than any band in Kansas City, even Bennie Moten and Jesse Stone.[3]

The Trent Orchestra, though known only in the Southwest, was a pioneer swing jazz ensemble, as was another seldom-recorded but nevertheless legendary territory band out of Oklahoma City, the Blue Devils.

The Blue Devils was famous for its competitive spirit—band members preferred battle dances and jam sessions to any other performing context—and its loose, free-swinging rhythmic approach. The Blue Devils band that recorded in November 1929 consisted of some of the greatest jazz figures ever gathered in one ensemble, though they were not yet famous. University of Kansas student Walter Page played tuba, baritone saxophone, and string bass. Texas-born reed player Buster Smith doubled on clarinet and alto saxophone and was matched by the incomparable trumpeter Lips Page, whose "infectious rhythmic drive, blasting tone, and ability to pile chorus upon chorus made the Blue Devils' brass section go."[4] Bill Basie, a New Jersey pianist who had studied with Fats Waller and toured the vaudeville circuit before becoming a Blue Devil, was fast developing into a leading swing pianist. Eddie Durham, guitarist for the

band, was experimenting with electrical amplification. Tenor saxophonist Lester Young, whom the Blue Devils recruited during a tour into the
Minneapolis area, possessed the rich but controlled tone, incredible exe-
cution, and advanced improvisational skills that made the Blue Devils'
reed section unbeatable. The singer, Jimmy Rushing, contributed a powerful, straightforward, unadorned vocal delivery that was a perfect match
for Lips Page's trumpet licks. When Kansas City bandleader Bennie Moten
could not beat the Blue Devils in jam sessions, he hired them all, and in
the process transformed his band's rather stilted rhythmic approach into
a more energized swing. When Moten relinquished control of his orchestra to Bill "Count" Basie in the mid-1930s, this same aggregate of former
Blue Devils formed the nucleus of Basie's "Big Swing Machine." 5

The Trent orchestra and the Blue Devils were but two of the many
southwestern jazz bands that possessed as one of their primary attributes
a good sense of swing. One reason that southwestern bands felt a four-
beat swing rhythm, while bands in the Northeast struggled with a rigid
and less liberated two-beat approach, may be traced to the loose-limbed,
highly improvised blues tradition that was fundamental to southwestern
jazz. Swing jazz probably originated in the rhythm sections of southwestern bands, but because of their limited recording opportunities and only
local recognition, they are afforded almost no credit for helping to invent
the style. Instead, northeastern bands, like those of Fletcher Henderson
and Benny Goodman, because of the frequency and national distribution
of their recordings, are usually associated with the rhythmic changes that
resulted in swing jazz.

The Henderson band was the seminal northern swing ensemble, in-
fluencing other groups seeking to escape the two-beat trap in favor of a
more fluid swing-four. But by late 1934 the Henderson organization was
in a state of collapse, and Benny Goodman hired Henderson to be one
of his arrangers. Almost immediately the Goodman band gained a hith-
erto missing rhythmic energy. Jazz historian Gunther Schuller gives Henderson's arrangements the credit for "revivifying" the Goodman sound:
"Henderson's arrangements of current or familiar tunes had a good beat,
were smartly orchestrated, cleverly setting off brass and reeds in complementary fashion: they had just enough daring (compared with the 'sweet'
commercial fare generally prevalent on radio) to capture the listener's
ear. Herein, then, lay the uncanny amalgam of success that precipitated
the Swing Era: spicing up familiar commercial, popular material with a

Harlem-oriented musical seasoning and selling it via a white band for a white musical/commercial audience."[6]

Because it delineated swing jazz as no other musical element could, the most significant shift for the Goodman band was the rhythmic adjustment from the older two-beat pattern to the smoother, more flexible swing-four. By the mid-1930s, most dance band rhythm sections throughout the country, in horn and string groups, had adopted a swing-four rhythmic basis, and the Swing Era was under way.

The rhythm section is literally the heartbeat of the jazz band, and though its exact instrumentation has changed, its function—providing a rhythmic background against which the frontline melody instruments work—has remained remarkably intact. Even the overall makeup of the jazz rhythm section has survived with only slight variation. A bass instrument of some kind lays down the harmonic foundation and articulates either all or some of the beats in each measure, while other instruments reinforce the beat pattern, either by playing chords or melodies in a rhythmic fashion or by eliciting various sounds from the drum set in association with specific beats.

In the pre–World War I jazz tradition of New Orleans, where marching-band musicians by day became jazz musicians by night, the bass role was often fulfilled by tuba or bass saxophone. But in cases where jazz music accompanied dancing, and as most dance bands were string bands, the string bass also found a place in early New Orleans jazz. The string bass was undoubtedly used in early jazz more frequently than recorded evidence suggests; but since string bass was hard to hear on acoustic recordings, a wind bass was used to cut through the horns. As jazz blossomed in cities like Chicago, Kansas City, and New York in the 1920s, especially after electrical recording technology was invented, the string bass emerged as dominant, causing many tuba players to convert to upright string bass.

In New Orleans bands before World War I, the rhythmic-harmonic filler was most often provided by a banjo. But by the beginning of the Swing Era, the banjo had been replaced by the guitar, and the piano had become a standard member of the jazz rhythm section. Horn bands had drums from the beginning, but string bands typically did not. Without the overpowering horns, string bands could derive sufficient rhythmic push from banjos, guitars, and sometimes a string bass. Bob Wills was the first string bandleader to hire a drummer because he had a few horns in his string band and was playing to large crowds in huge dance halls;

he needed drums to solidify the dance beat. To this day, western swing bands remain inconsistent in their use of drums.

Banjo

Since the banjo was a member of the jazz rhythm section from the beginning and survived in western swing even after being dropped from horn bands, it is a logical instrument with which to begin a discussion of individual rhythm players. The banjo, a plucked string instrument with a long fretted neck and round body over which a vellum, skin, or plastic membrane is tightly stretched, was invented by African American slaves and was modeled on African instruments. The banjo, its playing techniques, and its typical rhythm patterns were absorbed into the black-face minstrel shows of the mid-nineteenth century, whence they influenced the rhythmic character of ragtime.[7] Ragtime bands normally employed banjoists who executed highly syncopated single-string melodies as well as strummed chords.

Three kinds of banjos were available to ragtime and early jazz players: the five-string model in G or C (tuned g-d-g-b-d and g-c-g-b-d respectively), the four-string tenor banjo (tuned c-g-d-a), and the six-string "guitar banjo" (tuned E-A-d-g-b-e like a guitar). Apparently there was little difference in the playing techniques applied to these instruments, and eventually the four-string banjo emerged as the banjo of choice for jazz musicians.[8]

There were many competent banjoists who fulfilled their harmonic-rhythmic functions in jazz, but a few left indelible marks on the art of jazz banjo playing. One of these was Johnny St. Cyr, who recorded in the 1920s with Louis Armstrong's Hot Five and Hot Seven as well as with Jelly Roll Morton's Red Hot Peppers. A self-taught guitarist and banjoist from New Orleans, St. Cyr played on every New Orleans band of note before moving to Chicago in the 1920s and becoming the most sought-after banjoist in that city. For much of his career he played a six-string instrument that he built himself by attaching a guitar neck to a banjo body. St. Cyr developed both ensemble and solo styles. For ensemble work he played in the "relaxed, four-beat chordal manner associated with New Orleans jazz."[9] In feature solo choruses he developed a technique of playing single-string melodies on the low strings while punctuating with chords on the upper strings, usually on beats two and four. He added a further virtuosic touch to his solo playing with high-string tremolos. St. Cyr's solo approach combined trombone and bass licks with the left-hand chord patterns associated with ragtime. He was probably the best of the early jazz banjoists; certainly he set a standard for others to follow.

Western swing has produced its share of banjo legends. The first western swing banjoist of note was Ocie Stockard, who joined Milton Brown and His Musical Brownies in 1932.[10] Stockard's role with the Musical Brownies was primarily a harmonic-rhythmic one, with occasional melodic flourishes. He provided a steady four-beat chordal pattern against which the frontline players improvised impressive solos. With Stockard playing banjo, Brown had no need of a drummer.

In the history of western swing, Smokey Rogers (1917–1993) emerges as a true genius—singer, songwriter, comedian, and superb banjoist and guitarist. A Michigan boy, Smokey played banjo on his first amateur contest on radio station WJR in Detroit when he was only eight years old. A few years later he met three other talented musicians in Detroit—Larry "Pedro" DePaul (accordion), Andrew "Cactus" Soldi (fiddle), and "Texas" Jim Lewis (bass)—with whom he formed a quartet. The four young men went to New York City, where they auditioned for the show at the Village Barn and were booked for a full year's engagement. After this year in New York, they toured around the country and eventually settled in California.

By the late 1930s, Hollywood was showing a profit despite the depression because of its movie westerns and Broadway-style musicals. Talented musicians could find work in Los Angeles in movie and recording studios. Smokey and his three companions made several musical movie shorts with Charles Starrett and settled into steady freelance work.[11]

Spade Cooley was making a name for himself as a popular swing bandleader in Los Angeles. When Cooley's manager, Bert Phillips, decided to double his profits by splitting the Cooley band in half and moving the new band to the Riverside Rancho, Cooley was forced to hire replacement musicians. He hired Smokey Rogers and Deuce Spriggens (bass) to fill out his half of the band.

In late 1943 Cooley dissolved his business relationship with Phillips and signed a recording contract with Columbia Records. At its first recording session the Cooley band cut a song written by Smokey Rogers, "Shame, Shame on You," which became a major hit and the Cooley band's theme song. For the next three years Smokey contributed to the success of the Cooley band with his guitar and banjo playing, singing, song writing, and comedy routines.

When Tex Williams broke from Cooley in mid-1946, most of Cooley's musicians, including Smokey Rogers, joined Tex Williams and the Western Caravan, which opened at the Redondo Barn on July 4, 1946. Only a short time later the Western Caravan moved to a converted roller rink between Los Angeles and Glendale, which the band renamed the Palace Barn. On July 24, 1946, the Caravan made its first records on the Capitol label. In late 1947 Tex Williams and the Western Caravan made a series of feature films and musical shorts for Universal Studios. Always on the lookout for better business opportunities, Williams moved his band to the RCA record label in 1951, and when that proved unsuccessful, he signed with Decca in 1953. The Caravan began to feel the pressure of declining visibility and profits in the late 1950s with the upsurge of interest in rock music and finally disbanded in 1957.[12] For much of this decade, Smokey Rogers contributed to the Western Caravan as he had previously to the Spade Cooley band.

Smokey was a busy musician in Los Angeles, working not only with Cooley and Williams, but also with Cliffie Stone, Tennessee Ernie Ford, steel guitarists Joaquin Murphy and Speedy West, and many others. Later in the 1950s, he relocated to San Diego, where for several years he hosted a popular television show. Smokey bought the Bostonia Ballroom in San Diego and promoted western swing and country music acts. A gifted songwriter, he wrote, besides "Shame, Shame on You," such popular songs as "Spanish Fandango," "You Can't Break My Heart," "Tho' I Tried," "Long-Lost Love," and "Gone." Smokey Rogers remained active in western swing until his death from a stroke and cancer on November 23, 1993.[13]

Smokey added a strong melodic element to tenor banjo playing. He was a steady component of the rhythm section, often strumming chords on beats two and four and filling in the other two beats with melodic figures. A versatile player, Smokey matched his playing to the type of music being performed—strumming in a two-beat pattern on traditional numbers such as fiddle tunes and polkas, playing the more fluid swing-four on up-tempo swing numbers. He was also an outstanding soloist, fully capable of rapid-fire, single-string melodic lines, combined with the finger-picking patterns and upper-register tremolos idiomatic to the banjo. "Scale Boogie," recorded by the Western Caravan, features Smokey picking out a boogie-woogie melody line on the lower strings against chords and rapid tremolos in the upper register. Smokey's playing demonstrated great imagination in improvisation and an unflagging rhythmic drive.

Banjoist Marvin "Smokey" Montgomery Talks about Western Swing

MARVIN "SMOKEY" MONTGOMERY was born in 1910 in Reinard, Iowa, the heart of the agricultural belt. He claims that he never learned to milk a cow but spent plenty of time shucking corn. His bad experience with an overly aggressive turkey gobbler gave him a permanent distaste for all winged farm animals.

Smokey began teaching himself to play banjo when he was ten. As he relates it, his mother, who was a pianist, had purchased a small ukulele banjo for Smokey's younger brother, who showed no interest in it. Smokey assumed charge of the banjo, a great relief to the entire family, as he had been playing drums and, in his words, "driving everybody crazy." Smokey learned quickly and was soon playing duets with his mother. "She'd buy sheet music everytime she went up to Fort Dodge and I'd sit there and play the uke with her." Smokey absorbed the popular dance music of the day by tagging along with his parents. Though he was too young to enter the large dance halls they frequented, he could observe and listen to the bands from outside.

> I'd stand and watch these orchestras and saw a banjo player playing tenor style, so I ordered a chord book from Sears and Roebuck and just started playing tenor style—which is tuned like a viola. In the twenties they had the pit orchestras with lots of violin players, and the Dixieland jazz started taking over and the fiddle players started losing their jobs, so they bought banjos and tuned them so that the fingering would be the same, except there would be a fifth difference, like viola. All they had to do was learn to shake their hand real fast and they could play.

Smokey soon learned to play tenor banjo well enough that his mother formed a small dance band called the Iowa Orioles. Smokey built a drum case to fit on the back of their gray Chrysler, and the little group, consisting of piano, banjo, drums, and saxophone, played their own small territory for most of Smokey's high school years. When he graduated from high school, Smokey attended Iowa State College at Ames, where he studied industrial arts but continued to play his banjo at every opportunity. "I wanted to be a schoolteacher and make twenty-five bucks a week," he recalls. During Smokey's sophomore year at Iowa State, a tent show from Texas came through town and staged an amateur contest in which Smokey took second place and won three dollars. The manager of the tent show was impressed with Smokey's banjo playing and took his name and address. Two weeks later he telegraphed Smokey and offered him a job with the tent show.

Life as a tent show musician proved grueling: Smokey not only played in the orchestra but also helped raise the tent. When his hands became so blistered that he could not play his banjo, he was given the less strenuous task of checking and repairing the 2,000 folding wooden chairs used by the audience. Since Smokey had been studying industrial arts in college, the manager sometimes put him in charge of operating the electrical system for the show. The tent show orchestra played while people were being seated, then serenaded audiences between the three acts of the show. The year was 1934, the height of the depression, and Smokey earned about eleven dollars a week, out of which he paid for his meals. "I just lived in the gab house with all the roughnecks. I had my cot on the wardrobe trunk."

During his first year with the tent show, the troupe toured West Texas towns like Odessa and Wink, which were beginning to experience the oil boom. In the summer they returned north to Iowa and Illinois, but the following winter toured East and South Texas. Deciding that he was homesick and in need of a vacation, Smokey used the thirty dollars he had saved out of his wages to buy a train ticket that got him from Houston to Dallas.

> I got to Dallas about four o'clock in the morning. I had a little old battery radio, and I knew about WBAP and these fiddle bands because I listened to them all the time—the Wanderers and Blacky Simons and His Blue Jackets. So I walked down to the Adolphus Hotel from the depot and Blacky Simons came on about 6:30 A.M., and I waited until they were through. Blacky said, "Mrs. Davis [the manager of KRLD] is looking for a guitar player to go out and play with the piano player tonight for a party, and I'll introduce you to her." And it paid three dollars. I was making eleven bucks a week with the tent show, so three dollars was pretty good. I said, "Mrs. Davis, would you mind paying me in advance? My guitar and banjo are down at the depot and I don't have the money to get them." She

paid me. I went and got the instruments and got me a little one-dollar-a-night room in a little hotel up on Elm Street. I think it was one of those red-light-district houses. I only stayed about a week, but it was real funny. This piano player picked me up down at the hotel and we went out to the Dallas Country Club. It was a stag party, where the gal took off everything she ever had on plus a few more, and I thought, this Dallas is a wild town.

The piano player with whom Smokey played the stag party worked for the Wanderers and encouraged Smokey to audition, which he did the following day. They liked what they heard and put him on their 10:30 A.M. WFAA radio show. Smokey recalls, "They let me play a chorus on 'Sweet Georgia Brown.' I even remember what I played." That same night Smokey accompanied the Wanderers to a job in Kilgore, the middle of East Texas oil country. "We went to this place that had chicken wire in front of the bandstand. I asked the bartender, 'Why do you have this wire across here?' He said, 'We have a colored band that plays here during the week and these roughnecks come in here and drink and throw bottles at them, and we have to protect them.' We made twelve bucks that night."

Within a span of forty-eight hours Smokey had made more than he earned working a full week with the tent show, and he had not had to repair a chair or risk his life working the electrical system. There was no returning to the tent show for Smokey Montgomery. Though the band never officially hired Smokey, the Wanderers continued to use him on radio broadcasts and live performances. In June of 1935 several of the Wanderers—Smokey, Dick Reinhart (guitar/vocals), and Burt Dodson (bass/vocals)—were invited to join the Light Crust Doughboys band, which was being reorganized under the direction of Eddie Dunn after Burrus Mills president Jack Burrus fired W. Lee O'Daniel for allegedly pocketing extra money made from the band's theater gigs. The newly reconstituted Doughboys included new members Smokey, Reinhart, and Dodson, along with previous members Muryel "Zeke" Campbell (guitar), Kenneth Pitts (fiddle), and Clifford "Doc" Gross (fiddle). O'Daniel had given each Doughboy a nickname, and the three new recruits assumed the names worn by their predecessors. Smokey inherited the name Junior from the banjo player he replaced: "I had that name with the Doughboys until 1948, when we went on television on Channel 5. We were the first band on live television. We were the Light Crust Doughboys, but on television we were called Mel Cox and the Flying X Ranchboys. When I would play my banjo on fast things on that old TV, my hand would blur. Mel would say, 'Well, there's old Junior smoking it out.' But the first thing you know, he started calling me Smokey, and I was glad to get rid of the name Junior."

Life with the Doughboys involved a great deal of practicing: "We punched in at nine at the Burrus Mills studio, and that's the way I learned to play. Knocky Parker [piano] and myself and Muryel "Zeke" Campbell would sit around the studio and jam; we'd take a tune like 'Darktown Strutters' Ball' and everybody would play a chorus in the key of C and then we'd go to C-sharp, and on up through all the keys until we got back to C. You'll learn something doing that. We listened to records and tried to copy them. We were trying to imitate the big bands."

The Doughboys had a large following in Fort Worth, but the hottest and best band working the area in 1935 was Milton Brown and His Musical Brownies. Smokey had many conversations with Brown and ample opportunity to form an opinion of the man and his talent. "Milton didn't play an instrument. He was a good singer, and he had a personality that wouldn't quit with people. Personally, I think if Milton hadn't been killed in that car wreck, he would have been more popular than Bob Wills."

Milton Brown had just won a contract from Republic Pictures to do a film with Gene Autry, *Oh Suzanna*. When he was killed in 1936, the Doughboys took his place on the picture. They returned from Hollywood more determined to increase the size of their band and play swing jazz. Their first addition was pianist Knocky Parker, who was just a kid out of high school when he auditioned for the Doughboys.

> The Brownies had a good piano player by the name of "Papa" Calhoun because of "Fatha" Earl Hines out of Chicago. Everybody was trying to imitate Fatha Hines, so the Brownies called their piano player Papa Calhoun. When Knocky Parker sat down and started playing like Papa Calhoun, I said, "Knocky, play your own stuff, don't play like that; anybody can play that way." And so Knocky started playing. Of course, we hired him. His first day he came down with the measles, and his parents took his shoes and clothes away; but he wanted to come to the radio program anyway. Barefooted, he started walking to Fort Worth from his home in Palmer, Texas. He was a genius. He became known as "the wildman of the piano."

Smokey and fiddler Kenneth Pitts convinced young Parker to enroll at Texas Christian University, where he studied English literature and music. According to Smokey, Parker never learned to read music, despite his advanced training. When it came time to give his senior piano recital, he played his pieces (one of which was George Gershwin's *Rhapsody in Blue*) by memory while a fellow student turned pages to make it appear as though Parker were reading. In time, Parker became a professor of English literature at Southern Florida University in Tampa, but Smokey continued to work with him on various music projects, including a recorded history of ragtime on the Audiofile label.

Smokey and Kenneth Pitts also studied music at Texas Christian University. Smokey says, "I studied every music course they had out there. I'd go at seven o'clock in the morning and stay until eight-thirty and then go back out in the afternoon. I stayed out there for about three years studying music—conducting, arranging, music history." His arranging courses proved quite useful as Smokey began transcribing and arranging songs from records for use by the Doughboys, everything from old breakdowns and fiddle tunes to the jazz numbers recorded by Bob Crosby and the Bobcats and other big bands and the popular tunes of the day. Smokey developed a formula that fit with the Doughboys' instrumentation: "I'd write the lead for electric guitar, and we always had two fiddles then, so I'd write three-part harmony. Once in a while I'd write a fourth part for Knocky on the piano, and we'd have four-part harmony. The Doughboys would sound like a big band. We'd follow the big bands' arrangements as far as we could. That's what all the fiddle bands were trying to do; that's the reason you heard so many pop songs and things like that in those days."

Occasionally record company executives would suggest new songs to the bands they had under contract. Smokey remembers a time in 1938 when Art Satherley, A & R man for Columbia Records, called Smokey from New York and suggested that they listen to Bennie Moten's new release, "South." The Doughboys listened and then recorded their own version; quite to their surprise, since it was entirely instrumental, "South" became one of their biggest sellers. They copied the opening and closing sections of the Moten arrangement but added their own individual solo choruses, thus giving "South" a unique western swing flavor. "We did 'South' and all the other fiddle bands were listening to us on the air and they tried to copy us, and we listened to all the other fiddle bands and tried to copy tunes that we heard them do. Before you knew it, every western swing band was playing 'South.'"

Western swing bands shared not only repertory but also sidemen. In 1938 Doughboys bass player Jim Boyd left the group to join the W. Lee

O'Daniel band, which was part of O'Daniel's campaign strategy in the U.S. Senate race. Joe Frank Ferguson left Bob Wills's Texas Playboys to play bass and sing with the Doughboys. In 1940 Knocky Parker left the Doughboys to do graduate work at Columbia University, and Frank Reneau took his place as the Doughboys' pianist. The Light Crust Doughboys disbanded during World War II, as the military draft took its toll, but reformed in 1945, with Smokey and Jim Boyd as the nucleus of the reorganized band. The Doughboys continued to represent Burrus Mills, which sponsored the band's daily radio program until it finally went off the air in 1952. Remaining members of the Doughboys continue to play for various special occasions.

The popular music world has changed dramatically since Smokey first became a Light Crust Doughboy in 1935, and he does not welcome all of the changes. He is particularly disturbed by modifications concocted in Nashville, which he feels interfere with the performance and progress of western swing.

> What we were doing then [before World War II] was playing the best we knew how when the record producers would say to take a chorus; we'd give it everything we had. Then after World War II you'd go into a recording studio and they'd say to play like so-and-so in Nashville. From then on, you don't play what you feel, you play like they want you to play—like somebody else. Some said to hold it down, don't get all that hot jazz in there. Thanks to George Strait, we still get to do a little bit of improvisation; the Light Crust Doughboys do George Strait songs, but there aren't too many songs coming out now that we can do in our own style. Most of the newer songs have heavy drum beats, like rock 'n' roll, or no rhythm at all.

Smokey assumes that when the Light Crust Doughboys are hired, they are expected to play western swing, so they limit themselves to the standard repertory of the 1930s and 1940s and the few current songs that suit their playing approach. Smokey insists that this distinctive playing approach incorporates "our hot choruses in the middle of the songs, just like in the old days." If it is contemporary country music that an audience wants, the Light Crust Doughboys is not their band. For country music that sounds the way it does off the recordings, Smokey suggests another band of which he is a part, the Wagon Masters.

While Smokey has been a continuous member of the Light Crust Doughboys since 1935, he has also been involved with other musical activities. Over one hundred of his own songs and many of his arrangements have been recorded. Until the mid-1970s he worked as an arranger for a Christian music company, Rainbow Records. He also did the arrangements for five contemporary Christian albums released by Lulu Roman, formerly of the *Hee Haw* television show. Smokey relinquished this kind of work when he reached age sixty-five and could no longer tolerate the pressure of deadlines and restrictions associated with commercial recording. When he arranges and composes now, it is usually for the Dallas Banjo Band, which he directs, or for two jazz combos with which he performs—a trio called Smokey and the Bearkats and a band called the Dallas Hot Five.

Smokey also became involved in the publishing and producing end of music in 1957, when he and partner Arty Glenn formed Glendale Music. They never owned any monster hits, but they made good money. In 1990 the two decided to dissolve Glendale Music Company because it was no longer showing a profit. A year later they received a royalty check for $5,000 from England on their song "Percolator," released by saxophonist Boots Randolph in 1965. At the beginning of 1992 they received another royalty check for $3,000 on the same tune and had to reincorporate Glendale Publishing Company. The week before this interview Smokey had received a check for $7,257 from Germany for "Percolator."

In 1963 Smokey took the money from a club he had owned and operated for about eleven years and put it into a recording studio with partner Ed Burnett. Summit Burnett Recording Sound is still a busy studio today; in fact, Mark O'Connor's *Heroes* album was partially recorded there. Summit Burnett started in a leased warehouse, then in 1970 moved to a modern facility built to the partners' specifications. With several studios and state-of-the-art equipment, Summit Burnett Recording Sound turns out a quality product.

Smokey Montgomery has worked every angle of the music business, from playing to producing, and has received numerous awards, including induction into several western swing halls of fame and selection to participate in the World's All-Star Dixieland Jazz Band, an ensemble consisting of players from the United States and Europe, which concertized widely in the mid-1980s. He names Harry Reeser and Eddie Peabody as important influences for him.

Harry Reeser had a banjo club that broadcast on radio for Chiquist Club Soda. He had three or four banjos playing along with the orchestra, and they did some really flapperette tunes that were just a little complicated. I got every record of his I could find. I tried to copy his style—a real technical single-string style. He played clear up until he died in 1973. I saw Eddie Peabody in Denver when I was about sixteen years old. He was playing in vaudeville. He played his tune and said that he was going to imitate two banjos at once. The song was "Waiting for the Sunrise." He played lead on A string and put chords with it to make it sound like two banjos.

A plaque from the Western Swing Hall of Fame in Austin credits Smokey with introducing Dixieland style banjo playing into western swing. He insists that he plays basically the same, whether he is playing Dixieland or western swing, though he admits that, when playing swing for dance audiences, he accents all four beats equally in the swing-four rhythm. When playing Dixieland, Smokey uses the typical jazz two-beat pattern, accenting beats two and four in the 4/4 meter. Smokey Montgomery plays banjo so well that many people have asked him to describe his approach, and his response often is: "I played drums before I played banjo; I'm doing the same thing on the banjo rhythmwise as I'd be doing if I were playing drums."

Like most western swing musicians, Smokey has had to play some country music to survive, and he notes that the differences between country music and jazz are as much harmonic as rhythmic. "In a country band you would only use flatted fifths and pure seventh chords, but with Dixieland and swing I can play flatted ninths and nine-sixes. In country music you play plain old pure triads, in jazz you play those extra chords." Smokey prefers to play jazz, not only because of the wider chord choices, but also because of the opportunities for improvisation. "In a jazz chorus you follow the chord progression, but you play any notes you want that fit, and try to make it swing; that's fun. You're creating something right on somebody else's chord progression." Whether keeping time or playing a solo chorus, Smokey Montgomery is the consummate tenor banjoist, a true living legend, and still picking in his eighties.

Bass

The jazz rhythm section has always included a bass instrument of some kind, either tuba, bass saxophone, or string bass. In fact, the bass player has often been more responsible for maintaining a steady beat than the drummer. But because the bass instrument is seldom featured in a solo capacity, few listeners realize its importance. Jazz historian Leonard Feather stresses the significant role of the bass.

> The jazz unit can no more dispense with a bass than a house with its foundation or a ship with its hull. Since the motivating element in both written and improvised jazz is the harmonic structure of the composition, it devolves upon the bass to provide a constant guide to this structure, most often by playing the root of the incumbent chord, or its fifth, and by linking these notes together with other notes of the chord or with passing notes. At the same time, through the depth and penetration of its tonal quality, the bass provides the fundamental rhythmic beat. The pianist and guitarist may "comp" (fill in with rhythmic punctuations and syncopations); the drummer may invest in a variety of complex cross-rhythms, but through it all the bass provides the deep, rich four-to-the-bar *sine qua non* that gives the band, literally, its lowest common denominator.[14]

The instrument that has served these dual harmonic-rhythmic functions has varied over time and context. Ragtime and string bands in the 1890s and early 1900s included string bass players, who typically bowed on beats one and three in the four-beat measures and occasionally doubled the trombone or cello in playing melodic interludes in compositions having several themes.[15]

Pre-electric recordings generally required wind bass, most often tuba, because string bass was difficult to pick up with primitive recording equipment. It is likely that some early jazz bands used wind bass in live performance because it could cut through the rest of the horns. However, since ragtime and dance music heavily influenced jazz, it is also probable that string bass was used in live performance with horns, and there are documented examples of string bass being played on early jazz recordings. String bassist Steve Brown recorded with the New Orleans Rhythm Kings as early as 1922.[16]

When electric recording techniques were developed in the mid-1920s, the string bass began to replace the wind bass in most jazz ensembles. By the early 1930s, jazz tuba players had converted to string bass and were searching for ways to increase its volume. One approach was to install extremely high bridges that lifted the strings well above the fingerboard, producing a "high action" and a larger dynamic range. Other solutions included "slapping" the strings hard against the fingerboard, using aluminum-bodied instruments (Pops Foster with Luis Russell and Louis Armstrong), and attaching primitive electric pickups for sound amplification (Wellman Braud with Duke Ellington).[17]

Bassists have been instrumental in instigating and emphasizing stylistic shifts in jazz. In early or traditional jazz, bassists helped to maintain the common two-beat patterns; but players like Walter Page, John Kirby, and Bob Haggart laid the foundation for swing with their plucked, walking bass lines that distributed accents more evenly on all four beats of the 4/4 meter. While these bassists of the early 1930s were skilled players, they accepted the role of timekeepers, playing "endless strings of quarter notes or, occasionally in slower tempi, dotted eighths and sixteenths."[18]

Individual bass players have left highly influential legacies, as jazz bassists have built on the styles of John Lindsay (1894–1950), George Murphy "Pops" Foster (1892–1969), Wellman Braud (1891–1966), Walter Sylvester Page (1900–1957), Jimmy Blanton (1918–1942), Oscar Pettiford (1922–1960), Ray Brown (b. 1926), and Leroy Elliott "Slam" Stewart (1914–1987). Walter Page was one of the most celebrated and influential bassists of the late 1930s, largely due to his years as the backbone of the Count Basie rhythm section. Page was the founder of the talented Blue Devils band out of Oklahoma City, which included Bill Basie. When financial setbacks forced Page to relinquish control of the Blue Devils in 1931, he went to work for Bennie Moten in Kansas City. He was playing in Moten's band in 1934 when Count Basie became its new leader. Page then worked for the Jeter-Pillars Orchestra in St. Louis before returning to Basie's band (1935–1942, 1946–1949). Historian J. Bradford Robinson characterizes Walter Page as "a mainstay of Basie's celebrated rhythm section, where the solidity and swing of his playing enabled the leader (pianist Basie) to dispense with stride left-hand patterns and Jo Jones to transfer the pulse to the hi-hat cymbals."[19] Walter Page also played the first recorded string bass solo chorus on "Pagin' the Devil," by the Kansas City Six, a unit from the Basie Orchestra. He helped to popularize the walking-bass technique.

The pivotal bass figure in jazz history, Jimmy Blanton, shared a great many similarities with his guitarist contemporary, Charlie Christian. Both began playing in family bands; each altered the course of the development of his instrument; both participated in early bebop experiments; and both died young from the ravages of tuberculosis. Blanton was discovered in 1939 by Duke Ellington in a riverboat band and immediately hired.

Earlier Ellington had used bassist Wellman Braud, whose slapping of the strings to produce a larger sound sometimes interfered with the clarity of the rhythm section. Robinson writes that Blanton's playing

> stabilized the band's rhythm and greatly enhanced its swing. He [Blanton] possessed great dexterity and range, roundness of tone, accurate intonation, and above all an unprecedented sense of swing. His strong feeling for harmony led him to incorporate many non-harmonic passing notes in his accompaniment lines, giving them a contrapuntal flavor and stimulating soloists to their own harmonic explorations. Blanton also contributed to the earliest fully satisfying jazz solos on this instrument, which depart in their inventive melody and flexible rhythms from the walking bass style that was then prevalent. Despite his short career, Blanton left a large recorded legacy, not only in his 130-odd recordings with Ellington's orchestra, but also in many small-group performances with some of Ellington's sidemen, and especially in a remarkable series of duos with Ellington himself.[20]

Blanton's playing style provided the inspiration for all modern jazz bassists up to the 1960s and laid the groundwork for the bebop rhythm section.

Of the many bassists who built on Blanton's innovations, Oscar Pettiford, Ray Brown, and Slam Stewart probably had the greatest impact on swing bassists, especially western swing players, in the 1940s, 1950s, and 1960s. Through his recordings with Charlie Barnett, the Roy Eldridge Quartet, Dizzy Gillespie, Duke Ellington, and Woody Herman, Pettiford was a powerful emissary of the double bass as a solo instrument, fully equal in sound and importance to the horns.[21] Likewise, Raymond Matthews Brown, though associated early with bebop, made an impact on all bass players because of the "precision of his playing, the beauty of his tone, and the tastefulness of his solos."[22] Brown was heard frequently in performance and on records with such jazz greats as Charlie Parker, Dizzy Gillespie, Bud Powell, the Milt Jackson Quartet, the Oscar Peterson Trio, the L.A. Four, and Duke Ellington. He was also spotlighted as musical director and bassist for his wife, Ella Fitzgerald. This exposure and his natural talent led him to dominate the jazz popularity polls as a bassist during the 1950s. Slam Stewart, who at one time studied bass at the Boston Conservatory, was best known for his unique method of bowing and humming a melody in perfect unison. Stewart was renowned for his facile accompaniments in duos with Dizzy Gillespie and Don Byas and in combos fronted by Red Norvo, Benny Goodman, Art Tatum, Roy Eldridge, Bucky Pizzarelli, and others.[23]

Western swing bassists drew upon these jazz bass greats and older southwestern string band traditions. Although the bass was just as vital in western swing bands as in mainstream horn bands, western swing bass players rarely had the opportunity to develop solo identities because they were confined to a timekeeping function. Perhaps because the western swing band emerged out of the rural string band tradition, pioneer western swing musicians did not conceive of the bass as a solo instrument or of bass players as virtuosi. Whereas fiddlers and sometimes guitarists achieved an elevated status as technically proficient soloists, bass players remained in the background as rhythm players. Yet without the bass player steadily keeping time, there would be no swing. Modern bassists in western swing bands exert much more freedom in ensemble and solo playing than did their predecessors in the 1930s, 1940s, and 1950s.

A Few Good Bass Players Talk about Western Swing

LUKE WILLS, younger brother of the famous Bob Wills, relished his backup role as rhythm guitar and bass player in the bands of both Bob and Johnnie Lee Wills. Luke was born Luther J. Wills in 1920 in Hal County, Texas, about one hundred miles southeast of Amarillo. His father, John, was a prominent breakdown fiddler and a struggling West Texas cotton farmer, and Luke and his older brothers grew up plowing cotton fields behind mule teams and accompanying their father at country dances. Luke remembers one of the psychological ploys his father used to keep his sons hard at work on the farm. "Dad would put watermelon seeds in with the cotton seeds; you didn't know just where they'd drop. When the cotton would get ready to pick in the fall, well, you might run into a big fine watermelon lying under some of that cotton. You'd be surprised at the good little things like that would do."

Luke has vivid memories of his father's competing for prizes in fiddle contests around the state, especially when the main rival was another West Texas fiddle legend, Eck Robertson.

> At one time he had twelve violins under his bed that he'd won at fiddling contests. Eck Robertson was quite a fiddler from Amarillo, Texas, and he and Dad were good friends, but they were like the

old western gunfighters—competitors. My dad had a tune he called "Gone Indian." It was basically his tune. He could just completely mystify a crowd with it, because it's a real showy tune. He'd hit one high note and take his bow off the fiddle and put this fiddle over in the other hand, and that note would still be sounding. He had this high holler that he could do and it just got the crowd, then he'd go right back to fiddling. People didn't know where that long note was coming from. But the point I'm making is that in these contests they'd fiddle for blood. Dad won one contest, maybe another five-dollar fiddle. And Dad was kidding Eck. He said, "Well, you sure done good, Eck." Eck said, "You didn't win it. You just out-hollered me. That's all."

Bob Wills was considerably older than Luke and was on his own, working as a musician and a barber, long before Luke was old enough to leave home. Luke remembers the stock-market crash of 1929 and the ensuing depression, which was disastrous for the Wills family. When they lost their cotton farm in West Texas, they moved to Plainview, where John Wills eked out a meager living playing for dances, and then to a farm owned by W. Lee O'Daniel in Aledo, Texas, close to Fort Worth. Brother Bob had joined the Light Crust Doughboys and was able to convince his boss, O'Daniel, to allow his struggling family to work the O'Daniel farm. O'Daniel would eventually use the Wills family's presence on his property first to threaten and then punish the headstrong Bob Wills.

Luke began teaching himself to play guitar when he was twelve years old and living with his family on the O'Daniel farm. The year was 1932, and swing was beginning to be heard on radio and records. Luke wanted to duplicate the guitar playing of swing band stylists, with their more complex and percussive bar chords. But his father, John, insisted that his son "hit that long A," which meant playing a more rural-sounding guitar that allowed open strings to vibrate freely.

When Bob Wills left the Doughboys and his family was forced off O'Daniel's farm, they moved to a farm about seven miles south of the West Texas town of Muleshoe. John Wills had already put together a string band consisting of fiddle, bass, and tenor banjo, which he maintained in the move back to West Texas. Young Luke got his first professional band experience playing guitar in this group, which performed on a daily radio show on station KICH out of Clovis, New Mexico, and which, by 1935, had won a spot on radio station KFYO in Lubbock. All of the band members also worked on John Wills's cotton farm, but farming merely provided financial support for their musicians' lives.

About 1937 Bob Wills hired seventeen-year-old Luke to play tenor banjo in the Texas Playboys band that was working out of Tulsa, Oklahoma. When their cousin Son Lansford left the band for a brief time, Luke moved over to bass, which became his permanent instrument. By 1939, Bob Wills and the Texas Playboys included winds as well as strings, and it had grown to such a degree that Bob established a second Wills family band in Tulsa, with brother Johnnie Lee in charge. Luke went with Johnnie Lee while Bob and the remaining Playboys began spending more time on the West Coast. When Bob got the contract to make eight films with Russell Hayden for Columbia Pictures, he borrowed Luke and some other string players from Johnnie Lee's band. Luke made these movies with his brother Bob, and he explains that Bob was not always easy to direct on the movie set: "We were doing a scene loading big bales of hay on a wagon and singing at the same time. It's all playback singing, but Bob didn't like the idea. He said, 'You don't see somebody lifting a hundred and eighty pound bale of hay and singing.' Bob called the director, Billy Burk, over and said, 'There's no way you can get any reality this way. I haven't fooled with that much hay, but I know you don't sing.'"

World War II and the military draft took Luke away from the Playboys but not from the music business. He enlisted in the navy and ended up with a unit of Seabees. While stationed in the Admiralty Islands, Luke assembled a band that he called Luke Wills and the Admiralty Hired Hands, which included a music-reading trumpeter, a Cajun fiddler, four guitar players, and Luke on bass. The instrument Luke played was, in his words, "Navy issue, borrowed one midnight from the supply center and returned when I shipped out." Being an inventor and a clown, Luke outfitted this bass with a spring and footstand so that he could bounce it around the stage. "I'd just bounce on up to the mike and start singing with that bass still going." The act and the band were successful and much in demand. Sometimes they played in less than optimum conditions, as, for example, when their bandstand was built over ninety tons of TNT on a supply ship.

Early in 1946 Luke was discharged from the navy and returned to Tulsa to resume playing bass for Johnnie Lee; but later that year he rejoined Bob and the Playboys in Fresno, California, which became the band's headquarters. In 1947 Bob created another band, Luke Wills and the Texas Playboys 2, which soon changed its name to Luke Wills and His

Rhythm Busters. Luke explains, "Bob had an idea that Fresno would be the center of the San Joaquin Valley. South would be Los Angeles . . . north to Oakland, San Francisco, Modesto, and it was a good area. But Bob was on the road all the time and he decided to start this band to hold the territory while he was out touring." The Rhythm Busters played concerts, dances, and radio broadcasts and recorded first on the King label, then for RCA Victor.

Though Bob and Luke attempted to establish a territory in California like the one they had experienced in Oklahoma, Texas, Missouri, Kansas, and Arkansas, their mutual vision never materialized, largely because Bob was on national tours so much of the time and also because post–World War II America was a changed place. No longer in the grips of a depression economy, people had more money to spend on entertainment and were not dependent on affordable dances. Since the national economy was greatly improved, musicians expected large salaries, but insisted that bandleaders observe union rules regarding working hours and tours. Popular music had become big business, and Bob Wills had to think and act accordingly. In 1947 he purchased the old Aragon Ballroom near Sacramento, changed its name to Wills Point, and placed Luke in charge while he was away on tours. But Wills Point was never the financial success or the home that Luke and Bob had envisioned.

Bob and Luke Wills spent the years 1949–1961 in search of a home and a territory, moving to Oklahoma City, Dallas, Amarillo, Abilene, Tulsa, and back to the West Coast. For a time in Oklahoma City in 1949 Luke reorganized the Rhythm Busters, but disbanded it in less than a year to help Bob. In 1950 Bob Wills opened the Bob Wills Ranch House in Dallas and placed Luke in charge of the house band while he continued to tour. But unscrupulous accountants and business managers brought the Bob Wills Ranch House to ruin, and Bob himself to the brink of bankruptcy. Wills sold the Ranch House and returned to Wills Point.

In March 1953 Luke was recording with the Playboys at MGM in Hollywood, but the youngest Wills brother, Billy Jack, played bass on the last MGM recording session in March 1954. By this time Billy Jack Wills, who had started his professional career as a drummer and bass player in Bob's band in 1947, was in charge of the house band at Wills Point. While Bob and Luke toured and searched for a home, Billy Jack became firmly entrenched in the West Coast western swing scene, playing dances, broadcasting on radio station KFBK in Sacramento, and hosting a television show, the last western swing band leader to do so on a regular basis. Loyd

Jones, a friend and admirer of Billy Jack Wills, recalls an occasion when Billy Jack's band played back-to-back with Harry James's big swing band at Governor's Hall in Sacramento: "Although the James orchestra was more than twice the size of Billy Jack's band and they had arrangements charted for them, the Billy Jack Wills western swing band outplayed them, doing nothing but big band tunes with an unbelievably full sound using trumpet, mandolin, and steel guitar, belting out four- and five-part 'section' work." [24]

Billy Jack Wills remained the mainstay of the Bob Wills variety of western swing on the West Coast, while Bob and Luke carried their sound nationally and Johnnie Lee maintained the original Wills circuit out of Tulsa. In 1959 Bob and Luke and the Texas Playboys established their headquarters in Las Vegas, where they performed regularly at the Showboat and the Golden Nugget. This was a small Playboys band consisting of Bob Wills, Joe Holley, and Rufus Thibodeaux playing fiddles, Wade Peeler on drums, Millard Kelso at the piano, Gene Crownover on steel, Luke playing bass, and two singers, Laura Lee McBride and Darla Darrett. For six years the Playboys drew large audiences in Las Vegas, and when they relocated first to Tulsa, then to Fort Worth, they continued to book month-long engagements in Las Vegas.

In mid-1963 Bob Wills and company were back in California for a tour and a recording session for Liberty Hill Records. This time Luke played bass in a huge band that included five fiddles, one viola, two electric guitars, steel guitar, piano, drums, and six vocalists. Luke also played bass for the Longhorn Records sessions in 1964–1965 that produced Bob Wills's only folk album. After Bob suffered a second heart attack in 1964, he disbanded the Playboys, except for occasional recording sessions. Luke returned to Las Vegas, which became his permanent home. He remained active in western swing music until a recent crippling stroke left him partially paralyzed and unable to play.

Unlike his other two brothers, Johnnie Lee and Billy Jack, both of whom were able to create separate musical identities, Luke's musical life was closely intertwined with that of Bob Wills. Luke accepted his role as a background rhythm player and has never desired the solo spotlight. But he knows how important his role is in establishing the swing style and providing a good rhythmic foundation for dancing. His formula for playing western swing bass is simple but accurate. "How I play depends on the tune. If it's an up-tempo tune, I normally play four beats, 4/4 time [four equally accented beats as in a walking bass]. And depending on the tempo of the tune, I might play 2/4. It's up to the tune; an up-tempo tune, probably four beats, a slower tune like 'Faded Love,' probably two beats. You work with the drummer and the piano player. With a player like Joe Holley—he kicks all the time—I play four with him all the time, and on most of Bob's fast tunes, I'd go 4/4." Like swing bassists in general, Luke switched between jazz 2/4 and swing-four in accordance with the tempo and character of each tune and the soloist he was backing. Luke exemplified the best qualities in a western swing bass player: always rock-steady and dependable, closely attuned to the drummer and pianist, felt rather than heard, and never zealous for the spotlight.

JOE FRANK FERGUSON, like Luke Wills, grew up around farming and ranching before finding his way into the world of western swing music. He was born in 1920 in Fort Worth, where his father worked as a butcher at one of the many meat-packing plants located near the legendary Fort Worth stockyards. When Joe Frank was five, the family moved to West Texas, where his father worked as a ranch foreman. When Joe Frank was ten, the family moved again so that his father could assume a similar position on a ranch near Kaw City, Oklahoma; this was where Joe Frank spent the rest of his adolescence. As a high school student in Kaw City, Joe Frank's extracurricular activities included sports, one-act plays, and singing in a male chorus, a mixed chorus, various quartets, and solo performances. Though he briefly played clarinet in the high school band, Joe Frank felt that his primary talent was vocal.

With his limited musical background, Joe Frank never imagined a time when music would provide his family's income. In fact, he became a Texas Playboy quite by accident, in late 1935, while working as a flagman on a survey team near Tulsa.

> They had a contest going in a local club there in Tulsa, and we were there about six or eight weeks with that gang living in Tulsa. I went down to this club and won the first week, came back and won the next week, and finally won the whole thing. I was running out of money trying to stay with the contest and I missed my bus back to Pawhuska, Oklahoma, where I was living. The next morning after the club management paid my hotel bill and I got my five-dollar prize, and while I was waiting on the next bus, I wandered into radio station KVOO. A lady named Lydia White, who was playing organ and church songs, saw me outside with my ear up against the

glass and motioned me to come in. I went in and sang a few hymns with her, and she said, "You know, we have a staff frolic here in the afternoon. I believe I can get you a spot on there if you want to do it." "Man alive, get on the radio! You bet!" So I did a couple of numbers on the radio, and in about twenty minutes the phone rang in the control room. It was Bob Wills. He was going to Missouri to play a dance. He called back wanting them to keep me there until the next day, so he could talk to me. That was my start with Bob Wills.

Because of his clear, lyrical tenor voice, Joe Frank was the perfect vocalist for popular ballads, which was exactly what Bob Wills hired him to sing. At first he had no other job on the band, so when he was not singing he was left standing around the bandstand. But soon he began substituting for the bass player. Since Wills did not allow breaks or intermissions during four- and five-hour dance jobs, players had to sneak off the bandstand at opportune moments, and Joe Frank would step in and relieve the bass player. Joe Frank describes his introduction to the bass as "on-the-job training," explaining that "Leon McAuliffe would tell me what strings to pull and where to put my noting finger."

Joe Frank adapted to the bass quickly, and when Playboy bassist Son Lansford went out on his own in 1936, Joe Frank became the regular bass player. For the Playboys' recording session on the Vocalion label in Chicago in 1936, Joe Frank sang the popular numbers and played bass on all the rest. During the two years that he was the Playboys' bassist, Joe Frank formed a close working relationship with pianist Al Stricklin and drummer Smoky Dacus. It was this close mutual understanding that contributed to the legendary rhythm and swing of the Bob Wills band. Joe Frank does not attribute their success as a rhythm section to talent as much as to communication. "There have been technicians that played with Bob and could play rings around Al Stricklin, but there was no way in the world they could copy Al Stricklin, and Al did exactly what Bob wanted him to do and what Smoky Dacus and I wanted him to do. That was our rhythm section. We knew what each other was thinking, what little trick we were going to try on each other, like skipping a beat or hitting an off-beat. We couldn't fool one another."

Though working for Bob Wills was a full-time, demanding job, Joe Frank, like most of the other living Playboys, speaks idyllically of it as "the best job in the United States." Wills had his rules—everyone in the band dressed alike, hair and clothes were neat and clean, everybody on the bandstand smiled at the crowd and played well, nobody drank on the job, and no one dared to leave without greeting the folks. Joe recalls that people in the crowds knew not only Bob but also his sidemen on a first-name basis. In exchange for total commitment to the good of the band, Wills paid well, allowed his players much artistic freedom, and created a family atmosphere. When Joe Frank first started with the Playboys, he actually lived for a time with Bob Wills's family and was treated like a relative. Bob Wills also bought Joe Frank his first bass, and when Joe Frank left the Playboys to join the Light Crust Doughboys, Wills allowed him to take that bass for a minimal payment of twelve dollars.

Son Lansford returned to the Playboys, forcing Joe Frank to relinquish his bass job. Because he had played a little bit of clarinet in high school, he was moved to the saxophone section, where once again he received on-the-job training. "I didn't know what I was playing, but they told me what finger on the left hand made what note on the horn. Some of it didn't sound very good for a while, but it worked out all right. I practiced a lot. I got to where I could sightread anything they put in front of me."

Joe Frank continued as a singer and saxophonist with Wills until 1940, when he returned to Fort Worth and became a Light Crust Doughboy.

> Bob got me the job himself; that is, he told me about it. He said, "I know you don't like to play that sax," and the Doughboys' bass player, Jim Boyd, was leaving to go with W. Lee O'Daniel. They needed a bass player and a singer to take his place. "I'll let you go down there and audition for the job," Bob said. "You get it, no strings attached, no hard feelings. You just need to be there, because that's the type of thing you need to do." I'm the only one who ever left Bob Wills to go with the Doughboys. They told me if I could sing a tune that had a yodel in it and not crack that yodel, I had the job. "South of the Border" was the name of the tune and I didn't crack the yodel, so I got the job.

Life with the Doughboys was quite different from what it had been with the Playboys. The Doughboys worked for Burrus Mills, which managed and produced the band. It played more concerts than dances, appeared on a daily radio broadcast, and made recordings, for which each man received a salary. The band could not collect royalties from its recordings, as these were paid to Burrus Mills. Each program was recorded a week ahead of time, and the pressed discs were sent out to radio stations all around Fort Worth so that the transcriptions could be simulcast with the band's live radio programs. The band members traveled from concert to concert on a large bus with a platform on the back and a built-in sound system. Joe Frank recalls, "We could set up out in the middle of the pasture with that bus, at a rodeo or goat roping or picnic or anything. We set up our own power system and everything and broadcast, and you could hear us ten miles away."

There were also musical differences between the Doughboys and the Playboys, most noticeably for Joe Frank the lack of drums; but since the Doughboys did not play dances where thousands needed to hear the beat, there was no need for the heightened rhythmic effect of drums. Banjo, guitar, and bass could supply more than enough percussion. The Doughboys also emphasized three- and four-part harmony singing, as opposed to the solo, perhaps with vocal backup, that was characteristic of the Wills band. The repertories of both bands were identical—a varied collection of folk songs, popular songs, big band jazz arrangements, and even hymns. The Doughboys even performed numbers made famous by the Texas Playboys. Musically, then, Joe Frank experienced little difficulty moving from the Playboys to the Doughboys.

Joe Frank remained with the Doughboys until it disbanded in 1942 after the United States entered World War II. From 1942 to 1944, Joe Frank served in the U.S. Coast Guard and was stationed in Seattle. After his discharge, he returned to Oklahoma, where he supervised a ranching operation for an uncle. In 1949 he left the ranch to return to Fort Worth, where, except for a tour with Bob Wills in 1951, he has remained. He supported his family in Fort Worth through various jobs while continuing to make music at night. "I'd go home and clean my fingernails and get in my tux and go play club dates. I played big band, played bass, some saxophone, but I didn't like the horn as much as I liked the bass. I worked a lot of trio stuff, with piano and drums and bass, and I did the vocals. We had a route that we could go through here in Fort Worth a month at a time at each club. I'd sing country songs and I'd sing pop songs. I could sing 'San Antonio Rose' and 'Faded Love.' I'd do skits with different things. I didn't want to travel with two youngsters."

But Joe Frank did travel for a brief period in 1951 with Bob Wills and the Texas Playboys.

In 1951, we left Fort Worth. We followed Harry James; he booked in front of us. We covered nine states in nine weeks and outdrew Harry James in every spot over the same route. That was when we made the Telescriptions, the Snader Telescriptions, the forerunners of present-day videos. They were taped, and each was a tape of one song. They were used as spacers; this was before networks, and these telescriptions were used as spacers between local programs. If a program would run short, they'd use a spacer.

When the Original Texas Playboys was formed shortly after Bob Wills's death in 1975, Joe Frank became a charter member, and he remained with the band until it ceased touring and performing in 1986. Since 1986, Joe Frank has played more golf than bass, though he still appears occasionally at Playboys reunions. He remains extremely proud of what the Bob Wills rhythm section accomplished and insists that no other band, not even the nationally known horn bands, could swing like Bob Wills and the Texas Playboys. His favorite contemporary bands play some western swing—Ray Benson and Asleep at the Wheel, George Strait and the Ace in the Hole band—but Joe Frank feels that they have not fully grasped the secret of that great Playboy swing. Referring to a *Texas Connection* broadcast of July 4 and 11, 1992, during which he and Smoky Dacus played several numbers with Ray Benson and Asleep at the Wheel, Joe Frank made the following observation: "We hadn't been in that tune long, and I looked around and Smoky was looking straight at me. And that's how it's been working for us anyway. We can tell if it's not there. Smoky likes to say, 'That's in the crack. That sucker is not going to move.'" What made the Playboys' rhythm section move, according to Joe Frank, was the use of two-beat patterns in ensemble playing, alternating with swing-four behind solo choruses. Joe Frank's pride is well placed, for the Wills rhythm section was comparable to that of Count Basie's Big Swing Machine.

JIM BOYD was a pioneer western swing musician who participated in creating the style in the late 1920s and early 1930s. Like most western swing musicians, his background was rural and his outlet to the music world was the radio. Jim Boyd was born in 1910 and raised on a cotton farm in Fannin County, some five miles from the little Texas town of Ladonia. Rainy Saturdays were special days for the Boyd boys because they won reprieve from the normal farm chores. On one particularly wet Saturday afternoon, the two boys walked the five miles into town and were pleasantly surprised to find a traveling medicine show. Jim remembered,

> The first act out was a blackface comedian with some of those long toes on his shoes, and when he would dance he'd pop the floor with the shoes. Then he brought out a guitar, and I punched my brother Bill and I said, "Gosh, look at that guitar." And the first thing he did was make a chord that we later identified as what country boys call long A. And the first song he sang was "If You Want to Do Something Big, Go Wash an Elephant." I told my brother, "If I could make that chord like that on that guitar, I would never go back to that cotton patch."

It was not long before Jim's and Bill's lives began to change. With their cotton-picking earnings, they ordered a $3.98 guitar out of the Montgomery Ward catalogue. Many years later, Jim still remembered the day in 1926 that the postman, riding a horse because the roads were too muddy for a car, brought that package from Wards. Since Bill was older by four years, he spent more time playing with the guitar, but he would go out and listen to other guitar players, and come home and teach new chords and techniques to Jim. In this way, and through trial and error, the two boys taught themselves to play guitar.

With confidence high after a few months of practice, Bill and Jim hitchhiked into nearby Greenville, where they auditioned for a spot on radio station KFPM. The studio sat squarely in the middle of a warehouse on the second floor of a furniture store. "We got up there by way of a freight elevator. Both of us were scared to death. I was playing a doodle-bug mandolin and Bill was playing the guitar. We sang some old Jimmie Rodgers songs, 'T for Texas,' and some of those songs. After a while here came the freight elevator with a number three washtub full of telegrams. Then as soon as they read a few, well they brought up another tubful. Just people everywhere listening to that show, and so I thought we were getting pretty famous."

Soon KFPM was not large enough for the burgeoning young stars, and again they took to the road, this time thumbing rides to the Baker Hotel in Dallas, from which radio station WFAA broadcast. They auditioned and were hired at fifteen dollars a week each, which seemed an astronomical figure. With money in their pockets, they could ride the train home.

In 1929 the Boyd family moved to Dallas, and in that same year the stock-market crash sent the American economy plummeting. By 1930 the Boyd family's finances were so bad that Jim had to leave high school and go to work. He took a job with the Western Electric Company, but by 1932, when many banks closed, he was laid off. While employed, Jim had purchased a better guitar, which he now took with him to the White Plaza Hotel to audition for station WRR.

> I walked into WRR Radio and saw a fellow out in the hall. I said, "Mister, I'm hungry. I need to earn some money to eat." He said, "What can you do?" I said, "I can pick this guitar." He said, "Well, shuck it out and let me hear you." I said, "You mean out here in the hall?" He said, "Yeah." I got that guitar out, still scared to death, and played the best I could. He said, "Be here in the morning at six o'clock." I said, "I'll be here." So my little mother got me up in time to eat breakfast and walk back to that radio station four miles and carry that guitar every morning. You could ride the streetcar for a nickel, but I didn't have a nickel. So at the end of the week he gave me $2.75, and I said, "You just tickled me to death." I took that money home and gave it to my mother and she bought groceries as far as it would go.

Those were difficult times, but Jim, not yet twenty years old, had gotten a good start in radio. Shortly after he began performing on WRR, he formed a dance band that he called the Rhythm Aces. Besides playing a daily program on WRR, they worked dance jobs in small towns around Dallas, for which they received $1.25 each.

Jim's musical talent caught the attention of another area band, the Wanderers, and he was invited to join the eight-piece ensemble. About the same time, Jim's brother Bill organized his own band, Bill Boyd and the Cowboy Ramblers, of which Jim was a charter member. In 1934 Bill Boyd signed a contract with RCA Victor, and the band went to San Antonio to record. Jim explains, "I worked on every recording that he [Bill Boyd] made and played the bass fiddle on ninety percent of them."

Jim had started playing bass back in 1932 when he had first gone to work at station WRR. "There was a group of sidewinders came through Dallas and they signed on WRR. One of their members had a bass fiddle, and I had that guitar. So he didn't want to play bass; he wanted to play guitar. He said, 'Why don't you go to work with us? You can play bass and I'll play guitar.' I said, 'I don't know how to play bass.' He said, 'Well, the four strings on the bass are the same as the last big strings on a guitar—G, D, A, and E.' So I signed on and played some dance jobs with them, playing the bass. Sure did smart on my fingers. Tore 'em up!"

Jim never completely gave up the guitar, but he gained a reputation for playing good bass and singing. In 1934 he was working on radio and playing dances with the Wanderers, his own Rhythm Aces, and recording with Bill Boyd and the Cowboy Ramblers. His credits were already so impressive that WRR signed him on as staff musician, playing guitar, bass, banjo, and mandolin "with anybody, anywhere, anytime." One of the vocalists Jim backed on WRR was Kathryn Starling, whom the public later knew as Kay Starr.

Sometime in the mid-1930s, Roy Newman broke off from the Wanderers and formed his own band, using Jim Boyd's Rhythm Aces as its nucleus. Jim was quick to point out that western swing bands shared sidemen just as they did repertory. Jim had all the work he could handle, but he could not turn down an invitation that came in 1938 to join the Light Crust Doughboys at a salary of thirty-five dollars a week, plus all road expenses paid and uniforms furnished and cleaned. He did not hesitate to accept the job as bass player and vocalist, not only because of the money, but also because, as Jim put it, "the Doughboys were the most famous group in the country at the time."

Just as Jim was convinced things could not get better, they did, for in 1940 he received an offer from W. Lee O'Daniel that he could not refuse.

> The phone rang a little after one o'clock in the afternoon, and a voice said, "Just a moment for Governor W. Lee O'Daniel." He got on the phone and said, "Jim Boyd, I've been listening to you for a long time singing with those Light Crust Doughboys. The politicians stole my songbird, and I want you to take his place." I said, "Well, I'm pretty satisfied, pretty happy where I am." He said, "Would you come and talk to me?" I said, "Yes, sir." So I went down to Austin the next day and went to the Governor's Mansion. I really did have some reservations about joining up with his Hillbilly Boys because to me their music was real down-to-earth hillbilly, corny, off the cob, and wasn't anything like the western swing that the Doughboys were playing. I said, "How much money are we talking about?" He said, "I'll pay you $250 a month, and I'll furnish you a place to live with all bills paid." I said, "Well, I'll take that, Governor."

Jim became a Hillbilly Boy and remained one through O'Daniel's successful 1941 senatorial campaign. In order to draw his monthly salary from the state, Jim had to work for the state. O'Daniel made him a colonel in the National Guard and got him a job at Camp Mabry. When O'Daniel left to assume his newly won Senate seat, he put Jim in charge of getting the band members and their families moved to Washington, D.C. Jim was reluctant about making the move himself because he could not get O'Daniel to commit to a salary figure or to tell him what kind of a day job he would have. Finally, Jim refused to go to Washington with the rest of the band, and O'Daniel reciprocated by getting him kicked out of his free housing and having his pay reduced.

> The Adjutant General called me and asked, "What kind of money are you making out there at Camp Mabry?" I said, "Two hundred and fifty a month." He said, "You have your quarters furnished too, don't you? Well, today you're going to start making a hundred and twenty-five dollars a month, and I want you to move out of those quarters." I said, "That's fine, General Page. While I'm moving out, I'll just move back to Dallas, because I don't have to work for one hundred and twenty-five dollars a month and give up those quarters, too. I can beat that in Dallas."

The year was 1942, and Jim went back to work in brother Bill's band, which turned out to be a good business move. "Seemed like things just began to fit in place and started getting better. I was working around the clock; I've never had so much work in my life."

Shortly after Jim rejoined his brother in Dallas, the band went out to Los Angeles to record for RCA Victor; and when the thirty sides were cut, Steve Stone, A & R man for RCA, asked Jim to stay in L.A. and do session work with other artists at the rate of eighty-three dollars per session. There was plenty of money to be made as a studio musician, but with his pockets already full of cash, Jim decided to go home. He returned to Dallas with an RCA recording contract of his own; but a musicians' union strike prevented his actually cutting those records until 1949, when he played the sessions in Chicago with his own band, Jim Boyd and His Men of the West.

Jim describes this band as "the finest musicians that money could buy." They played a regular Saturday-night program, *Saturday Night Shindig*, on station WFAA, and they had a weekly television program as well. Jim also worked as a network disc jockey and sold radio time. "If I had a pocket without any money in it, I would cut it off," he said. "I had pockets full of money all the time, new cars."

Jim's long-standing affiliation with WFAA ended bitterly in 1952, when he refused to relocate the Saturday-night show to the Fair Park Music Hall. He and the producers could not agree on a format for the show, and there was little audience enthusiasm for it anyway. WFAA fired Jim from both television and radio, and suddenly his pockets were empty.

Always the entrepreneur, Jim contacted Smokey Montgomery, leader of the Light Crust Doughboys, and offered him a deal whereby they combined their two bands for different occasions. Montgomery was in charge of the Big D Jamboree band at this time, and Jim frequently worked on that show with him. From 1952 until his death in 1993, Jim Boyd and Smokey Montgomery worked together, sometimes as the Light Crust Doughboys, sometimes as the Wagon Masters.

In 1969 Jim got into the business of building houses, which proved lucrative until the housing-market slump of the mid-1980s. But he never gave up his music and, in fact, continued to play right up until his death. Jim had a special place in his heart for the last band he led, the Men of the West.

> I had six people, but five voices. We did special arrangements and quartet work. Most of it was western, cowboy, and some novelty. I had a fiddle man, Fred Casares, who was a charter member of the old Wanderers. Then I had the finest bass man. He played with the Dallas Symphony, and he also played good fiddle, and he played ocarina. And he sang in the trios and quartets. He could hear the part somebody else wasn't singing. Don Course was his name. And I had an accordion player, Red Gilliam. He's about the size of a peanut, and he sang bass. Then I had a guitar man, and one of the finest tenor singers that I ever had in my life, Jake Wright. Jake played rhythm guitar. Part of the time I played electric guitar, and part of the time I played a real fine acoustic Super 400 Gibson that I bought and fell in love with. Then I had a steel guitar man, Paul Blunt, and he sang wonderfully. So we just had singers running out our ears. Johnny Gimble worked with me a long time.

The Men of the West was a versatile band that could entertain with western swing standards, Sons of the Pioneers songs, popular tunes, and novelty skits. While the group did not have a significant impact as recording artists, they were seen three times a week on WFAA's Channel 8.

Though Jim had gained recognition as a bass player, the guitar remained his first love, and he played only guitar with the Men of the West.

Jim's remarks about those who influenced him sound remarkably like Cliff Bruner's; he insisted that he was working too young and too much to be influenced by other guitarists or bass players, though he named Dick Reinhart, guitarist with the Doughboys, and two New York figures, Dick McDonald and Carl Kress. Jim was already making his music when Bob Wills emerged in Tulsa, so he paid little attention to the Wills sound. "Really there weren't any guides and anybody to go by, and a lot of this we just had to figure out ourselves. That's with our playing and our selection of songs and our singing; you had to work up your own style." Jim tended to downplay his role as a bassist, explaining that he was always singing or doing comedy routines while he played bass, so he did not try to bring out the instrument. But he understood the need for a solid, steady bass to keep the ensemble together, and his bass playing, while understated, was consistently strong.

GLYNN DUNCAN, another singer-bassist who performed with several outstanding western swing bands, was born in Whitney, Texas, in 1925. As a schoolboy, he made his musical debut singing in amateur talent contests in Whitney and other small towns in the area. After graduation from high school, Glynn moved to Fresno, California, where he worked on his brother-in-law's large cotton farm. The year was 1942, the United States was at war, and Glynn soon joined the navy. He recalls, "The first trip I made overseas, it was over eighteen months before I put my feet on the dry ground." It was during this lengthy confinement on a navy ship that Glynn learned to play bass. "There was a bugler aboard ship who started me out playing bass. They formed a little band aboard the ship and they needed a bass player. He started me out, and from there I just taught myself."

Glynn had no intention of pursuing a musical career after the war; in fact, he returned to farming near Fresno. But when the opportunity to earn his living as a professional musician arrived, Glynn was ready. Being a musician was not as economically stable as farming, but it was a great deal more fun. Bob Wills was putting together a band for his brother Luke and contacted Glynn to come and sing with Luke Wills and His Rhythm Busters. Glynn explains, "We both sang and played bass. We just switched off and back and forth; I'd sing and Luke would play bass, and vice versa."

From Luke's band Glynn went with world champion cowboy Bob

Crosby. "A guy had formed a band for him; he had retired from rodeo-ing, but he would do a lot of exhibitions . . . with the rodeos. The band would play some of the old cowboy songs during his show and then we'd play for rodeo dances." When the Crosby band broke up after about a year, Glynn returned to Texas, settling temporarily in Cleburne, where he worked on a radio show with ex-Playboy pianist Al Stricklin. His next stop was Waco, Texas, and the locally popular dance band of drummer Doyle Brink. Late in 1948 Glynn's brother, Tommy, who had been the featured vocalist with Bob Wills and the Texas Playboys from the band's inception, left Wills to form Tommy Duncan and the Western Allstars. Tommy called Glynn to return to California and join his new group. Tommy was twelve years older than Glynn, and the two brothers had never been close. They began to develop a close relationship while Glynn worked on Tommy's band. Since Tommy and Glynn both sang, and by all ac-counts sounded very much alike, they alternated singing and playing bass.

Glynn decided that he could front a band and struck out on his own to form one in the oil-rich town of Lubbock, Texas. "A bunch of guys in Tommy's band and I were going to get rich in Lubbock, but we nearly starved to death." When his musical efforts in Lubbock failed, Glynn moved to Fort Worth, where he played in various clubs. But soon he was hired by the famed Merle Lindsey, whose big western swing band out of Oklahoma City was one of the best in the Southwest. After a time with Merle Lindsey and the Oklahoma Nightriders, Glynn began to be home-sick for California. Back in Los Angeles he quickly found work with the western swing band of Bob Wills imitator Oli Rasmussen.

Rasmussen was a direct copy of Bob Wills, from the makeup of the band and its repertory right down to the "ah-has." His twelve-piece group played at the 97 Street Corral in Los Angeles and at the Harmony Park Ballroom in Anaheim. In 1957 Glynn got what he considered the break of his entire musical career, when Bob Wills invited him to be a Texas Playboy; no more imitation, this was the real thing.

> That was the greatest time I ever spent. Everybody wanted to work for Bob Wills, and I thought it was an honor to be on the band that my brother had been on. I thought I knew a lot about the music business, but I learned more about music and about how to conduct myself on the bandstand working for Bob than I did with all the rest because there was something magic about his band. If he wasn't on the bandstand, the band would be playing all right, but when-

ever he walked on the bandstand, it was an altogether different atmosphere. A lot of people thought you had to be a great musician to work for Bob, but that wasn't true. If you could play, Bob Wills could get it out of you. You didn't have to be a great musician to start with, because there was something about the man whenever he walked on the bandstand you just wanted to give a hundred and twenty percent.

After his stint with Bob Wills, Glynn basically retired from the full-time music business. Having grown weary of the constant traveling and grueling performance schedules, he moved his family back to Southern California, where he took a regular day job and confined his playing and singing to weekends. Occasionally he still plays western swing festivals.

Glynn has strong preferences regarding the western swing rhythm section. As a bass player, he wants to work with a drummer who plays ahead of the beat and drives the band forward. And he wants the drummer to use sticks, not brushes, so that his driving swing rhythm will be both heard and felt. In fact, it was the lack of rhythmic drive that Glynn found disturbing in the bands of Spade Cooley and Tex Williams and that he still finds missing from many current western swing revival bands. In his opinion many present-day western swing rhythm players do not have a clue about western swing rhythm. Like most swing bass players, Glynn likes the variety of switching from 2/4 to swing-four. "I like the bass to play 2/4 on slow songs, especially behind my vocals. But on an up-tempo tune, I like the drive of a steady swing-four. To me western swing is a pushing, driving beat." To this day, Glynn would rather play for a dance than a concert. "Whenever people are just sitting and listening, you don't know whether they're pleased or not. But if they're dancing, you know that they're enjoying themselves." The western swing bass players interviewed for this study did not complain about their lack of solo spotlight opportunities; rather they were pleased to be part of rhythm sections that laid down the most danceable beat in jazz history.

LOUISE ROWE BEASLEY has the most unique story among western swing musicians. Not only is she the only female to have played an instrument in Bob Wills's band, she was also preceded into this world by seven musically gifted brothers who formed the first western swing band in which she ever performed. Their father, James Iker Rowe, was a singer and songwriter. He grew up with the Stamps brothers and sang in and wrote gospel songs for the Stamps Quartet.[25] Although the gospel quartet style in which he composed has become obsolete in today's Christian music scene, a few of his songs are still favorites, especially "Love Lifted Me." Louise remembers that music was always important to the Rowe family. "Father taught us to play music and sing. I wrote a song called 'Good Old-Fashioned Harmony'—it's a song about our family. It tells that he would gather us around and say, 'Kids, it's better to sing than fight and fuss.' He'd give us a part and say, 'Now sing it right, and it might make you a star.'"

The oldest Rowe brother, Henry (Hank), made a guitar out of a cigar box and screen wire strings, and he and the second son, Guy, learned to play it. When the homemade instrument no longer served their artistic needs, Hank and Guy sold Sears and Roebuck garden seed and Cloverine Salve to earn enough money for a real guitar. Observing their success at teaching themselves to play the guitar, their father bought them a fiddle, which they also learned to play by the trial-and-error method. This was the beginning of the Rowe Brothers band. At first Hank and Guy played their small repertory of tunes repeatedly for country dances—songs like "Lay Me a Pallet Down on the Floor," "Chicken Reel," "Comin' Round the Mountain," and "Ida Red." As each successive brother acquired a level of instrumental proficiency, he would join the Rowe Brothers, and both the sound and the repertory of tunes would increase. The Rowe Brothers really began in earnest in 1929, the year of the stock-market crash and the beginning of the Great Depression. Jack recalls, "Neighbors began to call on the Rowe Brothers to play for their country dances. Just about every Saturday night we had a dance somewhere in our part of the country (around Stephens County, Oklahoma). The host farmer or rancher would periodically stop the music and pass the hat around for money to pay the band."[26]

When the third brother, Earl, won a fiddling contest in Ardmore, Oklahoma, in 1935, the Rowe Brothers got their first radio show, on station KVSO, which billed itself as the "Voice of the Southwest." Though their daily radio broadcast paid them only one dollar each per broadcast, it broadened their exposure and greatly increased their dance bookings. Louise was five in 1935, when she sang "Chattanooga Choo Choo" with her brothers' band at a school concert in Geronimo, Oklahoma.

In 1941 all seven Rowe Brothers went off to war while Louise stayed home and attended high school. She sang in a high school quartet patterned after Fred Waring's vocal ensemble and briefly played clarinet in the school band. But every day after school she had a music lesson with her father. Rather than directing his daughter to a particular instrument, he encouraged her to "learn to play just a little bit on every instrument that was there at the house."

When World War II ended and the seven Rowe Brothers returned from Europe and the South Pacific, they resumed their dance band business; since they each played several instruments, they flipped coins to determine which brother would play which instrument permanently. The oldest brother, Hank, ended up playing drums. Guy won steel guitar. Earl and D. L. (Lightning) played fiddles. A. D. (Thunder) played bass. Luke won rhythm guitar, and Jack fronted the band and sang. California offered the liveliest music scene, and the Rowe Brothers headed west, where they experienced moderate success backing stars such as Tex Ritter and Texas Slim, playing for dances, recording, and performing on local radio and stage shows.

But after a couple of years in California, the Rowe Brothers returned to their roots, first settling in Wichita Falls, Texas. Here they worked for radio station KFDX and played a large dance circuit of several hundred miles; then they moved on to Dallas, which became their permanent home. For several years in Dallas they backed Al Dexter, whose best-selling record was "Pistol Packin' Mama," and they performed regularly at the Bridgeport Club, in which they were part owners. They also became guardians to their youngest sibling, sister Louise, after the death of their parents.

It was in Dallas that Louise had her first opportunity to perform professionally, when at the age of sixteen she began singing on the Big D Jamboree. And it was at her brothers' club that she got her first big break. One night in 1952 the Rowe Brothers and Bob Wills and the Texas Playboys were sharing a battle dance at the Bridgeport Club when Louise got up to sing a number with her brothers. Bob Wills liked what he heard and hired her on the spot as a vocalist on an eighteen-day tour. Louise feels that Wills had no intention of keeping her beyond the tour because she did not know how to yodel, but luck and talent prolonged her time with Wills to a full year. On the last night of the tour, guitarist Eldon Shamblin was unable to make the job, but there was a guitar on the bandstand.

> I went over there and picked up that guitar; my brothers were fans
> of Bob Wills, so I knew all of his songs and I could play the chords

on the guitar. When I played rhythm, Bob looked over at me and said, "I didn't know you could play guitar." I couldn't play it that well, but I played well enough to get through some rhythms that we needed. He gave me a smile of approval; and then when somebody else took the guitar, there wasn't anybody to play bass. So I just stepped back and played a song on the bass. Bob turned all the way around and smiled again. Then we got a request for "Faded Love." Bob said, "Well, Eldon's not here to sing the third part on the trio." I was so scared, but I mustered up the courage to say, "Bob, I can sing the harmony to that." He said, "Are you sure, child?" I said, "Yes, sir, I can." Because I could harmonize better than I could sing solo. When we played "Faded Love," I got the high part like Billy Bowman on the record. And Bob liked the sound and he hired me after that.

The Playboys returned to Hollywood for a recording session, and Bob Wills took Louise to get her musicians' union card, after which he declared, "Now you're really one of the Texas Playboys!" Wills had female vocalists, but Louise was the only woman who ever played an instrument, and a bass at that, with Bob Wills and the Texas Playboys. "I wasn't really a bass player. I didn't know that much about it. But Eldon Shamblin and Billy Bowman and Keith Coleman and the other guys would look back at me and say, 'Come on, girl, get it.' I really beat that bass out and, using my ear, I tried to find the notes I needed. I finally got some recordings of Glenn Miller and Billy May, the big bands, and I literally memorized the runs that their bass players made, and then I started playing those and pretty soon people thought they were mine. In fact, soon I had listened to enough to do my own runs."

After the year with Bob Wills, Louise went on to play bass and sing with other western swing bands, notably Billy Gray and the Western Oakies and Tommy Allsup's Southernaires. She was married to Tommy Allsup when she played bass in his band out of Odessa, Texas, and Moon Mullican was their pianist. This was, in Louise's opinion, "a super band," but since it did not record, it is little known except among other western swing veterans.

Louise went from her marriage to Allsup and from the Southernaires to play bass and sing with Billy Gray and the Western Oakies, which toured with the Grand Ole Opry as the backup band for country singers like George Jones, Little Jimmy Dickens, and Faron Young. In 1959 Bob

Wills asked Louise to join the Playboys in Las Vegas, but she had met and married fiddler Buddy Beasley, and they had decided to stop touring, settle down, and have a family. They have raised two musically talented daughters. Louise was a regular member of only three bands, but she has played bass with quite a few other acts. While she was still with the Southernaires, she substituted for the ailing bass player of the Inkspots. She played some with the Norman Petty Trio and with a jazz trio in Lawton, Oklahoma, fronted by pianist Jimmy Stewart. Louise recalls that after ten-thirty each night, Jimmy Stewart would play nothing but western swing because he was such a Bob Wills fan.

Louise contends that western swing musicians can easily fit into other swing bands, even those populated by reading musicians.

> Western swing musicians could sit in with those big bands that had reading musicians and could play the arrangements without the scores the other band members were reading. I've done it. I've played bass in a big swing orchestra. I didn't have any music. The band leader turned around and gave me a solo, and I took it! They couldn't believe I wasn't reading. Nearly all western swing musicians can fit in with whatever style they want you to play. And if they turn to you and say play a solo, you do it. They'd ask western swing musicians if they could read music. "Yes, but not enough to hurt me," they'd reply.

Western swing musicians can play in any kind of swing band because the language of swing and much of the repertory are the same, whether played by horn players or string players. Louise has definite opinions about achieving an authentic western swing sound, starting with the type of bass used: "The upright bass is felt, whereas the electric bass is heard. The upright blends in with the bass drum, and gives the depth to the real authentic western swing music. The western swing music that they play now is great, fantastic, but there's so much electronics with it that it does make it a little bit different from original western swing. We used to call it the rhythm section, and the fiddles, guitars, and the horn were the front line. Now, they've brought the electric bass up to the front line. I still prefer the upright sound."

Louise could write a method book for aspiring western swing musicians describing how each should approach playing his or her instrument. Starting with the drummer, she explains, "I can't play drums, but I can tell someone how to play western swing. Play closed high-hat behind the fiddles, and usually behind the vocalist. Usually we'd switch between 4/4 and 2/4, and the bass drum is matched with the bass fiddle. When the steel comes in for a solo, the drummer should make a roll and bring the steel player in and hit a high-sounding cymbal at the end of that roll. Sometimes you keep the cymbal going behind the steel player. The drummer should play semiclosed high-hat with the piano. Behind the solos (fiddle and steel), the drummer should always play 4/4. The heads on the snare drum should be tightened to where they thud rather than rattle. No rattle!"

Louise's instructions for the rhythm guitarist are just as explicit: "You do not ever play an open chord on guitar in a western swing band. You always play closed chords, bar chords. You chop; don't ever let a chord ring. Chop the chords, and there are certain ways to chop them. Eldon Shamblin knows exactly how to chop those chords perfectly. Ringing chords are used in hillbilly, country music, not in western swing. They're not big band either. When big band guitarists played in 4/4 meter, they chopped the chords, but not quite as much as in western swing."

Louise outlines the dual roles of fiddle players, both as soloists and backup: "The fiddles come in and do their swing and then each one takes a solo. If the steel is soloing, the fiddles will be holding chords. They'll play chords behind the steel or piano player." She describes the bandleader as the field commander who turns potential chaos into music. "The bandleader is calling solos, and pointing backup. A good leader appoints the backup, too." Louise would never remove the spontaneity and improvisation from western swing, but she insists that having a plan is a necessary prerequisite to performance, even if only the bandleader knows the plan, as was often the case with Bob Wills.

Louise Rowe Beasley does not play as much as she used to, but she still possesses sharp insights into the nature of western swing. She is justifiably proud of the honors that have been heaped upon her brothers and herself by western swing halls of fame in Colorado, Tennessee, Nebraska, Wyoming, Oklahoma, Texas, Nevada, and California. Louise takes no particular credit for the opportunities she has had; she is thankful that she was in the right places at the right times. A worn scrapbook bulges with pictures of the seven Rowe Brothers and Sister Louise and of the artists with whom they have worked along the way: Tex Ritter, Monte Hall, Fuzzy St. John, Al Dexter, Jim Reeves, Jimmie Davis, Ray Price,

Lefty Frizzell, Marty Robbins, Bob Wills, Hank Snow, Billie Walker, T. Texas Tyler, and Hank Williams Sr., to name a few.

Louise and her fiddler husband, Buddy Beasley, have created a color-coded self-study fiddle method that they market out of their home near San Marcos. When they are on the road these days, it is usually to direct fiddle workshops and sell their fiddle method. And there are still Rowe family reunions, at which western swing is always the main course.

SIX

The Western Swing Rhythm Section: Piano and Drums

Piano

The piano has not participated in every jazz ensemble, yet it has been a jazz instrument since the inception of the music. Jazz historian Leonard Feather says:

> Like the blind student who develops an uncannily keen sense of hearing, the piano throughout jazz history has compensated for its failures and absences in certain areas by showing amazing strength in others. Because of its immobility, it was absent from the early ragtime crews that played in street parades and rode on advertising wagons; but because a house is not a home without a piano, it was the first instrument available, the first studied and mastered for jazz, in thousands of houses (many of which also were not homes). New Orleans Storyville bagnios, the honky-tonks of Sedalia, and Washington and Brooklyn, relied on their "professor" to keep up a rolling, tumultuous background of rags, stomps and blues while the customers were entertained—upstairs or down.
>
> While the piano is incapable of the glissandi, "smears," and tonal distortions that lent jazz its original vocal and local color, it compensates by providing the soloist with the outlet for triply rich expression in the fields of melody, rhythm, and harmony, while all the horns, capable of but one note at a time, are limited to the first two of these.[1]

The first style of jazz piano playing was ragtime, and the rhythmic legacy of ragtime affected jazz well into the 1920s. Historians typically assign 1896, the year of the first published piano rag, as the beginning of the ragtime craze in the United States, but African Americans had been dancing and partying to ragtime music—performed by banjoists, guitarists, string or wind ensembles, and even vocalists—long before the music crystallized into its "classic" piano format in the hands of geniuses like Scott Joplin.

Classic piano ragtime composers melded African American rhythmic elements—syncopation, an innate metronomic sense, polyrhythm—to European ideas of musical structure and tonality to create a musical product that would sell in the white popular music market. And sell it did! Says Leonard Feather, "Keyboards all over America were resounding to ragtime. Since there were no phonograph recordings and only limited access to ragtime on player piano rolls, most of the interchange of ideas in the tidal wave of ragtime mania (ca. 1897–1912) took place when these musicians (professional ragtime pianists) went on the road, and through the vast quantity of sheet music that brought ragtime, amateur or professional, to every parlor during those heavily syncopated years."[2]

Many jazz historians treat ragtime as a precursor of jazz because, in its classic stage, it was notated and reproduced by pianists dependent on scores or by the mechanical means of the player piano roll. In either case, improvisation played no part. But jazz pianist Billy Taylor disagrees.

> Many writers regard ragtime piano compositions as fixed pieces, like Mozart and Haydn sonatas, and do not recognize the essential improvisatory aspects of the style. All jazz pianists of the era improvised often, using the score merely as a starting point. Many historians also ignore the fact that Bunk Johnson, Buddy Bolden, and many other musicians active before the turn of the century considered themselves ragtime players. Though their repertories included other types of material, the vocabulary, forms, and devices they used were definitely those of the ragtime style. Ragtime was, most emphatically, the first jazz style.[3]

Taylor's insistence that ragtime was the first jazz makes sense when one considers the different levels of participation in the music. For the vast majority of amateur pianists, ragtime was a challenging notated popular music, not jazz; but for those traveling professors exchanging musical ideas in "cutting" competitions and jam sessions all over the South and Southwest, the score was merely a starting point for improvisation, and for these pianists, ragtime was jazz.

The identifying features of ragtime were rhythmic in nature. The ragtime pianist's left hand provided a steady bass line consisting often of bass note to chord in 4/4 meter, against which the right hand played a highly syncopated melody. With this polyrhythmic juxtaposition of variable right-hand melody against invariable left-hand bass pattern, ragtime reflected African and African American origin. The ragtime pianist was also a veritable one-man band, with left hand functioning as the rhythm section against the right-hand frontline melody. Billy Taylor is even more emphatic when he writes, "The left hand sounded like a trombone or tuba, and the right hand sounded like a trumpet or clarinet."[4]

In the Northeast, especially in the Harlem district of New York City, a group of schooled pianists, notably Lucky Roberts, Willie "the Lion" Smith, and James P. Johnson, used ragtime as the basis for an energetic, virtuosic style of jazz piano playing labeled "stride." In their individual ways, Fats Waller and his student Bill "Count" Basie, along with Duke Ellington, Earl Hines, and the incomparable Art Tatum were formidable stride pianists.

Taylor connects the emergence of stride piano to the post–World War I migration of African American ragtime pianists to larger urban centers, where "cutting" contests became more competitive. In order to best their rivals, ragtime pianists had to demonstrate their virtuosity and invent new pianistic devices at increasingly fast tempos. Stride bass patterns tended to be more syncopated and varied than those of ragtime and could include such techniques as walking tenths and chromaticism. Stride pianists also expanded the harmonic vocabulary of jazz piano to include ninth and thirteenth chords, and they increased the excitement of right-hand melody by incorporating riffs (short, repeated melodic patterns), and rapid scale runs, both diatonic and chromatic. The stride pianist literally covered the entire keyboard, sometimes suggesting or even imitating a complete band (orchestral style) with sections of horns. In that the major musical events often occurred off the implied steady beat, stride piano playing tended to swing more than ragtime and, in fact, helped pave the way for the four-beat swing feel of the mid-1930s.

Whereas stride was a complication and refinement of ragtime, boogie-woogie was an unrefined piano version of the unsophisticated rural blues. Boogie-woogie was created in Texas in the 1920s by self-taught, itinerant pianists who incorporated elements of blues guitar and banjo accompaniments into their piano playing. Taylor describes the context in which boogie-woogie came to life.

In the Southwest there were powerful players who entertained the tough workers from the levee, turpentine and sawmill camps. They traveled on the "barrel-house" circuit. Because the camps were usually far from towns, the company would typically set up a shack where the workers could drink and relax. The bar was often just a wooden slab supported by barrels, but there was usually a beat-up piano in the corner for itinerant musicians to play. Since these pianists had no instrument to carry, it was easy for them to hop a freight and roam from place to place—mining camps, brothels, and so on. There was ample work for musicians willing to travel.[5]

Boogie-woogie pianists were capable of incredible independence between left and right hands. The left hand laid down an irrepressible rhythmic-harmonic foundation, over which the right hand improvised rhythmically complex, riff-filled melodies. The most characteristic feature of boogie-woogie was the left hand with its repeated bass figure (ostinato), which set the pace and tone for the tune. Boogie-woogie bass lines consisted of single-note walking patterns, repeated chords, or a combination of the two; they tended to subdivide the four beats of each measure into smaller units—quarters and eighths, sixteenths, or even triplet eighths. Right-hand melodies were improvised in a percussive, polyrhythmic fashion and were often based on ragtime, marches, popular tunes, blues, spirituals, and hymns. Among the many devices used to enliven borrowed bits of melody were riffs, sequential passages, chord repetition, chromatic figures, tremolos, and melodic harmonizations at intervals of a third or fourth. Since boogie-woogie derived from the rural blues, it retained the simple three-chord harmonic structure of the blues. To compensate for the piano's inability to play the blue notes, pitch bends, and slurs common in vocal blues, boogie-woogie pianists added seconds and cluster chords as well as keyboard glissandi to their melody lines.

Ragtime and stride pianists regarded their boogie-woogie contemporaries as folksy and second-rate because they could not read music, but they were, nevertheless, drawn to the energy of the style and incorporated boogie-woogie devices into their own playing. In the late 1930s and early 1940s, swing jazz arrangers transformed boogie-woogie into commercial, big band music that was extremely popular with audiences. When this happened, pioneer boogie-woogie pianists like Pine Top Smith, Pete Johnson, Meade "Lux" Lewis, and Jimmy Yancey gained new respect and began to influence swing musicians such as Count Basie and Benny Goodman.[6]

The blues was at the heart of jazz in Kansas City, Chicago, and urban centers of the Southwest, where, in the late 1920s and early 1930s, blues vocalists like Ma Rainey, Bessie Smith, and Mamie Smith gave the world its first taste of classic, or urban, blues. As they worked in clubs and theaters, these classic blues singers were often backed by ragtime, stride, or boogie-woogie pianists, who had to adapt their piano playing to the unique deliveries of the vocalists. In the process, both singers and pianists gained a new flexibility and intensification of expression. Stride pianist Bill Basie first discovered the blues when he was stranded in Kansas City after a show in which he was working disbanded. According to Taylor,

> When Basie heard the Kansas City blues players, he heard tremendous technical facility, subtlety, and much more. Pianists like Pete Johnson could play stride piano, shout piano (closely related to stride), and also the widest variety of blues styles, ranging from "skiffle" (a country style of playing) to pulsating boogie-woogie. It was a new dimension of piano playing for an Easterner, and Basie assimilated it well. The rhythmic discipline of stride piano and boogie-woogie styles solidified the Basie concept of jazz rhythm. That concept permeates both his piano playing and the way his bands swing.[7]

Through his combining of different styles, Basie became a pioneer of the swing piano approach. Swing pianists of the mid-1930s and 1940s worked in an environment different from that of their ragtime, stride, and boogie-woogie predecessors; whereas these earlier piano styles were first soloistic and then influential on ensemble jazz, the swing piano was, from the start, involved in collaboration with an ensemble. The job of the swing pianist was to underscore the four beats of the swing-four rhythm; but thanks to the presence of drums, bass, and rhythm guitar, the swing pianist was free to explore new and less mechanical means of accomplishing this task. Swing pianists used a lighter touch and incorporated more rhythmic, melodic, and harmonic variety. They could play chords on every beat or create left-hand countermelodies. They could play stride-like bass parts or boogie-woogie bass patterns. And, on occasion, swing pianists left the bass playing entirely to the bass instrument and played only right-hand melodies. For swing pianists chord choices became more interesting and complex, and dynamic changes wider. Working in close collaboration with the other rhythm players, swing pianists retained the flexibility and independence to function in the ensemble, back different soloists, or be soloists themselves.

These then were the main piano styles by which jazz pianists were categorized: ragtime, stride, boogie-woogie, swing. Several jazz pianists exerted tremendous influence on all jazz pianists, including those who played in western swing bands. Earl "Fatha" Hines (b. 1903) formed a bridge between early jazz and swing, making him one of the most important jazz figures of the 1930s. He was mentioned often by the western swing pianists interviewed as a dynamic force in their own approach to the keyboard. Hines assimilated several different styles of music—ragtime, classic blues, Dixieland—into the first truly individual style of jazz piano playing. He first came to the forefront of jazz through his recordings with Louis Armstrong's Hot Five. He led his own big band, which broadcast from the Grand Terrace Ballroom in Chicago, from 1928 to 1939. Jazz pianists as far away as Kansas and Texas heard Hines on the radio and benefited from his innovations.

Hines's playing was characterized by force, energy, and an unerring sense for beat placement. Basically a stride pianist, Hines would frequently cease the typical stride left-hand figurations to play walking tenths up and down a scale. In duets with horn players, Hines created hornlike right-hand melodies, often doubled at the octave, with ornamentation and tremolos, causing his approach to be labeled "trumpet-style." Even his phrasing attested to his familiarity with horn lines. Always on top of the tempo and relentlessly driving the beat forward, Hines was a master of surprise, especially in his solo playing, when he would take off in unexpected directions and yet never lose track of the beat.

Jazz historian Mark Gridley says that Hines provided new insights and a new direction for jazz pianists: "His playing is less flowery and more direct. It is less classically pianistic and more swinging. The Hines approach is more flexible than the rigidly structural ragtime and stride approach, and, because of this, Hines has greater capacity for conveying a broad assortment of musical feelings." [8] Leonard Feather concentrates on the rhythmic complexities of Hines's playing: "This Houdini of jazz piano, . . . emphatic both in his influence and in the vigorous flamboyant rhythmic nature of his approach, is capable of tying himself into the most baffling of rhythmic knots and of successfully extricating himself every time." [9]

Another influential and often-copied jazz pianist was Teddy Wilson (1912–1986), who modernized jazz piano by rejecting the notion that the left hand was primarily for timekeeping. He lightened his touch, streamlined his melodic and harmonic lines, and played with a grace and symmetry that caused some listeners to mistake him for a cocktail lounge entertainer. But though his playing was pleasant, it was never superficial. Says Feather, "His slow-tempo performances in particular evidence great warmth and an approach that compensated in dignified, swinging simplicity for what it lacked in Hines's brilliant and sometimes flashy variety." [10] As the pianist in Benny Goodman's small combos and large orchestra, Teddy Wilson became the centerpiece of an entire school of jazz piano playing.

The uncontested technical wizard of jazz piano, Art Tatum (1910–1956), summed up every jazz piano style that had gone before and delineated the future. Even concert pianists were awed by his virtuosity—cascades of clearly articulated notes racing down the scale at rapid tempos and in oddly devised but completely logical rhythm patterns. Tatum was an impulsive pianist, often disrupting the direction of his own lines to throw in a musical idea that seemed to have no place until he had molded it into the musical whole. Like his rhythmic sense, Tatum's harmonic vocabulary was both peculiar and advanced. He explored polytonality through key changes within single phrases, which he always managed somehow to resolve, and through chords with altered intervals that suggested alternate key possibilities. So far-reaching was Tatum's impact that it extended not only to pianists but to other instrumentalists, like guitarist Tal Farlow and saxophonists Don Byas, Charlie Parker, and John Coltrane. But in reality Tatum's style was largely incomparable, for as Feather explains,

> There was no Tatum school of piano, no Tatum style to copy, no neo-Tatum to compare with the original. The ideas of Waller, Wilson and Hines at least were potentially within reach of the aspiring youngsters while Tatum's remained the envy of the most gifted contemporaries. His brain and fingers moved so fast that he expressed in one measure more ideas, more subtleties of phrasing and dynamics and harmony, than could most of his predecessors in four. Tatum was not a standard by which jazz piano could be judged, nor an objective toward which others would aim; the cliché "in a class by himself" applied so clearly in his case that

other pianists, after sitting for hours in awestruck silence, would go home determined not to try to emulate Tatum, but to give up the piano forever.[11]

Not as gigantic as Hines, Wilson, and Tatum, but still important to the evolution of jazz piano in the 1940s and 1950s were Milt Buckner (1915–1977), Nat Cole (1917–1965), and Erroll Garner (1923–1977). Milt Buckner, pianist in Lionel Hampton's band, updated the orchestral approach to jazz piano with his so-called locked-hands style, which imitated the horn section's five- to seven-part chord voicings of big band swing arrangements. In contrast to the normal plan of right-hand melody and left-hand chordal accompaniment, Buckner used both hands, playing closed-position chords in parallel motion, with the main melody carried as the top note of each chord and duplicated an octave lower in the bass. This device was both percussive and melodic and especially useful in situations without drummers. Because he was often relegated to the role of accompanist in the 1930s, and because his style of playing lacked brilliance and flashiness, Buckner's contributions were not readily recognized by jazz audiences and critics, but other pianists, notably Nat Cole, George Shearing, Lennie Tristano, and Oscar Peterson, added their own distinctive voicings to Buckner's locked-hands technique.

Before he became one of the most popular singers of his time, Nat Cole was an inventive jazz pianist whose trio work from 1943 to 1949 placed him in the forefront of modern jazz activity. Cole created spare, lightly touched melody lines that he accompanied with equally sparse, briefly heard chordal bursts. In other words, he was among the first to perfect the modern art of comping. The trio he led was an extremely tight ensemble in which rhythm and bass lines were carefully coordinated between piano and guitar. While most of their performance was arranged and rehearsed, time was allowed for appropriately delicate and logically conceived solos. Modern pianists who drew heavily on Cole's style included Oscar Peterson, Bill Evans, and Horace Silver.

Erroll Garner is more difficult to describe than his contemporaries. Garner's approach was basically swing, but he avoided the lighter, simpler touch of Wilson and Cole and played chords on all four beats of each measure, like a rhythm guitarist. His rhythmic signature was his placement of each chord just after the beat, which gave his playing a fluid swing. Garner's highly ornamented melodies grew out of chords, many of which reflected his interest in the French impressionist music of Claude

Debussy—colorful, nonfunctional harmonic structures with myriad possibilities for resolution. Gridley states that Garner's main contribution to his own and later generations of jazz pianists was his focus on the harmonic movement of music rather than the linear.[12] And Leonard Feather notes the accessibility and appeal of Garner's playing for fans and critics.[13]

Western swing has had its share of outstanding and influential pianists. The first pianist to play in a western swing band was Fred "Papa" Calhoun, who helped transform Milton Brown's Musical Brownies from a fiddle band into a jazz band. Brown hired Calhoun in 1932 because of his jazz experience and improvisational skill, dubbing him "Papa" to show that he, like Earl "Fatha" Hines, was a starting point for the new style. Calhoun played on all of the more than one hundred tunes that the Brownies recorded over a two-and-a-half-year period. After the death of Milton Brown in 1936, Calhoun began to appear with other western swing bands, including Cliff Bruner's Texas Wanderers.

Calhoun's was a unique style that focused on the right-hand melody-chord work. His melody lines were harmonically conceived and were colored with frequent dissonant seconds and cluster chords in order to capture a blues flavor. Calhoun's rhythms were not driving or aggressive but rather characterized by the same kind of laid-back swing found among pianists who accompanied blues singers. Though Calhoun was not a virtuoso, he was an outstanding addition to the rhythm section of the Brownies; he was the first pianist to play with a string band.

Recording in Chicago in January 1935, the Brownies cut their hit single "Taking Off" for Decca. By this time Calhoun had probably heard recordings by both Earl Hines and Count Basie, but his playing was bluesier than theirs. His left hand was not especially active in this recording, as he relegated the bass-rhythm functions to the string bass. Behind the string solos he concentrated on the treble register of the piano, playing chords on all four beats, in close collaboration with the rhythm guitar and banjo. When he took a solo chorus, Calhoun played short melodic phrases and riffs sprinkled with seconds and cluster chords, all on the upper half of the keyboard. Many of his melodic phrases resembled trumpet lines, especially when he moved quickly to the top of a phrase and cascaded down gradually, much as Louis Armstrong did on "West End Blues."

Calhoun played in Cliff Bruner's Texas Wanderers for a Decca recording session in February 1937. One of the tunes from this session, "Milk Cow Blues," showed Calhoun to be a sensitive blues pianist. In a call-and-response duet with the vocalist, Calhoun created countermelodies replete with dissonant seconds that closely resembled vocal slurs and blue notes; and many of the melodic phrases started at the top and literally fell down the scale. Behind Bruner's violin solo, Calhoun chorded on every beat and occasionally embellished the violin line. When Calhoun took a solo chorus, his interpretation of the melody included a few runs, some tremolos, and his signature descending right-hand phrases with dissonant seconds. Fred Calhoun was not an overly exciting pianist, but he was reliable and steady. He also brought jazz improvisation and a strong flavor of the blues to Milton Brown's Musical Brownies. He might be regarded as the father of western swing piano.

A Few Good Pianists Talk about Western Swing

AL STRICKLIN, known as "Brother Al," the "Piano Pounder," is still the pianist most readily associated with western swing. Alton Meeks Stricklin was born in 1908 in the tiny Texas town of Antioch in Johnson County. Al's aptitude for music appeared early, and by the time he was five, he was chording at the piano behind his breakdown-fiddler father. His older sister taught him to play a few melodies, and the rest he acquired by listening to the radio. By the age of twelve, Al could play most of the popular tunes of the day and add his own improvised accompaniments.

Antioch was a conservative, religious community, where local ministers regularly inveighed against all popular music and dancing, so Al confined his public piano playing to hymns and folk songs. But at home Al's father encouraged his interest in popular music and jazz. The Stricklin family moved to the larger town of Grandview, where Al finished high school. After high school he attended Weatherford Junior College and then Texas Christian College in Fort Worth before receiving his teaching certificate from Baylor University in Waco. Al supported himself in college by playing for school functions and teaching piano. He did not make allies of the local music teachers because he taught as he had learned—strictly by ear with large measures of improvisation. He could have played dances but had difficulty escaping the puritanical notion drilled into him by the preachers of Antioch.

When the stock market crashed in 1929, the social atmosphere in small-town Texas loosened up because people were desperate for affordable entertainment, and dancing was highly affordable. Dancing and dance music gained a sudden respect, and Al could play for dances with a clear conscience. Al was working in Fort Worth as pianist for radio station

KFJZ's staff band, the Hi-Flyers, when he first met Bob Wills. It was at a dance engagement, and Al recalls:

> We were playing the Cinderella Roof dance hall in Fort Worth when Bob Wills walked in, wearing expensive cowboy boots and an expensive tailored western suit. His pants were tucked inside his boots and he was wearing spurs. He had on a little black tie with a large diamond stickpin in it. He had on a big western hat. He was tall and straight. He walked up to me and said, "Hi, Mr. Stricklin." He said he wanted to talk to me when I got a break. So when we finished, Bob and I sat down in a booth. He said, "Strick, I've hit it pretty big up in Tulsa. I've got a radio program and it's going pretty good. We're making about $2,000 a week. I got an old boy who sings. His name is Tommy Duncan. He also plays the piano, but he doesn't know too much about it. He gets a lot of laughs but I'm looking for a better piano player. I'm going to need one in September."
>
> "Are you offering me a job?" I asked.
>
> "Yeah, I am," he said.
>
> "How much does it pay?" I asked.
>
> "Thirty bucks," said Wills.
>
> "A month?" I asked.
>
> "No, a week," he replied.[14]

That was a lot of money during the depression, and Al grabbed at the chance. With twenty dollars in their pockets, Al Stricklin and his wife climbed into their battered 1931 Chevrolet and headed for Tulsa. Al was apprehensive that morning of September 6, 1935, when he stepped out of the cheap motel room where they had spent their first night in Tulsa. Wills was not yet a celebrity in Texas, and Al was not certain that he was going to be able to make a living with this band. But he quickly learned that in Oklahoma Bob Wills had already become a culture hero.

Al found Wills and the band at their daily radio show, which was broadcast from a large supermarket called the Barrel Food Palace. The show was already in full swing, and Al was amazed by the size and enthusiasm of the crowd gathered to watch. When Wills spotted Al, he immediately introduced him not only as the new Playboy pianist but as "the greatest piano player you ever heard."[15] Determined to prove his new boss correct, Al made his way to the battered piano; but much to his dismay, Tommy Duncan had already been there. "A good third of the hammers were off. Many of the strings were broken. The tuning was so bad that I could barely make one chord, much less a run or a melody. I felt like the guy with the rope around his neck waiting to fall through the trap door. But I couldn't back out now. So I just played. Rather I played at playing." [16]

Al's discomfort continued to mount. Not only had Tommy Duncan demolished the piano, but the repertory the band was playing was completely unknown to him. "It reminded me of some of the modern musicians today. They call it different things, mostly rock. And loud as that. And everybody seemed to have amplifiers except the piano. I got back there and I don't know whether I was playing or not because I couldn't hear anything, but the piano was pretty bad. I had the impression that I didn't belong in that outfit. It wasn't my kind of music. I'd never played that. And it went very badly. I worried. I thought, this is probably the first musician Bob Wills has ever had that lasted a day." [17]

At the rehearsal that afternoon Wills welcomed Al into the band and promised to have the piano repaired for the next day's broadcast. Wills wanted to transform his fiddle band into a commercially successful swing band. He had already acquired trombone and saxophone players and a drummer, but he needed a pianist with an interest in popular music and a knowledge of modern chord structures. That pianist was Al Stricklin.

For the next seven years, Al was the pianist for Bob Wills and the Texas Playboys, and his name, like Bob's, became a household word with thousands of adoring fans. Al was constantly amazed by the crowd recognition he received, even though he had been with the band only a short time; but he attributed his instant success to Bob's complimentary introductions and to the numerous solo choruses Bob called upon him to play. Al discovered that there were people who even dreamed of being Al Stricklin, like the young hitchhiker Al and his brother picked up in Cleburne, Texas.

> I was down on a little vacation visiting my brother and riding around with him. And somewhere out there a nice-looking young man was thumbing a ride. We put him in the back seat. . . . He was a conversationalist type of young man, and he said, "What do you fellows do?" And my brother said, "I work for a newspaper and my brother here is a musician." This young man said, "Well, what do you know? I'm a musician, too. I play for Bob Wills and the Texas Playboys. My name is Al Stricklin." I waited for the laughter to come and no laughter came. He was serious. I never did tell him

different. We got out and started to let him out, and I reached in and I had a musicians' union card from Local 94 in Tulsa. I said, "By the way, you might be interested in this." He looked at it and he just handed that card back to me, and started running.[18]

Al was well aware that Wills had hired him because of an upcoming recording session, and he had been with the band less than a month, barely enough time to become familiar with the band and its repertory, when they went to Dallas to record on the Brunswick label. The Wills band at this point was rough and unpolished in its sound, but this home-spun quality appealed to the rural clientele that made up the Playboys' primary audience. The piano was little heard on these first recordings, coming through only on medium- to slow-tempo tunes such as "Maiden's Prayer," "Mexicali Rose," "Old-Fashioned Love," and a blues number, "Sittin' on Top of the World." The Playboys at this point was a cross between a country fiddle band and a Dixieland jazz band. The Dixieland flavor derived from the insistent 2/4 meter, collective improvisation, and Al's steady ragtime left hand and syncopated right-hand melody work. Al played with a great deal of rhythmic excitement and energy and with a more percussive attack than Fred Calhoun. His brief solo on "Old-Fashioned Love" reflected his strong ragtime piano background.

The Playboys band that recorded a year later in Chicago was a more competent ensemble. In his effort to turn a fiddle band into a swing band, Wills had added more musicians and was stressing arrangements, which required reading musicians. Al was concerned.

I had taught piano before coming to Bob, but I knew very little about reading music. I knew I was going to have to change.

I managed pretty well until we got a new arrangement. It was "Beat Me Daddy, Eight to the Bar." This was a new kind of beat that Tommy Dorsey had inserted into this arrangement. The left hand had to hit eight beats to a measure.

Until this time I had played what was called a two-four beat with my left hand. In other words, a bass note and a chord in that order, and only four beats to the bar. To double up and play eight beats to a bar, was to me, just about impossible. It would be like telling an old country boy to go up and make love to some movie star.

We didn't play that "Daddy" business for a couple of weeks. I'll bet that I worked on that thing at least two hundred hours. It still didn't sound right. I just couldn't make that left hand go. But, I

finally played it for Bob. He came over afterwards. I just knew he
was going to say, "Al, I need a good bus driver." He didn't. "Al,
you did great," he said.[19]

All of the big swing bands were playing boogie numbers like "Beat
Me Daddy, Eight to the Bar" as well as arrangements of popular songs
and original jazz compositions by Duke Ellington, Fletcher Henderson,
Don Redman, Count Basie, and others. Al wrestled with Basie's "One
O'Clock Jump," a particularly difficult number that opens with a sixteen-
measure introduction played by piano and drums. "I was supposed to
play it note for note, just like Basie did. I worked my tail off on that one,
too. Hundreds of hours were spent working on it. Practicing it. Perfecting it. Dreaming about it. Nightmares they were. I finally got it down
pretty good, or so I thought, on the piano."[20]

However, when the band first played this new number on a radio
broadcast from Bixby, Oklahoma, a small town south of Tulsa, there was
no piano for Al to play, only a pump organ. The piece was difficult
enough on the piano, but next to impossible on pump organ. Al pumped
furiously with both feet and flailed away at "One O'Clock Jump," while
Dacus hammered wildly on his drums. By the time the interminable six-
teen-measure introduction was over and the horns were supposed to
come in, the horn players were laughing too hard to blow, and Al and
Smoky Dacus had to finish out the tune.

It was 1938, and the Texas Playboys were drawing larger crowds and
making more money than most of the big horn bands. In this expanding
market, Al found his responsibilities increasing. He was given charge of
auditioning the numerous people who wanted to be in the band. He heard
a few pianists whom he thought better than himself and told Wills about
them, but Bob insisted that there was no better pianist for the Playboys
than Al. He was also given the job of screening the hundreds of compositions that were submitted to the band.

The year 1938 was productive for the Playboys in terms of successful
recordings. On May 6, they cut their western swing version of the popular song "I'll See You in My Dreams," with a large band consisting of two
fiddles, banjo, two guitars, steel guitar, bass, piano, drums, trumpet, clarinet, and saxophones. Eldon Shamblin had joined the band as lead guitarist, and Joe Ferguson had also joined the group as pop vocalist and
bass player. As for Al Stricklin, he had made the transition from ragtime
to swing piano, comping nicely with well-placed, modern chords and

countermelodies. The horn section assumed the lead in this number while the strings improvised countermelodies and fills.

In late November 1938, the Playboys were back in the studio in Dallas recording a variety of tunes, some of which used only strings. One of these, "That's What I Like about the South," was a swing arrangement that used three fiddles like a horn section against Eldon Shamblin's big bar chords and Al's piano fills. Both Al and Eldon took hot choruses based on the larger chord structures and freer rhythms of swing jazz.

By 1940, Bob Wills and the Texas Playboys was the most successful swing band in the country, judging by record sales, audience draw, and profits. On April 15, 1940, the Playboys were in Dallas again with their largest band to date, a seventeen-piece ensemble with a complete horn section plus strings. It was at this recording session that they cut the tune that put them over the top in popularity, "New San Antonio Rose." The tune was by Wills, and he had been trying to fit words to it for some time. Finally, just before the April 15 recording date, with the help of Tommy Duncan and other band members, "Rose" was outfitted with two verses and a chorus. Bing Crosby covered "New San Antonio Rose," the Irving Berlin Company published the sheet music, and Hollywood made a movie by the same title. The Playboys' success was no longer confined to the Southwest; they had gone national.

Other successful tunes from this recording session were the traditional country blues number "Corrine, Corrina," sung by Wills in his inimitable out-of-meter manner, the pop ballad "Time Changes Everything," featuring the vocals of Tommy Duncan, and the swing instrumental "Big Beaver," played almost entirely by the horn section and including brilliant horn solos. Al's piano styling had become light and rhythmically free, rather like that of Teddy Wilson. He was making close musical connection with the chord work of guitarist Eldon Shamblin, the rhythm playing of Smoky Dacus, and bass player Joe Ferguson.

The Playboys band that recorded in Dallas on the Okeh label in February 1941 was still large, with full contingents of strings and horns. On the blues number "Honey, What You Gonna Do?" Al proved himself the master comping pianist with blues-tinged dissonant chords, runs, short melodic fills, and beautifully placed single notes. "I Found a Dream" featured the horns in section work and solo breaks, Tommy Duncan's vocals, and Al Stricklin comping skillfully in the background. "Take Me Back to Tulsa" was a simple, earthy number that featured Wills playing breakdown fiddle against Louis Tierney's jazz violin. Al's chorus on this number harkened back to his ragtime piano days, but his background playing was all modern swing piano. Al had discovered the freedom of swing piano; he could leave the timekeeping to the bass and drums while using the piano for chordal punctuations and countermelodies.

In July 1941 the entire band went to Hollywood for the making of the movie *Go West, Young Lady*.

> We did our music on tape first. Later, when they were filming, you would follow the tape and synchronize the sounds with the motions. We surprised Morris Stoloff, the music director, the first day.
>
> He had some regular musicians standing by to play the music score for us. We told him there wasn't any use for him to hire them. He looked apprehensive until we started playing. Then he began smiling and keeping time with the music.
>
> "You boys really surprised me," he said. "I thought I was really going to have some problems. I thought you were just a bunch of . . . well, I hate to say this, but a bunch of hicks."
>
> We played for Miss Singleton and she sang several numbers. Then we played while Ann Miller sang and danced. Then it came time for several of our country numbers. Bob gave me the chorus on "Liza Jane." I hit it. Mr. Stoloff screamed, "Hold it. Hold it."
>
> I thought he was going to run me off. I just knew I had fouled up badly. But he had some stage hands bring out an old upright piano that had been fixed to sound rinkydink. Then he said, "Now, Mr. Piano Man, let's hear you go."
>
> I went. He loved it.[21]

The Playboys recorded while they were in California and took in the sights before returning to Tulsa. They were back in their usual dance and broadcast routine on December 7, 1941, when the Japanese bombed Pearl Harbor. It was a Sunday morning, and the band members gathered, all in a state of shock, to hear the broadcast in which President Roosevelt asked Congress to declare war. Everybody knew that life would never be the same for Bob Wills and the Texas Playboys.

Al went to the draft board in Tulsa and tried to enlist, but he was thirty-three and a widower with a young daughter to raise. He was turned down. But as other members of the band left for military service, Al knew he too had to do his part for the war effort. He resigned as the Playboys' pianist and returned to Texas, where he had family to help with his daughter. He went to work in a defense plant. After the war he played and even recorded with Wills on several occasions, and when the Original Texas Playboys formed shortly after Wills's death, Al was the natural selection as the pianist. Al Stricklin died in 1986, and, as they had promised to do, the Original Texas Playboys disbanded. More than any other pianist who ever worked for the Playboys, Al Stricklin, "Brother Al," was Bob Wills's piano player.

CLARENCE BUELL CAGLE was born on April 19, 1920, in Oklahoma City, a middle child out of six children, two girls and four boys. His father was an auto mechanic and an entertainer, with his family band billed as Uncle Charly and His Boys. When he was nine, Clarence began playing banjo in his father's band; a younger brother played guitar, and Cagle Sr. played fiddle. Clarence also learned to play guitar, and by the age of eleven, he had gravitated to fiddle. Uncle Charly and His Boys played for house parties, but they also had a daily noon broadcast on station KFXR.

Uncle Charly and His Boys had gained a following in Oklahoma City and were working regularly when Clarence's father suffered a back injury that forced him out of mechanic work and music. Young Clarence, age fourteen, left school and went to work full time playing Oklahoma City nightclubs as a pianist, though he had never played the piano before.

> I heard they needed a fiddle player out at one of the clubs, and so I went out there. They said, "Well, we just hired someone. What we need is a piano player." So I thought, well, maybe that's a good way to get my feet wet—not that I could play the piano, but my mother could play the piano a little. I told them, "I'll be back tomorrow night. You can see I'm kind of young, and Momma wouldn't know why I was out." I found out that I couldn't learn to play piano in one day, so I went back out that next night and I had put on a wrist band—my wrist was kind of messed up. I told them it was. I didn't tell them it was several weeks old. They took me on the strength that I told them, "I believe I could play accompaniment with anything the band plays." I had spent all night getting the chords off the guitar and putting them on the keyboard. But that's the way I slipped in the back door playing piano. And until 1941 I took my fiddle with me although I went out to play piano. They'd let me play a breakdown or a waltz or something on the fiddle.

Clarence was a natural musician with an innate ability to learn the piano, and soon he had mastered the keyboard with the same facility he had already applied to banjo, guitar, and fiddle. He learned jazz piano styling on the job and in jam sessions with guitar giant Charlie Christian and his pianist brother, Eddie, also teenage boys growing up in Oklahoma City. Clarence recalls, "For several months Charlie Christian and I played just next door to each other. And every time I'd get a break I'd slip over next door and stand at the back of the door and Charlie would pull the microphone down between his knees and play his guitar. He didn't have an electric guitar. He played just through the PA system of the microphone. We really tried to learn from each other."

Because of the social barriers that prevented racially mixed bands, Clarence Cagle and Charlie Christian could work together only in informal jam sessions, which took place after each would get off work, around three o'clock in the morning. It did not matter to Clarence that his was the only white face in the crowd at these sessions; he was learning jazz with one of the great jazz guitar talents of the century. "I was a fourteen-year-old kid trying to make it in a man's world, and Charlie was too. I knew they were playing things I didn't play. I played a different kind of music than what they were playing. I just thought they might help me know a little more."

Clarence also began playing piano for daytime radio shows, and it was not unusual for him to spend eight to ten hours a day at the keyboard, working radio and then his nightly club jobs. When he was fifteen, his parents moved to a farm near Shawnee, Oklahoma. Clarence remained in Oklahoma City to work, and he sometimes lived out of his car.[22]

In 1938 Clarence joined the newly formed house band of the Swing Time Night Club. Calling themselves the Swing Billies, the band signed a contract with the Anderson-Pritchard Oil Company to sponsor a daily radio program on station WKY. With the financial support of the sponsor, the band bought a car, trailer, PA system, and instruments and began to play a dance circuit around Oklahoma. In April 1940 Clarence left the Swing Billies to join another club band in Amarillo; and a year later he moved to Coffeyville, Kansas, where he became the pianist for Herb Goddard and the Oklahoma Wanderers. Goddard had a daily radio spot on station KGGF and played nightly dances in all of the states reached by the station's signal—Kansas, Oklahoma, Arkansas, and Missouri. According to Clarence, Goddard had a nice singing voice and the band was populated by good musicians. In addition to playing piano with the Oklahoma Wanderers, Clarence also became a member of the radio station's staff band, playing different instruments and assuming different personalities for each show. "I would be Elmer playing fiddle on the 'Manamar' program. They called me Bob playing bass on the Ralston Purina program. I also played a show by myself, 'Cagle at the Keyboard,' a fifteen-minute spot."

The Oklahoma Wanderers broke up due to World War II, as one by one the musicians left to enlist. Clarence was classified 4F because of an injury to his leg suffered when he was fifteen months old. He was not out of work for long. In fact, Bob Wills was auditioning instrumentalists for a new Playboys band that he was putting together after his brief stay in the army, and he was planning a trip to the West Coast. Clarence auditioned and was hired; but when Bob informed him that his brother, Johnnie Lee, needed a pianist, Clarence decided to remain in Oklahoma. For sixteen years Clarence Cagle was Johnnie Lee Wills's piano player and close friend. Johnnie Lee played dances in a five-state area and broadcast daily over station KVOO in Tulsa. "We had a regular itinerary, like Oklahoma City every other Tuesday. Every other Friday we alternated between Fort Smith and Seminole. Every Thursday and Saturday we were at Cain's Academy. Monday nights in Fairfax or Coffeyville, Kansas, or someplace close in. And then Wednesday night sometimes Wichita, Kansas. That was a long one. But we always drove back the same night."

During the war years the distance the band could travel was governed by the rationing of gasoline and tires as well as by the radio station's broadcast signal. The Johnnie Lee Wills band became as popular in Oklahoma and surrounding states as Bob Wills and the Texas Playboys had been; in fact, they maintained and built upon Bob's former contacts. They also recorded over two hundred fifteen-minute transcriptions for General Mills that were played daily at noon on 176 radio stations. The Johnnie Lee Wills band assumed the status formerly reserved for Bob Wills and the Texas Playboys as the western swing institution of the Southwest.

Johnnie Lee Wills's band was a musically creditable organization, though his management style differed markedly from that of his brother Bob. Clarence explains:

Johnnie Lee was not a show person. Bob was more of a showman than he was a fiddle player. Johnnie Lee wanted the band to do real well. He'd leave it up to us. He'd say, "Now let's work something out." Bob would say, "This is the way it's going to be." Bob would say to a musician, "You sell it to me. Look at me, sell it to me, and I will sell it to the public." He would never let you play a song the same way twice. He didn't want the boys to know when they were going to get a chorus. He would kick off a song with his violin, then give Clarence the first chorus this time. The next time he'd give it to the steel man, the next time to the guitar man; you, men, were supposed to be looking at him. That kept the boys on their toes, because they had to keep their eyes on the boss. Johnnie Lee did this in a sense, but he wasn't as strict as Bob. Johnnie Lee was much easier to work for. The guys loved John and most of them who went to California with Bob didn't stay long. Bob had quite a changeover in musicians all along, but if he really needed somebody, he'd give John a call and say, "John, I need so-and-so." And there they would go. Bob Wills hired and fired six hundred musicians. In the same length of time I would say it would have been a hard press for Johnnie Lee to have gone through sixty or seventy. You had a job and a home with Johnnie Lee Wills. He was a prince of a man.

With the end of rationing after World War II, the Johnnie Lee Wills band could tour more widely, but it was still constrained by the daily noon broadcast. About 1955 Bob Wills left California and returned to Tulsa with a small group of musicians. It was his idea to combine his and Johnnie Lee's bands and tour the western states. Johnnie Lee agreed and resigned from KVOO. With a growing family in Tulsa, Clarence had no desire to join a tour band, and so, with his and his wife's savings, he bought a dump truck and embarked on a successful sand and gravel business.

In 1959 Johnnie Lee left the Playboys and returned to Tulsa to resume his band activity there. The first musician he recruited was his good friend Clarence Cagle, who happily returned. By the late 1950s the show business game had changed drastically, making it almost impossible to freelance. Johnnie Lee was forced to hire a talent agency, which booked the band at military bases all over the South and Southwest.[23] Clarence compares the band's schedule to a dart throw: "Look here, Hobbs, New Mexico, travel, open in San Diego, California, Modesto, Rosewood, California. Travel. Arizona, Las Cruces, New Mexico. El Paso. Lubbock, Colorado Springs, Colorado. Arrived in Colorado 8:45 P.M., then play Chickasha the next night. I drove all these miles, and not only drove it, but I played it." Over a span of twenty-one months, with Clarence at the wheel of the band bus, the Johnnie Lee Wills band covered over

226,000 miles playing mostly one-nighters. Two-night jobs were considered vacations.

After sixteen years with Johnnie Lee Wills, and with deep regret, Clarence resigned in 1961 and went with Leon McAuliffe's Cimarron Boys. Clarence felt the need to remain closer to home, and Johnnie Lee completely understood; but he never hired another pianist. Working for Leon McAuliffe was a different experience for Clarence, who notes that Leon emphasized modern arrangements and a great deal of rehearsal. "We had all these arrangements, the 'String of Pearls,' and all those things. We just played them night after night, but people still wanted to hear 'Steel Guitar Rag.' If they wanted Glenn Miller, they would have bought one of Glenn Miller's records." The music scene was in turmoil in the late 1950s and early 1960s; big band swing was no longer popular, rock and roll was making waves, and rural or small-town audiences in the South and Southwest were clinging to familiar traditions in a world that seemed constantly changing. In order to survive, western swing bands had to emphasize those tunes that were regarded as western swing standards; they had little room for experimentation. McAuliffe made the necessary adjustments and pieced together an outstanding band, which also toured extensively, something Clarence had not wanted to do. But McAuliffe had an airplane. "I had my flight number," says Clarence, "and every time my number came up I got on the airplane, whether for six hundred miles or two hundred miles or what. I thought, this is better than going down the highway all those miles."

Easier or not, Clarence was still gone from home much of the time, and with both children away at college, his wife was spending many lonely hours. Sensing Clarence's dilemma, Leon McAuliffe offered to sell the Cagles a music store in Rogers, Arkansas: "We had talked about getting some kind of business, something that we could work in together. Leon called us down one day and said, 'I have a music store in Rogers, Arkansas. Would you be interested in going down and seeing about having it?' And this is what we did from June 1 of 1963 to August 1 of 1982. For nineteen years we operated and worked our music store side by side. Then we took our retirement and moved back to Tulsa."

Retirement has been a busy time for Clarence Cagle. In 1982, when Johnnie Lee Wills and his band were asked to perform in Washington, D.C., for the Folklife Festival, Johnnie Lee would have no other pianist with him but Clarence. Clarence continued to work off and on in Johnnie Lee Wills's band until Johnnie Lee died in 1986. When Al Stricklin became terminally ill and died in 1986, Leon McAuliffe hired Clarence to play piano on the thirteen remaining concerts for which the Original Texas Playboys had contracts. Since 1986, Clarence has freelanced, playing a variety of jobs largely of his own choosing. He appears at Former Texas Playboy reunions and at western swing festivals and still practices the piano a couple of hours each day.

Clarence claims as his major influence Eddie Christian, piano-playing brother of Charlie Christian. He also learned a great deal by listening to the recordings of Teddy Wilson. Guy Logsdon, who profiled Clarence for the *Western Swing Society Music News*, described him as "the finest western swing pianist in the business; other piano men played and performed with flashy style. Clarence quietly played with tasteful, stylistic quality. He was essential to the Johnnie Lee Wills sound."[24]

Clarence never learned to read musical notation, but his exceptionally fine musical ear, his keen sense of swing, and his contagious good humor have more than compensated for his lack of music-reading skills. Clarence Cagle epitomizes the superb rhythm player—a member of the ensemble rather than a featured soloist. His piano touch is light and agile, full of nuance; he could never be described as a piano pounder. At the same time, his playing is highly rhythmic, as he frequently places melodic notes and chords just ahead of the beat and thus pushes the rhythm section forward. Clarence is also a melodic pianist, and even in chordal passages, the tune is never far away. He is an economical pianist, never over-elaborating on melodies. His linear movement over the keyboard is simple, direct, uncluttered, and perfectly adapted to the context. Clarence avoids most of the blues colorations that characterized the playing of Fred Calhoun. His elegant but no less emotional approach to the piano is comparable to that of his teenage idol and mentor, the jazz solo genius of the guitar, Charlie Christian.

CLIFF "SKEETER" ELKINS earned his nickname because he weighed barely five pounds when he was born in Denison, Texas, in 1922. His introduction to music came early through his mother's piano playing and the radio. Skeeter was not really as interested in the piano, however, as the accordion. When he was nine years old, his mother began taking him to Dallas for accordion lessons, and a little later she also put him with a piano teacher in Denison. Skeeter preferred the accordion because his teacher started him off playing tunes that he liked, unlike the typical beginner piano music fare. At the age of fourteen, Skeeter "graduated" from accordion study and received a certificate that allowed him to assist his accordion teacher.

After six months of teaching accordion, Skeeter was hired for his first band job, playing in Knight's Happy-Go-Lucky Cowboys, which was sponsored by Knight's Furniture Company in Sherman, Texas. This was a typical fiddle band with added accordion. The Cowboys played a noon broadcast and advertised for the furniture store. Skeeter was still in high school, so special arrangements had to be made. "They picked me up from school. Study period was the noon hour, so I got my study period arranged. Instead of going to study period, I'd go over there, because I did pretty good in school. I usually made straight A's."

When the Happy-Go-Lucky Cowboys disbanded, Skeeter joined Hack Reynolds and the Dixie Rhythm Boys, a western swing band modeled after Bob Wills and the Texas Playboys. While working in this second band, Skeeter switched from accordion to piano and never really played accordion in a band again. The Rhythm Boys played two nights a week at a rough honky-tonk in Sherman. It was not a glamorous job, but it provided Skeeter on-the-job training in the style of music that would become his livelihood.

When Skeeter graduated from high school in 1940, he and other members of the Rhythm Boys joined forces with local bandleader Leonard McRight, playing a six-nights-a-week job in another Denison honky-tonk. McRight's band included a saxophone player, guitarist, pianist, drummer, and bassist. Skeeter had recently married and had a young family to support, so he worked nights with the band and during the day sold newspapers and magazines at a Chief newstand.

About 1942 Skeeter moved to San Angelo, Texas, to work in a dance band fronted by Lowell McManes; the band toured throughout Oklahoma. He next went to work for Don Reese, then back to McManes for a tour of East Texas. Skeeter was making his living in territory bands, with only local followings and no recording contracts. But this was to change when he became the pianist for saxophonist Pud Brown, who worked out of Shreveport, Louisiana. "Pud Brown was a very good saxophone player. It was more of a jazz kind of Dixieland group. We played a place downtown in Shreveport, and then we played at a gambling place about fourteen miles out." This was a more professional band, with a larger draw and a different kind of music, and it provided Skeeter with valuable musical experience.

In 1947 Skeeter left Louisiana to rejoin Lowell McManes, who had organized a good western swing band in San Angelo. The fiddle player was the legendary Preacher Harkness. When McManes returned to Oklahoma, Skeeter kept the band together at the request of the club owner who employed them. At this point in his career, Skeeter began writing band arrangements based on the popular tunes of the day.

In December 1949, Skeeter heard that Bob Wills was auditioning piano players: "I went to Dallas. Bob had the Bob Wills Ranch House there. I went to Dallas and practiced with him, played with him, and they liked what I played, and so he took me out to his house and introduced me to Betty and all the kids. He had three at that time. So he hired me. I told Robbie (the club owner in San Angelo) I was going. We played two weeks, and then I came back and started working for Bob in Dallas."

Skeeter was Bob Wills's pianist from December 1949 to 1956. These were difficult years for the Playboys, as they were moving about looking for a home and attempting to recreate the glory years in Tulsa. After only a year at the Bob Wills Ranch House, the band relocated to Houston and then to Amarillo. All this time, Wills was scheduling tours; the band would tour for three weeks and spend two in whatever town was their temporary headquarters. The turnover of musicians was rapid, and Skeeter saw a lot of players come and go. From Amarillo, Wills moved the band to Altadena, California, near Los Angeles, and then up to Sacramento. It was 1956, and Wills was about to relocate the band again when Skeeter quit. "I didn't want to move, and Billy Jack Wills didn't want to move. I wanted to be home with my wife and kids. We had moved them all over the country."

Billy Jack Wills organized his own band in Sacramento, and for two years Skeeter was the pianist. When Billy Jack decided to move to Redding, California, Skeeter resigned and went to work for Sears, Roebuck and Company, but he remained active in music, playing in different local bands. "There were western swing bands, and pop bands—little trios, quartets, whatever. Tiny Moore and I had a trio for about a year. Then I went to a bigger band, a reading band, and they had anywhere from eleven to twenty-one pieces, whole sections. It was like an old Glenn Miller band that you listened to years ago. Five of the guys in the big band made another little group. We played spots where they wouldn't hire the big band, small spots. We played jazz, Dixieland, and enjoyed that."

Like most of the other western swing musicians interviewed, Skeeter Elkins learned by listening.

At first the only songs I heard were the cowboy bands. Then I started listening to some of the other bands—Wayne King, Guy Lombardo, Charlie Spivak, Carmen Cavallaro, Benny Goodman (I loved Benny Goodman's band). Benny Goodman had some good jazz musicians. He had a guy named Charlie Christian who played guitar real well. I liked his style. I tried to imitate his style. I think that's how Bob Wills's band got started. Bob developed his own style as a musician. He played mostly fiddle tunes at first, then started playing the jazz stuff. He hired musicians, and they played jazz like they heard from other bands. Then they started playing and developed their own style. It all became a western standard. Maybe you could hear some of it in the old Benny Goodman style, but it was changed. It still had the same jazz flavor that everybody liked. Then I listened to all the other jazz bands: Gene Krupa, Harry James.

Skeeter explains that western swing bands and horn bands played much the same repertory in the 1930s and 1940s, but with stylistic differences. Western swing musicians, probably because many could not read music, ignored arrangements and depended on feeling and instinct. And riffs and licks that were idiomatic for horns had to be varied for strings, and the use of strings as front-line instruments gave rise to new ways of thinking about melodies, chords, and keys in stock jazz arrangements. Skeeter insists that the western swing bands in which he worked were as polished and proficient as the major horn bands, but their sound was more earthy and their rhythms more driving and danceable.

Skeeter Elkins has experienced the gamut of band work, from the small no-name bands that proliferated in Texas and Oklahoma to the bright lights and fame of Bob Wills and Tex Williams, with whom he worked for about two weeks when Williams's regular pianist was ill. He made movie shorts with Wills and appeared with the Playboys on television shows hosted by Jimmy Wakely, Tennessee Ernie Ford, and Cliffie Stone. He has contributed to the bands with which he worked not only as a pianist, but also as an arranger and idea man.

RAY "CURLE"[25] HOLLINGSWORTH is one of the most sought-after of current western swing pianists. Though he was never a member of Bob Wills's Texas Playboys, he plays with the Playboys II band fronted by Johnny Gimble, because Gimble prefers Curle's piano styling. Curle was born in 1932 near the Central Texas town of Clifton. His mother played piano, his father fiddled, and his uncles played guitars and fiddles. There was never any doubt that the Hollingsworth children would be musically inclined. Family reunions are still musical events. Curle's only music lessons were with his mother, and he admits that even now he plays entirely by ear. "I can't read anything other than numbers and chord charts. My mother could read, but I didn't see the use in it until now." Curle combined his family musical traditions with what he gleaned from radio and recordings. His mother played ragtime, and he listened to the jazz piano playing of Erroll Garner, Oscar Peterson, Teddy Wilson, and Earl Hines. "I came up in the big band era—Frank Sinatra and the Ellington people and Glenn Miller. When I was going to school, that was the popular thing. I listened to them late at night. They'd come in from New Orleans, and we used to have great Dixie coming from Chicago at night."

Curle was fourteen when he started jobbing with local bands, playing joints. "I went to work for the Sutters Band when I was sixteen. I worked in the Austin area, then moved to Corpus Christi and went to work for the Rhythmaires—Johnny Gimble's uncles by marriage—they had a swing band, a good one at the time." After two years in Corpus Christi, Curle moved to Dallas to work in the big swing band of Dewey Grooms, proprietor of the Longhorn Ballroom, formerly the Bob Wills Ranch House. Later he moved to Lawton, Oklahoma, where he played in Tommy Allsup's famed western swing band. Curle's next step was a giant career leap that launched him into the musical limelight: in the mid-1950s he signed on with the Red Foley band, based in Springfield, Missouri. The Foley band played on the popular television show *Ozark Jubilee* and also toured widely. Foley had a good swing band, and Curle enjoyed the year he spent with him; but the show was canceled and the band folded, probably because of the pressure from rock and roll.

Curle's next band job was with the Miller Brothers out of Wichita Falls, Texas. Curle explains, "They were originally a hotel band. They played pop music and heavy horns and fiddles, then they went strictly fiddles and used one horn, a trumpet, and then went out on the road. It was better bookings, and, of course, the swing and the pop music lingered on in the band. All their arrangements were years old. They were a show band, too."

Many touring bands in the mid- to late 1950s were, of necessity, show bands rather than dance bands. They worked in an atmosphere in which the visual element was becoming as important as the musical performance, and they incorporated comedy routines and skits. Curle was on the road with the Miller Brothers for four years, traveling in forty-eight states and Canada. The band played numerous military bases as well as frontier days festivals and regular shows at the Golden Nugget in Las Vegas.

When he left the Miller Brothers, Curle returned to Central Texas, where he jobbed frequently with local bands and went to work for a Waco construction company. It was the early 1960s, and Johnny Gimble was beginning to spend a great deal of time recording in Nashville. Gimble had known Curle since the early fifties with the Rhythmaires and began to hire him for recording sessions. Curle has played piano on practically every Johnny Gimble album and has also performed regularly with Gimble on stage. When Gimble formed the Playboys II band, he wanted Curle to be the pianist, even though Curle had never been a Texas Playboy. "I never did work regularly for Bob Wills when he had his band. They came through one time and they wanted me to go to work with them, but I had a day job and just didn't go. We worked a bunch of jobs with Bob, just two or three nights at a time. At one time he just had Tag Lambert playing guitar, and driving him around. He used pickup musicians, really. And he could go almost anywhere and pick up some of his old band. Gimble and I worked some jobs with him that way."

Curle has recorded with country artists Merle Travis, Mack Wiseman, Chubby Wise, and Willie Nelson. He also worked on several radio and television shows with Nelson and was part of the musical cast of Nelson's 1980 movie, *Honeysuckle Rose*. Curle admits that he has had to play music he did not like in order to get work. The sixties were especially difficult years for swing musicians, and Curle survived by playing rock and roll. "It wasn't like Top Forty now, where you have to sit down and learn exactly what everybody's done in rock. If you played the beat, and that's about all it amounted to, the beat and the lyrics, you could get by." With the renewed interest in swing over the last two decades, Curle has had plenty of playing activity without having to play rock.

For Curle, jazz piano playing is based entirely on feeling, not on method, and in order for interesting improvisation to occur, the players must communicate with one another. Though a capable soloist, Curle prefers to play rhythm and claims that this has gotten him many jobs. "In the era I came up that's what you did. That's what you were hired for. You might get to take a chorus every once in a while, but you were hired to support the rhythm section."

Curle admires the great stride pianists, with their busy left hands coursing over the entire bottom half of the keyboard in varied and interesting patterns. His own approach resembles stride style in that his left hand plays chords to accentuate the beat while his right provides melodic fills. Watching Curle play, however, conjures visions of both Milt Buckner, with his hands close together in his famous lock-hands style, and Erroll Garner's signature technique of playing chords just after each beat. Like Buckner and Garner, Curle is a vertical pianist, thinking in terms of chords and melodic outgrowths of chords. This may account for the ease with which he has been able to learn from and work with guitarist Eldon Shamblin, who in the 1930s brought new harmonic resources to western swing. Curle Hollingsworth is still the backbone of any rhythm section with which he works.

Drums

Unlike the piano, which has not always been part of the jazz ensemble, the drum set is a charter member. Drum sets (traps) and drumming methods have evolved over the years. The trap sets available to New Orleans Dixieland drummers before World War I incorporated fewer instruments. Every trap set had a large, marching-size bass drum, constructed out of a wooden shell to which double calfskin heads were attached by means of tension rods. It was struck by a metal toe pedal invented by the Ludwig Drum Company in 1909. Holders or racks attached to the bass drum rim held cymbals, wood blocks, cowbells, and tom-toms. These early drum sets also had a snare drum, either laid in a chair or mounted on a stand. The snare drum had changed little since the mid-nineteenth century. Its shell and rims were made of wood or metal; it had gut snares; and its skin heads were held in place by ropes or tension rods. By 1918 snare drums with wire snares and quick snare releases were available.[26]

Early jazz drummers also had a small cymbal attached to the rim of the bass drum and played by a striker connected to the bass drum pedal. In time the cymbal striker was made to swivel so that the bass drum could be struck without engaging the floor cymbal. Smaller cymbals were suspended from a T-shaped stand clamped to the bass drum rim. Much of this equipment was used for special effects; cowbells, wood blocks, and the rim of the bass drum were hit to produce staccato sounds, and large cymbals were used at climactic points in a tune. The bass drum was generally struck on beats one and three, as a background, while most of the rhythmic pattern work was carried out on the snare drum.

In early jazz the drummer's role was felt to be backup—but nonetheless essential. In a conversation with Leonard Feather, Arthur "Zutty" Singleton (1898–1975) commented, "We just kept the rhythm going and hardly ever took a solo. But when we did, the drummers had all kinds of different sound effects; a bucket gimmick that almost sounded like a lion's roar; skillets, ratchets, bells, everything." [27] Pioneer drummers like Singleton and Warren "Baby" Dodds (1898–1959) perfected the New Orleans drumming style before World War I and then combined it with what they learned in Chicago and New York in the 1920s. Early jazz drummers devised an approach that was supportive of, but not dependent upon, the frontline players; though they drew upon the frontline rhythm patterns, they were free to alter these patterns. Pioneers like Singleton and Dodds were less timekeepers and more embellishers of the frontline rhythms produced by horns and strings.[28] They added an independent, though related, rhythmic layer.

In the 1920s Chicago drummers like Frank Snyder and Ben Pollack shifted more of their pattern playing from snare drum to the suspended cymbal, and they struck the bass drum on beats two and four and sometimes on all four beats of the measure. While they maintained the drummer's independent, nontimekeeping function, they built a bridge to the next generation of swing drummers. Swing drummers, in the 1930s and 1940s, added more instruments to their trap sets—additional cymbals of various sizes and timbres, floor tom-toms and mounted toms with adjustable tension rods for tuning, and the high-hat cymbal (two cymbals brought together by means of a pedal apparatus). The bass drum was technically improved in the 1930s with the addition of plastic heads, external mufflers, adjustable spurs for support, and tension lugs, and it was made more eye-appealing through colorful plastic lamination of the shell. Some swing drummers further surrounded themselves with timpani, tubular bells, and vibraphones.[29]

Whereas drummers from the previous jazz era had experienced a degree of independence but had developed little individuality (one drummer sounded much like another), swing drummers emerged as distinct personalities while being more dependent on the frontline instruments and the written score. Except during solo breaks, the swing drummer was a presence to be felt, not heard. The organization of the big swing bands made it necessary for drummers to avoid complex rhythmic patterns and independent rhythmic activity lest they clash with the frontline instruments. Jazz historian Mark Gridley summarizes swing drumming:

> With the exception of striking cymbals and gongs for dramatically timed effects, many of the big band drummers played lengthy passages without doing much more than stating each beat on the bass drum and reinforcing this with a simple time keeping pattern played on the snare drum with wire brushes or on a closed high-hat with sticks. Sometimes the second and fourth beats of each measure were emphasized by striking the snare drum with sticks. Deviations from these patterns usually constituted simple embellishments of the beat or busy patterns that were quickly played when the horns were pausing between ensemble phrases. Swing drummers tended not to play new and provocative rhythms that ran counter to the horn lines.[30]

Swing drummers did play solos, usually on the snare drum, occasionally on tom-toms, and normally accompanied by the steady four-beat pulse on the bass drum. As a display of technique, drum solos usually included cymbal crashes and strokes to cowbells and wood blocks, all generating high levels of excitement.[31] The legendary swing drummers—Dave Tough, Gene Krupa, Jo Jones, Cozy Cole, Sonny Greer, Chick Webb—made their reputations by individualizing the restrictive formula of swing drumming and, in so doing, paved the way for the liberation that was bop drumming, in which the drummer, once again, became an independent agent, creating a unique, but complementary, line of rhythmic activity.

Drummers in western swing bands were less likely to have solo choruses than drummers in big horn bands. In fact, they were less essential to western swing rhythm sections. Small western swing bands consisting entirely of strings could generate enough percussion and swing with rhythm guitar, banjo, bass, and piano. But the moment horns were added to western swing bands, drummers became necessary. All the drummers interviewed for this study worked for Bob Wills, the first western swing bandleader to add horns and drums to his string ensemble. It should be noted, however, that drummers like Krupa and Jones popularized the drum set to the point that every dance band needed drums in order to sound current and stylish. Thus, even western swing bands without horns often hired drummers in order to be in step with the times.

A *Few Good Drummers Talk about Western Swing*

W. E. "SMOKY" DACUS (b. 1913) is the undisputed godfather of western swing drummers, having been the first drummer to play in a string
band. When Smoky joined the Wills band in 1935, it was quite a contrast
to the life he had lived before in his hometown of Blackwell, Oklahoma,
where his father operated a barbershop. The elder Dacus expressed nothing but contempt for musicians and once pulled Smoky off a bandstand
with the words "I'm trying to raise a decent family, and I'm not trying to
raise any musicians. Anytime I find out that you're taken with that, I'm
coming after you." His attitude was not all that unusual among rural
southwesterners in the 1920s, many of whom viewed dancing and playing for dances as sinful activities. But treating music as a leisure pastime,
separate from dancing, was acceptable, so Smoky shined shoes at his father's barbershop and saved enough money to order a $12.50 banjo and
a $2.50 instruction book out of the Sears and Roebuck catalogue. He
learned to play banjo, though he did not like its sound, and, more important, he learned to read chords from the manual. From banjo Smoky
went on to guitar but ultimately settled on drums.

At Blackwell High School, Smoky played percussion in the concert
band, where his reading skills were further improved. When he graduated
from high school at the age of fifteen (he had been advanced several
grades), he went to work at a local glass plant. Then he was approached
by a man who had heard of his reputation as a dance drummer, despite
his father's objections, and offered him a job that would put him through
Tulsa University. "We're organizing a dance band called the Eight Collegians at Tulsa University," the man told Smoky. "You could pay your way
through school. We'll get all the school dances, and book civic club
dances, while you go to college."

This was a dream come true for a young man who had never expected to be able to afford college. Smoky registered at Tulsa University,
first majoring in petroleum engineering and then switching to English and
behavioral psychology. "My reason for the behavioral psychology was
that I wanted to see what made people tick; why they did certain things.
It never occurred to me that I couldn't figure out without finding out the
same thing about me." He was also playing drums in the Tulsa University
Marching Band and, after convincing the conductor to purchase timpani,
in the Tulsa University Symphony Orchestra. The Eight Collegians, besides playing dances, worked a sit-down job at a hotel, for which Smoky

had, in addition to his trap drums, a vibraphone and cathedral chimes. "We played luncheon and dinner music. I had, by far, the best job in Tulsa, fifteen dollars a week! But as soon as I'd get through there, I would go to these little clubs at the edge of town, and I would play Dixieland until daylight. Dixieland was what I loved to play, with its two-beat rhythm."

It was because of Smoky's experience and reputation as a Dixieland drummer that Bob Wills sought him out and offered him a job. "It was unheard of—a fiddle band—that's country music. I said, 'What in the hell do you want with a drummer in a fiddle band?' And Bob bit his cigar and poked me in the chest. He said, 'I want to take your kind of music, my kind of music, put them together, and make it swing.'"

Going with Bob Wills and the Texas Playboys was not an easy decision for Smoky. First of all, a drummer playing in a fiddle band was so unprecedented that Smoky had no idea what or how he was supposed to play. Second, the Texas Playboys, like all fiddle bands, was stigmatized as a hillbilly band, and Smoky knew that he would suffer criticism if he gave up playing "real jazz" to play in Wills's band. But the year was 1935, the height of the depression, and Wills's offer of sixty-five dollars a week assuaged most of Smoky's doubts.

It did not take Smoky too long on the Wills band to realize that he had made a wise decision; not only did his pay increase steadily, but he also experienced a musical freedom he had never known before. "I didn't have to read anything. I didn't have to pull out three or four tools at a time and play them. I just sat back there and watched the crowd, and it was something that I liked to play. And Wills let me play whatever I wanted to play."

Smoky also learned quickly why Wills needed a drummer; his band's rhythm section was weak. "Bob didn't know what a rhythm section was, but he wanted a beat that anybody could find, and if you can't dance to a two-beat, you can't dance. You might just as well go home." After Smoky was hired, it became obvious to the Playboys that Wills was moving in the direction of jazz, and some of them quit. This allowed Wills to hire musicians who fit into his scheme, and soon the rhythm section began to jell.

The bull fiddle player slapped those strings. The frequency of that click is so much higher than anything else going on in the band, you can hear that click three blocks away before you get to the dance

hall. So I put a brush in my left hand and played a 2/4 beat with the
guitar, and I sat on my trap case. Turned it up on end. And I would
take a stick and slap the side of my trap case. I'd get the same click
he was getting slapping that bull fiddle, and the same thing with
brushes the guitar was playing. And it just took off.

Smoky believed that his playing should mesh with the rest of the
sound, not dominate it, that he should be more felt than heard, and that
he was only part of a greater whole. He was influenced in his playing and
thinking by Sonny Greer, drummer with the Duke Ellington band. Smoky
had occasion to hear the Ellington band when it came through Tulsa on
tour; it was a memorable event.

Sonny was a little bitty African American man. He didn't weigh a
hundred and thirty pounds, but he played like I wanted to play. The
first time they were in Tulsa, I was out in the crowd. The second
show, I was back behind Sonny Greer. Duke Ellington was sitting
down there in front with a nine-foot Steinway, and playing it. Little
Sonny Greer was sitting back there with a pair of brushes, just
walking. I thought to myself, if that's good enough for Duke Ellington, it's good enough for me. So that show I'm behind Sonny. I
stayed back there, and I told him what I thought. Sonny and I are
very good friends to this day. Now that was the influence he had;
but he refused to show me how to play anything. He said, "I can
give you a lot of good advice. The more drums a man has, the less
he is apt to play. He's got all this stuff up here. Well, everybody
out in the audience can see he has all this stuff, and they wonder
when he's gonna hit all that stuff. He knows they wonder when he's
gonna hit all that stuff. He can only stand it so long, and he's gonna
hit all that stuff. Smoky, I'm fixing to give you some good advice.
It's important to know when to play, but it's more important to
know when not to."

Smoky listened and learned. While swing drummers were amassing
larger trap sets, Smoky stuck to the basic Dixieland set of bass, snare, a
ride cymbal, and crash cymbal, and he added a high-hat. He also devised
a playing style that was forceful yet understated. He rarely struck the ride
cymbal because its ringing tone was too loud and tended to blur the clear
beat pattern, but he used the tightly closed high-hat frequently.

For the first couple of months with Wills, Smoky worried most about what to play with each type of song and behind each soloist. Being basically a Dixieland drummer, he felt that he had to draw rhythmic ideas from individual soloists and back each of them differently. He devised a formula that worked well for the six years he spent with Wills. To back the louder horns, he played rhythm patterns with sticks on his trap case, which was also his stool. Behind a fiddle solo he used brushes. When Al Stricklin played a piano chorus, Smoky accompanied with a brush on the snare and a stick on the closed high-hat. On slow ballads, he used his brush-in-one-hand and stick-in-the-other technique. The ride cymbal made an appearance only in the ensemble-out choruses of up-tempo numbers. Smoky was a clear and precise drummer who did not permit holdover cymbal sound to impede the motion of the rhythm. It was this approach that contributed significantly to the drive and swing of the Wills rhythm section.

Smoky left the Playboys in February 1941 because he had a premonition that war was coming, and he did not want to be caught without a marketable skill. He had already observed a large migration of southwesterners to California to work in the defense industry; he decided to do the same, but first he wanted training. He went into Bob Wills's office and presented an irrefutable reason for leaving the highest-paying dance band in the entire country.

> Jim Rob, a musician is a musician because he wants to be, he enjoys it. It's an expression that he can't find anyplace else. It's an emotional outlet for him. But he stays there until, when he gets through with a job, he doesn't want to go jam. He wants to go home. And he begins to think about getting out of this business, and he goes to town and applies for a job. The man says, "What do you do?" He says, "I play guitar." He says, "Well, what else do you do?" He says, "That's all. I've played guitar since I was a kid." He says, "We don't need any guitar players here." He makes about three or four stops like that, and gets the same answer every time because he can't do anything but play a guitar. Jim Rob, from that point on he's a musician because he has to be, not because he wants to be. He can't get out.

Smoky was so determined to get out that he sold his drums so that he would not be tempted to play again. He went to Spartan Aircraft Company to take a sheet-metal course, and he excelled because of his outside research into the properties of metal. When he finished the course, he intended to go to California and work in the aircraft industry; instead, he was hired to teach the sheet-metal course at Spartan. And while he was teaching, he earned a private pilot's license, a commercial pilot's license, airframe certification, engine certification, and a propeller specialist's certificate. Smoky knew everything about airplanes; he could build one, maintain it, and fly it. He was quickly snapped up by Carter Oil Company, a subsidiary of Standard Oil of New Jersey, as a copilot and airplane mechanic. This was Smoky's other life, and it was his until he retired to Rogers, Arkansas, to fish off the banks of the White River.

Smoky played drums as a regular with only one western swing band, Bob Wills and the Texas Playboys. He worked briefly with Leon McAuliffe after McAuliffe returned from the war and started his own band. "Leon wanted a modern band, but he still wanted to keep the country flavor in it. So he had an awfully good band, but it was right out in the middle. It wasn't pop and it wasn't country. It was right out there in no-man's land. Ted Adams was playing bass, good bass man. And Moe Billings was playing piano, fine. I would go over there to the Cimarron Ballroom in Tulsa and sit in, and Ted would move his bass right up beside me, and we'd sit and ride for two hours." But Smoky was never the official drummer with the Cimarron Boys, nor did he want to be. When McAuliffe's drummer left, Smoky helped audition potential replacements, ultimately selecting young Tommy Perkins to play for McAuliffe's band.

Smoky was the only drummer Bob Wills would consider for the 1973 recording session that produced the album *For the Last Time*. Wills had hired flashier drummers, but none who suited his style of western swing like Smoky Dacus. Smoky marveled at the ease with which these musicians who had not worked together in forty years could recall the style, the songs, recreating everything as though no time had elapsed.

The key to the success of the Wills band was swing. Everything, every type of tune, had to swing. Smoky said, "The only thing we were zeroed in on, it didn't make any difference what the tune, . . . it had to sit there and swing. Any tune had to have that beat to it. We were playing dance music. That was our only concern." Some swing rhythm sections were truly magical—Count Basie's, Jimmy Lunceford's, Duke Ellington's, and Bob Wills's—and Smoky Dacus was among the great swing drummers of the era.

TOMMY PERKINS, born in Oklahoma City in 1934, was a youngster when he began to play drums professionally in a western swing band. Before that time he had grown up in a musical family and worked as part of a family trio. When Tommy's parents divorced, his mother married a musician. Tommy began playing drums at the age of twelve and was ready to participate when his mother and stepfather formed a trio consisting of piano, guitar, and drums.

Tommy's new family moved to Clinton, Oklahoma, where Tommy entered junior high. When his mother and stepfather went to Amarillo to work in a band, Tommy remained in Clinton, attended school, and played six nights a week in a hotel trio. By the age of fifteen, Tommy Perkins was a seasoned professional. He was ready musically in 1950, when Bob Wills blew through town on his way to California, minus a drummer. It was Tommy's first year in high school, and Wills had to seek the permission of the Oklahoma attorney general's office to take the boy out of school and out of state. As the attorney general was a fan of Bob Wills, he readily agreed to the plan.

In his wildest dreams young Tommy Perkins could never have imagined being hired to play drums on the most famous and popular of all western swing bands. And how did Wills treat his fifteen-year-old drummer? Did he tell him what to play and when? Tommy says, "No, you were free to play or he wouldn't have hired you. He wanted what he heard when he hired you." Tommy spoke the drum language that Wills wanted to hear—a strongly accented 2/4 dance beat, close collaboration with the other rhythm players, and being felt more than heard. "I felt comfortable playing what felt right for the band, because everybody was thinking alike. Sometimes I'd play closed high-hat when the piano player was playing, because back then they didn't use the sound systems like they use now. You had to be able to hear the other players. If you couldn't hear the other guys, you were playing too loud."

Wills never wanted a tune to drag, not even a slow one, and preferred a gradual accelerando toward the end. As the drummer, Tommy had to adjust to play a little ahead of the beat, to push, or play slightly behind the beat if the tempo threatened to get out of control. For the Wills band, everything, including rhythm, was based on feeling.

This was a ten-piece band that Wills took to California on tour in 1949–1950. He had been working with a small group, but with the competition in California—Spade Cooley, Tex Williams—he had to present a formidable force. Tommy was hired as auxiliary drummer, to play when

Billy Jack Wills left the drum set to sing. While they were in Hollywood, the Texas Playboys cut a number of records on the MGM label. Their greatest success from this session was "Faded Love," an old fiddle tune Bob Wills had learned from his father, with lyrics added by Billy Jack. Tommy Perkins played drums on this hit record.

After six weeks on tour with Bob Wills and the Texas Playboys, Tommy returned to Oklahoma and the family trio until after high school graduation. Then he got his second chance of a lifetime when Hank Thompson hired him. "That was an experience. First band I ever worked with that had two steel guitar players. It was a big band. He had three fiddles. That was a high-intensity band. It was a show band; lots of show stuff went on—antics, that kind of thing. That was a loud band, the loudest band I ever worked on. I cracked the top of my high-hat the first night on the band, I played it so hard."

Thompson's people picked up Tommy Perkins in Stillwater, Oklahoma, and transported him to Coffeyville, Kansas, for the first job he would play. Tommy was amazed when the entire band checked into a downtown hotel as a baseball team rather than a band; it seems bands were acquiring reputations for being destructive, and many hotels did not want to serve them. On the bandstand Thompson's people were consummate music professionals. They played first to warm up the crowd for Thompson, then again between and after his sets. In Tommy's opinion, Thompson had an excellent western swing band, though he himself was not a western swing musician.

In late 1952 Tommy moved out to Sacramento to work for Billy Jack Wills. "This was a six-piece band, a really good band. We did a lot of jazz tunes on this band. We did 'Summer Ritz Drive' and just a bunch of tunes like that." Tommy had by this time played drums in three of the best western swing bands in the business. Where could he go from here? To the small backup band of country artist Lefty Frizzell. Tommy played on several of Frizzell's hit records from around 1954 and toured extensively with the singer for a year and a half. Tommy was seldom home during that time, as they toured up and down each coast and most places in between. The list of one-nighters runs on and on, and in most of these places, even in the North and Northeast, Frizzell was well received by audiences. The depression and then World War II had dispersed rural southerners all over the country, so audiences for country music existed everywhere.

From Frizzell's band, Tommy returned to Oklahoma and western swing, auditioning for Leon McAuliffe's Cimarron Boys. For Tommy, working for McAuliffe was another great experience. Leon McAuliffe was on the outward fringe of western swing, encompassing more complex, less accessible musical ideas. When he nearly went broke, he had to rein in and reach out to audiences again. McAuliffe had a more hands-on approach to band management than either Bob or Billy Jack Wills, and Tommy remembers one day in particular when McAuliffe called him in for a drum lesson: "I was young then, nineteen or so. He said, 'I wish you'd play a little less bass drum, more left-hand, more high-hat, not too much cymbal. But feel free to play the way you want to.' "

After leaving Leon's band, Tommy stayed in Tulsa and worked at the Stardust Club, backing strippers. Then in 1962 he moved back to Oklahoma City and worked in several local bands, often with his friend since childhood, guitarist Benny Garcia. Like Smoky Dacus, Tommy Perkins is a drummer who thinks and functions as a part of the rhythm section, not as a flashy soloist. He explains,

> It's a certain type of rhythm that you hear and connect with; everybody has to be thinking the same. A lot of that comes from working together. I worked with the Texas Playboys II, that's Johnny Gimble's group. We don't get to play that often together, but when we do play, people come up and say, how much do you all get to work together? Maybe we hadn't worked together for six months, but it never sounds that way. We're all of the same mindset as to how it's got to sound. You know how it's supposed to sound, so you work for that sound and that feel.

Tommy has serious reservations about newer western swing bands, like Asleep at the Wheel, and he senses that it's the rhythmic aspect that is not quite right with these groups. He notes that since they play concerts and shows rather than dances, they have no obligation to maintain the solid 2/4 beat that, to Tommy, identifies western swing. He is also annoyed by the use of microphones on every instrument, even the drums, because this brings the drummer too much into the forefront, like a rock drummer. Says Tommy Perkins, "You're supposed to feel it, not hear it."

JOHNNY CUVIELLO, born in Fresno, California, in 1915, is the only western swing drummer to record a drum solo. His love affair with the trap set started when he was a teenage boy attending movies at the Wilson Theater in Fresno. "I heard this drummer drumming a short rhythm. The roll is what I fell in love with, the snare drum roll." Johnny used fourteen dollars he had saved from his newspaper route to purchase his first set of drums. They were Ludwigs—a small bass drum, an old wooden-shell snare drum with ropes for tension, a large ride cymbal, a tiny crash cymbal, a high-hat, and his prized possession, a fourteen-inch Indian tom-tom attached to the bass drum rim. He scoured local hock shops for sticks and brushes and was soon ready to play. But play what?

Johnny went first to the band director at his high school; the man decided he needed a drummer and would teach Johnny the rudiments. Each morning before classes started, Johnny was in the band hall learning to play drums. He spent the first three weeks playing nothing but bass drum. They moved next to the snare drum. "The band director taught me to read snare drum off of flute notes. He played the flute. It was all eighth notes and sixteenth notes, very few quarter notes." Johnny's band director was teaching him the rudiments of military drumming, one of the main elements of which was the press roll, Johnny's favorite drum stroke and the hallmark of his personal style.

When word spread that Johnny was learning to play drums, he began to be in demand for school dances. He formed his own seven-piece jazz band, in which he learned a great deal about swing from horn players who were more knowledgeable than he. "We were playing 'It Had to Be You,' and 'You're Driving Me Crazy,' the old standards, and 'My Confession,' and 'I Love You,' and waltzes and 'Springtime in the Rockies,' and they were showing me what to do, how to swing."

When he was sixteen years old, Johnny began to play professionally, mostly in small combos and in vaudeville and burlesque orchestras. But he loved to hear the big swing bands that came through Fresno. And one day, quite by accident, he got to play in one. The year was 1945, and the band was Bob Wills and the Texas Playboys.

> I met him at radio station KMJ in Fresno. I was playing tom-toms with a guy named Jack O'Neil for a weekly show, and imitating horses and sounds like that for this radio program. I heard there was going to be a western band up there at the station. So I walked up there one afternoon, and the band was setting up. I went to the drummer and said, "I'm a drummer also." He said, "Well, I'm drumming. Would you mind tuning up my snare drum—tighten the rods?" I said, "No, I don't mind." It was Billy Jack Wills. I tuned them up, and then he said, "Would you mind sitting in and playing?" I said, "Well, I've never played with a big band like this."

He said, "Go ahead and play." Meantime Bob showed up. He picked up his fiddle. He took off and we did all kinds of transcriptions. They were promotional transcriptions for Oakland, for Fresno, for everywhere he went. When he got through playing, he said, "Would you like to work with our band?" I said, "Yeah, sure I would." The band was so good. But I told Bob I had no boots or hats. "We'll have all that for you." And that's how I got started with Bob Wills.

While with Bob Wills, Johnny recorded the drum solo for which he is still famous.

I wrote this song "Texas Drummer Boy," and I wrote some words to it, but we didn't use words. I went to Bob and said, "Bob, I did a little drum solo." He said, "Oh, that's nice." I said, "Could I do a drum solo?" He said, "It's yours, it's yours." I went in the studio at the Wrigley Building in Chicago to do this solo. Bob said, "We're going to do this solo for Johnny." Bob named it "The Texas Drummer Boy." I didn't name it. And we started off and I started off naturally and picked up on a tom-tom. I felt it swinging. And Tiny filled in and took over, and then back to drums. Then it just became a natural feeling.

It was unprecedented to have a drum solo on a western swing band recording, but Wills was not afraid to experiment. Johnny admits that "Texas Drummer Boy" was not original but rather his interpretation of the popular "Hawaiian War Chant."

Johnny was with the Wills organization during a time of critical change. He played on the last recording session for Columbia and the first for MGM, and he saw a great many personnel changes. When he left the Playboys in 1947, he jobbed around for a while, then dropped out of music completely. He went to work for Lockheed Aircraft Corporation and did not touch his drums for some twelve years. When he returned to music in the early 1960s, it was to play with local bands that, much to his chagrin, knew little about swing. Johnny has also participated in Texas Playboy Reunions and Bob Wills Days in Turkey, Texas, and he has played various engagements with Truitt Cunningham and his San Antonio Rose band and with Luke Wills. At home in Fresno he sometimes plays drums in a local western swing band called the Lonestar Playboys.

Johnny Cuviello was influenced by some of the best swing drummers in the business—Gene Krupa, Buddy Rich, Dave Tough, Sidney Catlett, and Chick Webb. He probably got the idea for playing a drum solo on tom-toms from Gene Krupa, who first did this in 1937 with Benny Goodman's band on "Sing, Sing, Sing." All of the drummers Johnny listed as his heroes advanced the drum set to greater prominence as a solo instrument while solidifying the swing style of drumming. These were transitional drummers who prepared the way for later big band drummers, who, in their time, placed more emphasis on cymbal playing and moved drumming into bebop. Johnny was certainly an early swing or transitional drummer who did most of his playing on snare and closed high-hat, avoiding the hot ride cymbal except to build tension toward the end of the ensemble-out chorus.

Like Tommy Perkins, Johnny bemoans the present state of western swing rhythm and blames the problem in part on the fact that putting on a show takes precedence over making the music. For the sake of appearance, drummers are routinely separated from the rest of the rhythm section and set up on raised stages at the rear. The rhythm section is spread out, and if the bass player or rhythm guitar player happens to be the featured singer, he or she leaves the time-honored spot close to the drums and moves to the front. The result of this showmanship is a lack of communication among rhythm players and a lessening of the rhythmic drive; the music no longer swings. For Johnny, the best part of working for Bob Wills was the emphasis Wills placed on rhythm, that driving 2/4 dance beat with swing to spare. What's missing for Johnny in modern western swing bands is that tightly coordinated, driving swing that identified a Bob Wills rhythm section. And for Johnny Cuviello, as for other western swing rhythm players, there's no point in making this music if it does not swing.

SEVEN

The Rest of the Western Swing Band: Horn Players and Vocalists

Horns

Since western swing is jazz made predominantly by string bands, horns have played only a minor role. But two western swing band leaders, Bob Wills and Spade Cooley, at particular points in their careers, built large horn sections around the nucleus of strings. Many western swing bands have operated exceptionally well without horns, and others have used only one or two, usually trumpet or saxophone or both. For the most part, the horn players who have passed through western swing bands have come from and returned to the big horn bands. The reason for their sojourn in western swing bands has been strictly financial—at the height of western swing's popularity, western swing bands drew larger crowds and paid better salaries. It is difficult to find horn players who have specialized in western swing, but two were interviewed for this study.

A Few Good Horn Players Talk about Western Swing

GLENN "BLUB" RHEES (1925–1995) became interested in playing saxophone when he was six years old. He had two older brothers, one of whom played organ and piano, and the other, drums. Glenn's mother attempted to teach him to play piano, but Glenn was more interested in a saxophone that his drummer brother owned. To quiet little Glenn, the older brother relinquished his saxophone, and Glenn began to practice. "I'd practice that horn—I didn't care what it was, I'd try to blow on it. I'd turn on the radio and try to play with the bands on the radio. Back then there was all kinds of music on the radio—like the big bands: Glenn Miller, Tommy Dorsey, Benny Goodman. I'd just honk on that saxophone trying to play those songs."

Glenn began serious study of the saxophone in seventh grade band in Jennings, Oklahoma, but it was at a summer band camp in nearby Oilton that he knew for certain that the saxophone was going to be his life's work. The band director in Oilton, impressed with Glenn's natural talent and excellent musical ear, convinced him to transfer to Oilton for eighth grade and promised to place Glenn in the high school band. Glenn spent the next two years playing in the Oilton High School band and, when his teachers chided him for doing poorly in his other classes, telling them that he would not need those subjects when he grew up to be a dance band musician.

During his junior year in high school, Glenn's family moved to the big city of Tulsa, and he transferred to a larger band program run by a schooled German musician. Though this man knew nothing about improvisation or jazz, he helped Glenn to improve his technical and reading skills. While attending Webster High School in Tulsa, Glenn joined a student band called the Swing Sessions. This was a pop band that played the latest hits at school and civic dances. Young Glenn was also working as an usher at the Tulsa Theater. The theater owner regularly hired small bands, mostly country string bands, to entertain audiences before the movie feature and during intermissions. Glenn would mingle with the string players and discuss music, but he refused to sit in with them because they played in sharp keys, and saxophonists preferred flat keys. Still, he had grown up with western swing; the music appealed to him, but all those sharps daunted him.

When Glenn graduated from high school in 1943, he went to work for an oil exploration company that prospected in Oklahoma, Texas, Louisiana, Wyoming, and Montana. Everywhere he went, Glenn carried his horn. "I'd find bands where I was working, prospecting for oil. I'd get with a band in that territory and I'd play with them at night. I had a big following because all the guys on the crew would come hear me. They were always asking me, 'What are you doing this kind of work for when you can play like you play?' I'd say, 'Well, I'm trying to learn.' At the time I was self-conscious about my playing. I wasn't really sure. But I was trying to get with western bands at the time, to learn to play in those hillbilly sharp keys."

In 1946, after three years of oil prospecting and learning in territory bands, Glenn returned to Tulsa and took a job playing at the Uptown

Tavern. This was an after-hours club that stayed open long after others had closed. Musicians getting off their jobs would gather at the Uptown Tavern for jam sessions. One of the regulars at these sessions was the singer for a western swing band called Art Davis and the Rhythm Riders. Davis had made films with Gene Autry before moving to Tulsa and forming his own band. The singer spoke to Glenn one night during a break. "'Glen, would you like to go on the road?' I said, 'I'd give anything to go on the road.' That's like telling a baseball player, would you like to go with the New York Yankees. He said, 'I think I can get you on Art Davis's band. He's got a pretty good band playing out of Tulsa here.' So that was my inauguration with Art Davis. He had a radio broadcast every day on KAKC in Tulsa, and also on KTUL."

Glenn began working in a western swing band and confronting all those hillbilly keys. Besides the daily radio show, Davis played a dance circuit that ran north to Wichita, Kansas, and south to Wichita Falls, Texas. For two years, from 1946 to 1948, Glenn gained further experience in Art Davis's eight-piece western swing band. Davis was a fine fiddler, but could also double on clarinet, and he and Glenn devised interesting horn duets.

In 1948 Davis decided to run for the office of sheriff of Tulsa County, and he enlisted the band to help him campaign, much as Jimmie Davis did in Louisiana. After losing the election and most of his money, Davis decided that he would take his band to Florida, which he called "virgin territory." But Glenn had already experienced one dreadful "virgin territory" trip with Davis to Nebraska, and he was not interested in relocating to Florida. Instead, Glenn joined a band in Oklahoma City, Lucky Moeller's Western Oakies, which played at the Trianon Ballroom on Friday and Saturday nights and worked radio and a dance circuit. Glenn was not really expecting much when he joined Moeller, but was pleasantly surprised to find that he had stumbled into an excellent western swing band. Two of the best fiddlers in the business—Keith Coleman and Bob White—were already in the band, and Glenn spent a happy 1949 working with Moeller. But when Bob Wills hired Moeller to be his band manager, and Keith Coleman and Bob White to play fiddles, the Western Oakies was history. Glenn was out of work.

He attended the Playboys radio show broadcast from the Criterion Theater in Oklahoma City and was literally awed by what he heard. "I'll never forget the way Bob kicked off 'San Antonio Rose.' He kicked it off like it was real slow, like a ballad. And when they got to the middle of the song, that band hit that—Billy Jack Wills was on drums at the time, and he put a roll into the middle of that song, and it made me feel like I was in a rocket heading for the moon. That's just the way that band sounded. I thought, oh my gosh, I wish I was in Keith's and Bob's place right now, so that I could get on that band."

Glenn heard of job opportunities for musicians in the numerous clubs near the oilfields of New Mexico and West Texas. He went to work for the Eddy County Barn Dance in Carlsbad, but there were so many bands booked on the show that Glenn could not get enough playing time to earn a living. So he moved on to Pete's Club in Gallup, where he remained for nearly a year before returning to Carlsbad and landing a good job at the Lobby Club. Things went well for Glenn at the Lobby Club, so well, in fact, that he almost turned down an opportunity to go to work for Luke Wills and His Rhythm Busters.

> This was 1950. I was making good money in Carlsbad, but my new wife just hated it. She was a twin, and that was the first time she'd been away from her sister. There was a telegram for me from Luke. "If you're interested in going to work for me, you can come to Oklahoma City." I was doing good in Carlsbad, making good money. I just took the telegram and threw it on the dashboard. Later on that day Shirley got in the car to go shopping. She said, "What's that on the dashboard?" I said, "That's a telegram from Luke Wills." She said, "When are we leaving?" I said, "We're not leaving. I'm making good money here." She said, "No, the divorce is coming if you don't go back to Oklahoma City. Let's get close to home, that's where we're going."

Glenn joined Luke Wills's Rhythm Busters and remained until the group disbanded after a year. Glenn felt that they had a great band, per-haps in some ways better than those of Bob or Johnnie Lee Wills, but Luke was not the leader his brothers were and could not make the band work. Glenn next joined the Southernaires, a fine western swing band that played at the Southern Club in Lawton, Oklahoma. "There were some good musicians on the band: the steel guitar player, Bob White. The fiddle player from Jimmie Davis's band down in Louisiana, Preacher Harkness—he was tired of traveling with Davis. We had a very good band. Bob Wommack, who later made it pretty good in the western swing field, played trumpet. We played two horns on that band. Donny Mc-Daniels was the piano player, and he later went with Hank Thompson. Bob White also went with Thompson for several years."

The owner of the Southern Club booked top acts, so the band backed Lefty Frizzell, Jimmy Dickens, Webb Pierce, Hank Williams, Tex Ritter, Homer and Jethro, and other Nashville stars. More important for Glenn's career was the fact that Bob Wills played the Southern Club often, and Glenn and Wills became friends.

After two years at the Southern Club, Glenn decided to form a duet with his organ-playing brother. They played their repertory of pop songs, like "Tenderly" and "Stardust," to disinterested audiences at joints from Missouri to Minnesota. Finally, audience apathy got to both musicians, and they quit the freelance business. Glenn returned to Tulsa and hired a booking agent to keep him busy playing. He worked with different bands and had just returned from playing a job in Salina, Kansas, when he was contacted by Johnnie Lee Wills. Glenn joined Johnnie Lee's band in late 1955 and remained there for the next two years. These were good years for Glenn and for Johnnie Lee Wills. It was an excellent band, and all of the musicians enjoyed working for Johnnie Lee. And when in 1957 Bob Wills arrived in Tulsa wanting to hire Glenn away from Johnnie Lee's band, Glenn did not want to leave. He had heard false rumors that Bob Wills was a difficult man to work for, and he was too happy with Johnnie Lee. But Glenn agreed to play one dance job with Bob, not knowing that, by doing so, he had made a commitment to the band. "I ended up on tour. They kidnapped me off of Johnnie Lee's band. We wound up in Seattle, Washington. We were working one-nighters all the way. When you go with Bob Wills, you hit the road. That was a band that really played everywhere, coast to coast."

Though "kidnapped" at first, Glenn spent the next four years happily following Bob Wills anywhere he wanted to go. Shortly after Glenn joined the Playboys, Bob Wills and singer Tommy Duncan reunited, and they all went to Hollywood to record the *Together Again* album. Glenn played on two other albums, *Living Legend* and *Mr. Words and Mr. Music*. The recording sessions were good and the money excellent, but the touring schedule was grueling. On a Christmas holiday trip back to Tulsa, Glenn approached Johnnie Lee about getting his old job back, only to find that Johnnie Lee was breaking up his band and combining a few musicians with Bob's. That combined band would be based in Las Vegas and play a thirty-three-week stint at the Golden Nugget, plus shows at other casinos on the Nevada circuit. Glenn stayed on with Wills until February 1961, when Bob dismissed his horn players at the insistence of the owner of the Nugget. "Bob told me and Jack Loyd [clarinet], 'I've got to tell you boys something that I hate to tell you, because I think you are two of the greatest horn players that I've ever had on my band. But Bill Green [the casino owner] has talked to me, and he wants to go strictly strings. I've got to hire more fiddles.' I actually didn't get fired, I was just sent back to Johnnie Lee."

Johnnie Lee had left a few months earlier to reorganize his band in Tulsa, and Glenn rejoined him. He never felt any rancor toward Bob Wills, but he was irritated at the casino owner, who occasionally booked Johnnie Lee's band, with horn players, at the Golden Nugget but insisted that Bob work there with only a string band. Glenn left Johnnie Lee Wills in October 1963 to go to work for the Tulsa parks department. Having been on the road since 1946, he decided it was time to stay home. But he did not stop playing his saxophone. In fact, for the next seven years he worked weekends at the Caravan Ballroom in Tulsa on a band that also featured Eldon Shamblin, Amos Hedrick (previously a fiddler for Hank Thompson's band), and Tommy Perkins. He has also played in pickup bands with Hank Thompson, Speedy West, Herschel Clothier, Ferlin Husky, and others who came through Tulsa. In 1982 Glenn went to Washington, D.C., with Johnnie Lee Wills to represent Oklahoma at a Diamond Jubilee celebration sponsored by the Smithsonian Institute. He also played frequently with Truitt Cunningham and the San Antonio Rose Band and was much in demand on the local music scene in Tulsa.

It is rare to find horn players who have willingly dedicated their talents to mastering the sharp keys—unusual to horn players but required in string bands. Glenn demonstrated his musical ability early on by doing just that. Playing in string bands did not inhibit Glenn's technical prowess or his creative bent at improvisation. He was as much the consummate jazz saxophonist in those "hillbilly keys" as others in the more familiar tonal territory of typical horn bands. He proudly wore his nickname, the "Sax Maniac," because he had truly earned it.

BILLY BRIGGS, born in Calvert, Texas, in 1925, is another saxophonist who has sought opportunities to work in western swing bands. Billy says that he was born loving music. As a child he would walk up the street a short distance and sit on the lawn for hours listening to a neighbor playing her piano. He did not begin to study music until his freshman year in high school, when he started playing clarinet in the school band. The next year Billy was invited to join a fiddle band. Billy began his professional music career at the age of fourteen, playing clarinet in a fiddle band that was working in a honky-tonk near Hearne, Texas. He made two dollars per night, not bad wages for a child at the end of the depression.

When he was fifteen, Billy got his first saxophone, a tenor, and he also acquired an alto saxophone. He learned by listening to the fiddle bands he heard on the radio. "The fiddle bands played pop tunes. Most of them would add one horn, which inspired me. There was a saxophone player out of Fort Worth, and I met him. His name was Earl Driver. He played with a group called the Crystal Springs Ramblers out of Fort Worth." Billy Briggs does not talk about listening to the big horn bands, which could also be heard on radio, but about his fascination for western swing bands. Billy's love affair with western swing began early. Perhaps this western swing background explains why Billy never felt intimidated by the so-called "hillbilly keys."

The summer after Billy graduated from high school, he worked in a little six-piece band out of Temple, Texas, called the Southerners. In the fall he started college at Sam Houston State, but the United States had just entered World War II, so rather than finish the spring semester, Billy went to work in a defense plant in Fort Worth. In late 1943 Billy enlisted and was sent to Blackland Army Air Field in Waco, Texas, where he was assigned to the band. After two and a half years in Waco, he was transferred to Sioux Falls, South Dakota, to attend radio school. Billy ended his tour of duty in 1946 at Drew Air Field, playing in the band.

After the war, Billy joined a friend in building a band in Rock Island, Illinois. He spent three and a half years playing pop music in hotels and lounges. All the band members had grown up listening to western swing, so this was a swinging little combo. From Rock Island, Billy moved to Baton Rouge, Louisiana, to play in a band fronted by Arty Glenn. Glenn owned a grocery store, liquor store, and dance hall that catered to the bayou residents, many of whom reached the place by boat rather than automobile. After eight months with Glenn, Billy moved his family to Dallas, where he planned to attend telegraph school.

Dallas was a musically active place after World War II, and Billy soon found all the playing work he could handle. "There's an old club down here on South Irving, the Roundup Club. Seven nights a week, full every night. I went out there and I had my horn, and the drummer who worked there came around one day. He said, 'You a tenor player?' I said, 'Yeah.' He said, 'Won't you bring your horn and come sit in?' So I sat in, and after that, they hired me. Ted Daffan was there. I worked with Ted some. I played down there while I was going to telegraph school."

After telegraph school Billy went to work for the railroad, but it was not a job he liked. So he was ready for a change when his old friend from Illinois called and offered him a job with a wholesale grocery company in Lamesa, Texas. One Saturday night Billy took his horn and drove to the American Legion hall in Brownfield, not far from Lamesa, and before the night was over, he was playing on another dance band. But the best was yet to come.

> My friend from Illinois got a phone call. It was Johnny Gimble. He said that Mancel Tierney, the piano player with Bob Wills, was leaving, and they wanted a replacement for him. Well, Lou knew he wasn't going to leave, but anyway, we went over to Hobbs, New Mexico. At that time Bob had a sax player. So when Lou was sitting in, they asked me to sit in, too. I did. Bob liked what he heard, and it wasn't but about a month later till the phone rang one day, and it was Johnny Gimble again. He said, "Billy, Bob wants you to join him." Now this was about Thanksgiving 1950. I told him, "Well, let me think about it overnight." So I was telling Lou and he said, "Well, you know you want to go." So the next morning I called, and I joined Bob Wills and stayed on with him through June of 1951.

Billy's stay with Bob Wills was short but thrilling. Wills had put together a ten-piece group for a tour of the West Coast. The band played to sell-out crowds at the Riverside Rancho and basked in the popularity of Bob Wills. But Billy's most memorable moment occurred back home in Texas at a show the Playboys worked in Beaumont. "When my time to solo came, since it was a show, instead of a dance—I laid down on the floor. I was holding that horn up and really romping. They said Bob liked to have dropped his cigar. They said, you should have seen the look on his face." Wills may have been surprised by Billy's antics, but he was not angry. And when Billy went to resign, for he had already grown tired of the constant touring, Wills released him with these words: "Billy, you're the best we've ever had. Anytime you want to come back, you've got a place."

Billy returned to Dallas and for thirty-two years worked in the purchasing department of the Mobil Oil Corporation laboratory. He continued to fill his weeknights and weekends with a variety of music jobs. He has played in western swing bands and Dixieland bands. For years he played the country club circuit with his own jazz trio. He played on

Smokey Montgomery's band for the Big D Jamboree. He has played Texas Playboy Reunions and recorded with the Playboys II band. And now he is a regular member of Dave Alexander's big western swing band out of Dallas. Most of the sidemen in Alexander's band play from written arrangements, but Billy, fiddler Bobby Boatright, and the piano player (Pee Wee Lynn until his death in 1995) do what they have always done in western swing bands—improvise hot solo choruses. Billy says that his ability to improvise was the reason Alexander hired him.

Though Billy can play the hot solo choruses, he prefers to think of himself as part of the rhythm section, an unusual role for a horn player. "I just like to swing and push, and I play on top of the beat all of the time." Despite his age, Billy Briggs is still one of the most driving saxophone players in western swing. He does not play as much as he once did, not because he is unable but because musical styles have changed and he refuses to change with them. Billy was a swing saxophonist from the moment he picked up a horn, and he will be a swing saxophonist until he can no longer play. And do not call western swing "hillbilly music" in his presence. He has lived it, and he knows that some of the best jazz playing to be heard anywhere occurred in western swing bands.

Singers

Most people understand jazz to be instrumental music. In the 1930s and 1940s, however, when listeners were less interested in improvisation and more in entertainment and escape, jazz took on a strong vocal component. Most of the big bands, wind and string, had featured vocalists. It was the swinging beat that kept people dancing, but it was the song lyrics that kept them content.

Milton Brown (1903–1936), organizer of the first western swing band, was also the first western swing vocalist. Milton did not play an instrument, but was a gifted pop singer and an engaging stage personality. His use of a megaphone before the universal availability of microphones ensured that his vocals were important in his total band sound. Brown stressed improvisation from his sidemen and also demonstrated that he was a capable improviser with his scat singing on tunes like "Four or Five Times."[1] Bob Wills once said of Milton Brown that he had "the finest voice I'd ever heard."[2]

But because of his early death, Milton Brown is to western swing singing as Fred Calhoun is to western swing piano playing—the first but not the best remembered. The honor of being the most legendary of all western swing vocalists goes to Tommy Duncan, who was for many years associated with Bob Wills and the Texas Playboys. Tommy left the Light Crust Doughboys with Wills in 1932 and was a charter member of the Texas Playboys. Before Al Stricklin joined the band in 1935, Tommy was also the piano player, though he played very little piano. He put on a humorous show at the piano, banging away with his fists and feet and leaving a trail of demolished instruments in his wake. But there was nothing slapstick about Tommy's singing—with his fine tenor voice, his ability to deliver a feeling and a lyric. Wills himself sang many of the blues numbers, but Tommy was responsible for most of the rest of the tunes, and it was quite a variety of types of songs that he sang. In all, Tommy Duncan was the featured vocalist on close to five hundred Texas Playboy recordings.

When the United States entered World War II in 1941, Tommy was the first to leave the band and enlist. Earlier in the year, on February 24, 1941, at a recording session in Dallas, the Playboys had re-released "Maiden's Prayer," a number Wills had recorded six years earlier as a fiddle tune. But this time the only string instrument on the recording was Eldon Shamblin's guitar accompaniment to Tommy Duncan's vocal stylings with the newly added lyrics. "Maiden's Prayer" had become an updated swing rendition of an old favorite.[3]

When Tommy was discharged from the service, he immediately rejoined Wills. He participated on the dance tour billed as Bob Wills and His Great Vaudeville Show in late 1944 as well as in the first Columbia recording session of the new year, 1945. In September 1948 Tommy Duncan left the Texas Playboys to form his own band, Tommy Duncan and His Western Allstars. Tommy had a good band and did well for himself, but never attained the status he had enjoyed with Wills. As for Bob Wills, he hired numerous singers but never found a replacement for Tommy Duncan. Finally, in 1959 and largely by popular demand, Bob Wills and Tommy Duncan reunited. They signed a contract with Liberty Records and cut their hit album *Together Again*. Wills and Duncan also made several successful cross-country tours together and drew large crowds in Las Vegas before Tommy left the band permanently sometime in the early 1960s. Tommy retired to his ranch in California to tend his prize-winning quarter horses and pedigreed Black Angus cattle.

The first female vocalist to work on a western swing band was Laura Lee Owens (1920–1989), whom Bob Wills hired for his Great Vaudeville Show. Laura Lee had a great deal of show business experience before Wills made her the first Texas Playgirl. She came from a show business family; her father was the songwriter and western singer Doie "Tex" Owens, and Laura Lee began performing in a trio with him and her sister. By 1936 the Owens family trio had its own radio show on station KMBC in Bridgeport, Oklahoma. After graduation from high school in 1938, Laura Lee formed her own band, Laura Lee and Her Range Buddies.

When Bob Wills contacted Laura Lee in 1944 about going to California with the band, she insisted on a contract; and when Wills informed her that he never used contracts, she reminded him that he had never hired a female.[4] Before leaving on the tour, Wills and the band, now with one Playgirl, appeared in three movies, two with Russell Hayden and a third entitled *Melody Master, the Story of Bob Wills and His Texas Playboys*. Coming off the tour in January 1945, the Playboys and Laura Lee recorded in Hollywood on the Columbia label and made radio and television appearances.

In November 1945 Laura Lee Owens married Dickie McBride, a South Texas western swing bandleader who had moved out to California. She performed with her husband and continued to appear in Hollywood films, making thirteen movies with Gene Autry. She worked as a disc jockey, ran a dinner theater at Mountain View, Arkansas, for Grandpa Jones and wife Ramona of the television show *Hee Haw*. She appeared on shows with Hank Williams, Willie Nelson, Hank Thompson, Tex Ritter, Ernest Tubb, George Jones, and others.

When she was inducted into the Sacramento Western Swing Hall of Fame in October 1987, Laura Lee McBride was the uncontested "Queen of Western Swing." In her acceptance speech she reminded the audience that she was not the only female vocalist Bob Wills had hired, but she was the first. She died in Bryan, Texas, after a long battle with cancer, on January 25, 1989.

Bob Wills and all of his singers were well known and much loved on the West Coast, but West Coast western swing produced its own vocal genius in Tex Williams. As a young man, Williams had a gift for yodeling. But as he matured, his voice dropped to the deep, rich baritone for which he was known, and his yodeling days ended.[5] Williams's was a flexible voice, capable of delivering quite a range of song types. The tune that made him famous, "Smoke, Smoke, Smoke That Cigarette," required fast rhythmic speech on the verses. Then he could turn around and croon his way through slow ballads such as "Leaf of Love." With his friends Deuce Spriggens and Smokey Rogers, Williams displayed his talent for novelty and comedy songs. Williams was a vocal stylist with a smooth delivery, a warm baritone timbre, and an expressive way of molding melodic phrases.

A Few Good Vocalists Talk about Western Swing

When Laura Lee McBride left the Texas Playboys, Wills decided to replace her with EVELYN and DEAN McKINNEY (b. ca. 1928 and 1930), two sisters who, like Laura Lee, already had years of show business experience. The McKinney sisters had begun their professional careers on radio stations WBRC and WAPI in Birmingham, Alabama, in the 1940s, when Dean was only twelve and Evelyn fourteen. At first they performed with better-known radio personalities, but because of their great popularity with listeners, they soon had their own show, which was broadcast over thirteen stations of the Southern Transcription Network.[6]

Dean describes their repertory as "a broad middle-of-the-road type of music. We never did the Carter Family or the Grand Ole Opry style of music; we did things like the Andrews Sisters, the Denning Sisters. We worked in harmony; that's what we looked for, songs that would lend themselves to harmony."

The McKinney sisters moved to radio station WSB in Atlanta to appear on one of the South's leading late-night programs; then they worked on a few Grand Ole Opry shows with Eddie Arnold and with Eddie Peabody, the Banjo King. After four years of successful radio work in their home state of Alabama, the McKinney sisters, ages sixteen and eighteen, made a big career move to St. Louis, Missouri, and station KWK's *Shady Valley Network* program, where they worked with a band called the Buckeye Four.

From St. Louis the sisters went to Chicago to sing with Ted Weems and His Orchestra, a big swing band that broadcast over station WBRC.[7] They were working for Weems when they auditioned for Bob Wills. Dean explains,

> When Bob Wills came through, I believe he must have done an interview or brought the band and played at WBRC. Our managers and program director there at WBRC wanted Bob to hear us sing.

So we did a little fifteen- or twenty-minute program in one of the studios. Bob sat in the control room and listened. Afterwards he came out and said, "I really don't have an opening for you right now, but I'm working on an ABC network program for a major cereal company. If that program comes through, I will send for you girls." We thought, don't call me, I'll call you. We never expected to hear from him again.

But they did hear from him again, on February 12, 1946, and the telegram simply said, "Come at once." Going to work for Wills was quite a brave move for these two young women. Fresno, California, was a long way from home and parents, and they were not at all familiar with Wills, his Texas Playboys, or his musical style. But the McKinney sisters, with their pop and big band vocal experience, were exactly what Wills needed to continue his updated sound. Dean recalls,

So we came to Fresno, and that began one of the happiest periods of our lives, because we felt that we had made it in the music field, and we were very career-oriented and dedicated. We wanted to go just as far as we could go, and we felt that the fact that we had done radio and had regional network shows, and that we did Mutual Network and Armed Forces radio, and then were in Chicago—we felt that this would be a new medium for us. So we came to Fresno and began touring with Bob, and fairly soon after we joined Bob we went to Hollywood, and that was one of the most exciting experiences of our lives. We got to make a musical short entitled *Frontier Frolics* with Bob Wills and the Modernaires. And then from there we went on the road with the band and toured. We worked with Bob until about 1948.

Tommy Duncan was the band's featured vocalist—of that there was no doubt. Dean explains that "Tommy got the good popular songs before we'd get a chance at them. I remember when 'Oh What It Seemed to Be' came out. That was just a perfect duet. And 'My Happiness' and those things, and Tommy would get them before we would get a chance at them. He had first choice." Dean and Evelyn never sang with Tommy Duncan, but they did a great deal of trio work with mandolin and fiddle player Tiny Moore, and they sang in a quartet with Tiny and Eldon Shamblin. One of their quartet numbers, "It's a Good Day," was recorded on the Tiffany Transcriptions.

Evelyn married first, then Dean married Tiny Moore and both women left the Wills band, though they continued to work occasionally with the Playboys. About 1950 Tiny Moore decided to get off the road, and he and Dean remained in California to manage Wills Point. The McKinney sisters sang with the portion of the Playboy band that stayed behind to perform at Wills Point. In 1951 a daughter was born to Dean and Tiny, and they moved from Wills Point to Sacramento. Evelyn was already living in Sacramento with her family. The two sisters were much involved in the musical life of the city. They were often seen on the four local television stations, most often on *The Ranchhouse Party* and *The Billy Jack Wills Show*. The duo experienced a temporary hiatus when Evelyn went to work for the California Board of Tourism. But now that Evelyn has retired and Dean has been widowed, the McKinney sisters are singing together again.[8]

One of the better-known western swing vocalists today, LEON RAUSCH was born into a musical family in Springfield, Missouri, in 1927. Rausch feels that it was inevitable that he became a professional musician: "My daddy and mother were good musicians. My daddy was a band leader for a little town band—every little town had a brass band. He was also a vocal teacher and a violin teacher, and he was very good, and he was the head of the choir at church. When I got old enough to sing with my daddy and momma, we became a pretty popular trio around my hometown and we played for all the pie suppers and functions and never did get paid, but we were appreciated."

Leon made his solo singing debut at the age of three on a Springfield radio program called *The Kiddy Club*. When he was about twelve years old and his hands had grown sufficiently large, his father began teaching him to play guitar and upright bass. He particularly enjoyed "thumping" that bass and has kept at it all these years. Like so many southwestern musicians coming of age in the 1930s and 1940s, Leon practiced with the radio, which was his connection to the world of music. Having one's own radio program was perceived as a goal by every aspiring musician, as a certain level of stardom to be attained. As Leon began to master guitar and bass, he was hired at two dollars per job to play for local square dances and eventually began to broadcast on the radio with local bands.

During World War II Leon was in the military, and after he was discharged in 1947, he used the G.I. Bill to pay for job training. He learned glass cutting and was working at the Pittsburgh Glass Company in

Springfield and playing in local bands, when he got his first big break in the music business. He was hired to sing on a Sunday-night television show that originated in Tulsa. Sundays were spent driving to Tulsa, doing the show, and driving home. On one particular Sunday night in March 1958, Bob Wills and some of the Playboys were watching the show. "Bob took a liking to my singing and through his brother, who recommended me also because I'd sung with him a couple of times at Cain's Academy doing dance jobs. Bob thought it might be a good idea to hire me and try me out, see if I was going to make it."

Leon made it as a singer and rhythm guitarist with the Texas Playboys for four years, until 1961. It was his first taste of western swing, and he was completely enthralled. He enjoyed working the dances and watching people move to the snappy dance beat. He enjoyed the recording sessions and playing the stage shows at the Golden Nugget in Las Vegas. He even enjoyed the traveling. "Rock 'n' roll had more or less taken over. It meant we had to work harder for less money to pay the band; that's the reason we were working hard. Bob was desperately trying to hang on; that put us on the road for less money." Leon had to leave the band when his elderly parents began to require more of his time. He moved back to Tulsa and spent the next three years playing in the Johnnie Lee Wills band. This, too, was a touring band; but, except for the month spent working in Las Vegas, it played a circuit that put the musicians home every night. On the Johnnie Lee Wills band, Leon sang and played his favorite string bass.

In 1963 Bob Wills moved his band and his family to Fort Worth. He had only a year earlier suffered a heart attack and was trying to find a way to live in semiretirement. He sold the band to an ardent fan in Fort Worth and essentially went to work for the new owner. In 1964 Bob suffered a second heart attack and was limited in the amount of time he could devote to the band. At this point Leon was hired away from the Johnnie Lee Wills band to manage the Playboys in Fort Worth. Bob Wills appeared with the band whenever he felt well enough, but otherwise the Texas Playboys went on without him. Leon feels that they kept Bob going by keeping the band together.

Leon also sang with the Original Texas Playboys, though he was not an original. He also fronts his own band, the Texas Panthers, which works dances primarily in the Austin, San Antonio, and Houston areas. In all his years singing and playing western swing, Leon has seen many changes, but he is certain that there is still an audience for western swing.

The repertory has been altered somewhat to include more current country music, but western swing continues to live and grow. Leon bemoans the fact that audiences today, imbued as they are with commercial rock and country music, place so much emphasis on vocals—he prefers the exciting, improvised instrumentals.

Leon listens to a great deal of jazz, and though too humble to call himself a jazz musician, he knows that western swing is jazz. Like most western swing musicians, Leon does not read music. He sings and plays according to how he feels, from the heart, and he interprets and improvises according to the context. Western swing, as he so simply and eloquently explains, is just "a good mixture."

Leon Rausch can be heard playing electric guitar on the *Together Again* album, released by Bob Wills and Tommy Duncan in 1959, and on all of the Liberty Hill recordings from 1960 to 1961. When Wills invited a few of the Playboys to make *For the Last Time* in Dallas in December 1973, Leon Rausch was called to sing and play some bass. He has also recorded with Johnny Gimble, Tommy Morrell, and with his own band and has appeared at Playboy Reunions and western swing festivals. There is no room today for a single dominant western swing vocalist, as Tommy Duncan was in the 1930s and 1940s; but for sheer versatility, beauty of tone, and vocal styling, Leon Rausch is one of the top vocalists in modern western swing.

West Coast swing fans today enjoy the voice of TRUITT CUNNINGHAM (b. 1931), who was only seventeen years old when he got his chance to work for Bob Wills in 1948. Tommy Duncan had just left to start his own band, and Wills needed a quick but good replacement. Truitt grew up in Muleshoe, Texas, and at one time lived next door to John Wills, Bob's father; the Wills and Cunningham families were friends. Bob had also heard Truitt sing with the band he was working for in 1948, the Alabamans. Truitt recalls how he got the word that Bob Wills wanted him to audition. He and his new bride were staying with friends in Modesto, California, and Truitt was in the shower when fellow musician Chester Smith barged in and asked,

> "Truitt, did you know that Bob Wills is looking for you?" I said, "Oh, yeah. I'll bet he's been looking for months." I got out of the shower, and he said, "No." He was just shaking; he was so excited. He said, "No, Bob Wills is looking for you. He wants you to sing."

I said, "Well, how did you know this?" He said, "Fred Maddox talked to Luke Wills, Luke told Fred and Fred told me. I'm telling you, Bob Wills is looking for you." So the next day Bob and the Texas Playboys were on KFBK. I thought, I'll just wait until the show's over and call Bob. I put a call in to KFBK, and a girl came on the phone and said, "Can I help you?" I said, "Yeah, I'd like to speak to Bob Wills, please." I had no idea that he would come to the phone, and it was less than a minute, and here Bob came to the phone. I said, "Bob, this is Truitt Cunningham." He said, "We've been looking for you." And I liked to have fallen down. "Can you come down here tomorrow after the show and do us a little audition?" I said, "Yes, I can."

The next day at the radio station in Sacramento, Truitt sang for over an hour, and Bob Wills offered him a job starting immediately. But Truitt was newly married and was not ready to go on the road. Wills had just purchased the old Aragon Ballroom near Sacramento and converted it into Wills Point, so he sent Truitt to work there as part of the house band. After six months, Truitt left Wills Point and went out on his own to work the club circuit.

Truitt had been working in the house band of Mortimer's Club in Monterey for some eighteen months when he decided, for personal reasons, to quit and seek out Bob Wills once again. The Playboys were appearing in Redwood City, not far from Monterey, and Truitt went to Bob and asked for a job. Truitt officially became a Texas Playboy at Alturas, California, in July 1954.

After six months and some financial setbacks, Wills returned to Wills Point. Truitt returned to Mortimer's Club, and then in 1956, he went to work at Aerojet in Rolsom, California, while continuing to play in clubs at night and on weekends. In 1957 Truitt went with Billy Jack Wills as a regular on his television program; this lasted until 1960. Since 1960 Truitt has worked with his own bands, including a trio that performed on the *Country Corners* television show out of Sacramento and played a daily radio broadcast.

Truitt recorded one Top Ten hit in the 1960s, "The Truck That Peter Built," written by his good friends, Liz and Casey Anderson, whose daughter Lynn Anderson made her singing debut on the *Country Corners* show. Truitt fronted various television and club bands in the 1960s and 1970s.[9] In recent years he has organized the San Antonio Rose Band, consisting of former Texas Playboys—Truitt Cunningham (bass/vocals), Bobby Koefer (steel guitar), Bobby Boatright (fiddle), Curly Lewis (fiddle), Glenn Rhees (saxophone), Casey Dickens (drums), Eldon Shamblin (guitar), and Clarence Cagle (piano). The group records and performs at Playboy Reunions, western swing festivals, and even jazz festivals, playing the old arrangements of Bob Wills's favorite tunes.

Western swing audiences, particularly older ones, have become protective of the old Bob Wills arrangements and do not care to hear anything else. Truitt remembers that Wills performed everything that was popular during his long career as a bandleader, putting his personal signature on all kinds of tunes that were not, technically, his or other Playboys' creations. "I remember we used to do 'Release Me,' and current hits of the day. When they were done by Bob Wills, they were Bob Wills's tunes, but he did everything. Now, if you get up and do anything except a Bob Wills tune (one he wrote or introduced), they'll whisper to each other, 'Why are they doing that? That's not Bob Wills.'"

Like all forms of jazz, western swing is not a repertory but an approach, a way of playing and singing any repertory. Bob Wills, Spade Cooley, Tex Williams, Cliff Bruner—all the western swing bands transformed the most current popular music into western swing. These were not hillbilly bands playing country music; they were swing bands playing the popular dance music of an era in American entertainment. And the singers who performed with these western swing bands were not country singers but pop vocalists, sometimes crooners, stylizing songs much as did Bing Crosby and Frank Sinatra, who began their careers singing with swing bands.

Conclusion

From approximately 1932 to 1955, western swing was the entertainment and dance music of the Southwest and of places like California to which rural southwesterners migrated. Western swing was created by self-taught, nonreading musicians who populated innumerable local bands that played for countless daily radio broadcasts and in myriad dance halls spread all across this vast territory. Each band was unique, and yet all were the same. At the heart of every western swing band was its component of strings—fiddle, guitar, steel guitar, banjo, bass—to which various additions were made. Some bands used two or more fiddles, some several guitars, some one or more horns, some whole sections of horns. All had featured vocalists.

Western swing bands shared a repertory that included oral-tradition fiddle tunes, blues, and all the popular songs and jazz arrangements of the day, plus numerous newly created western swing standards. Western swing fused country music, blues, jazz, German polkas and waltzes, Mexican dance music, popular songs, Cajun tunes—in effect, all the music that coexisted in the vast rural landscape of the Southwest.

The heroes of western swing were the fiddle, guitar, steel guitar, and piano players, who improvised their hot jazz choruses over a rhythmic background so solid and energetic that audiences had to dance. Western swing was and is dance music! Most important, western swing was and is jazz—southwestern jazz—built upon the same principles of improvisation and interpretation that have turned all types of music into jazz. All efforts to classify western swing as country music will fall short upon further examination of the process involved in creating it.

Current attempts to recreate western swing do not begin to capture the original atmosphere and spirit of this music. Most western swing revival bands limit their repertory to the few western swing standards, usually those by Bob Wills or his sidemen, which are recognized by general audiences. And they learn solos from recordings and even written scores. This defeats the purpose of western swing, for if the western swing pioneers were making their jazz today, they would be improvising and reinterpreting all of the music they had heard and creating new music as well. Current western swing revival bands also fail to understand the rhythmic nature of western swing. And they perform in concerts and shows rather than in the dance halls for which the music was designed.

This book is only a beginning, an oral history told from the perspectives of a few living western swing musicians. It has focused upon some individuals and bands who made western swing music. No effort has been made to be inclusive, and literally hundreds of bands have been excluded. What must follow is theoretical research into the nature of western swing improvisation, with comparisons between individual efforts of western swing musicians and those of mainstream jazz figures. It is my belief that such a study will reveal a plethora of advanced harmonic and melodic ideas coming from this most unlikely source, the untutored, rural musicians of western swing. But then nobody told Louis Armstrong what to play or how to become the first great jazz soloist. He followed his instincts, as have all of the great western swing legends.

Notes

Introduction: Western Swing and the Texas Mystique

1. Betty Casey, *Dance across Texas*, 49–52.
2. T. R. Fehrenbach, *Seven Keys to Texas*, vii–viii.

1. Western Swing: Description and Development

1. *Western Swing Society Music News* 9, no. 1 (January 1994), 6.
2. Gunther Schuller, *The Swing Era: The Development of Jazz, 1930–1945,* 564–565.
3. Bill C. Malone, *Country Music, U.S.A.,* 31–34.
4. Charles R. Townsend, *San Antonio Rose: The Life and Music of Bob Wills,* 51–57.
5. Larry Willoughby, *Texas Rhythm, Texas Rhyme: A Pictorial History of Texas Music,* 12.
6. *Western Swing Society Music News* 9, no. 1 (January 1994).
7. Malone, *Country Music, U.S.A.,* 160; Willoughby, *Texas Rhythm, Texas Rhyme,* 50.
8. Townsend, *San Antonio Rose,* 55–60.
9. Kevin Coffey, "Is Bob Wills Still the King?" *Fort Worth Star Telegram,* March 9, 1992, sec. E2.
10. Ibid.
11. Townsend, *San Antonio Rose,* 149–150.
12. Quoted in ibid., 232.
13. Ibid., 285.
14. Ibid., 287.
15. Tom Dunbar, *From Bob Wills to Ray Benson: A History of Western Swing,* 67.
16. Ken Griffis, liner notes, *Tex Williams and the Swinging Western Caravan,* American Folk Music Archive and Research Center, record album AFM 711.
17. Dunbar, *From Bob Wills to Ray Benson,* 69.
18. Griffis, liner notes, *Tex Williams and the Swinging Western Caravan.*
19. Ibid.
20. Willoughby, *Texas Rhythm, Texas Rhyme,* 49.
21. Dunbar, *From Bob Wills to Ray Benson,* 94–95.

2. Western Swing Fiddlers

1. Matt Glaser, "Violin," in *The New Grove Dictionary of Jazz*, ed. Barry Kernfeld; hereafter cited as *NGDJ*.

2. Frank Tirro, *Jazz: A History*, 2d ed., 101–102.

3. Ibid., 102.

4. Ibid., 160, 149.

5. Matt Glaser and Alyn Shipton, "Violin," *NGDJ*.

6. Ross Russell, *Jazz Styles in Kansas City and the Southwest*, 61, 165.

7. J. Bradford Robinson, "Venuti, Joe," *NGDJ*; Glaser and Shipton, "Violin," *NGDJ*; Vincent Pelote, liner notes, *Jazz Strings*, Greatest Jazz Recordings of All Time, record 29/30–31/32.

8. J. Bradford Robinson, "Grappelli, Stephane," *NGDJ*; Glaser and Shipton, "Violin," *NGDJ*; Pelote, liner notes, *Jazz Strings*; Mark O'Connor, liner notes, *Heroes*, Warner Brothers, compact disc 9 45257-2.

9. Matt Glaser, "Smith, Stuff," *NGDJ*.

10. Pelote, liner notes, *Jazz Strings*.

11. John Morthland, liner notes, *Texas Music: Western Swing and Honky-Tonk*, Rhino Records, compact disc R2 71782.

12. The side is reproduced on Rhino's *Texas Music: Western Swing and Honky-Tonk*.

13. This recording of "Taking Off" is also included on the Rhino CD.

14. Rupert N. Richardson, Ernest Wallace, and Adrian N. Anderson, *Texas, the Lone Star State*, 3d ed., 337–338.

15. Tony Russell, *Blacks, Whites, and Blues*, 81.

16. Glen Tarver, "Profile: Johnny Gimble," *Western Swing Society Music News* 6, no. 6 (June 1991).

17. Ibid.

18. Johnny Gimble, *Still Fiddlin' Around*, MCA Records, compact disk MCAD-42021.

19. O'Connor, liner notes, *Heroes*.

20. "Profile: Bobby Boatright," *Western Swing Society Music News* 8, no. 6 (June 1993).

21. Keith Coleman spent time as one of the fiddlers on the Bob Wills Texas Playboys band in the late 1940s and early 1950s. He was acknowledged for his music-reading ability. According to Johnny Gimble, Coleman could "read the music and they could put a chart in front of him and he could read it" (Gimble, Oral History Interview). Gimble also remembers Coleman as a versatile musician who could double on saxophone. Coleman did session work in Nashville and also toured and recorded with Ray Price.

22. Bobby Boatright, *Among My Souvenirs*, cassette tape produced by Tommy Morrell, Garland Recording Studio.

3. Western Swing Guitarists

1. Tony Bacon and Jim Ferguson, "Guitar," *NGDJ*.

2. Norman Mongan, *The History of the Guitar in Jazz*, 6–8.

3. Mark C. Gridley, *Jazz Styles*, 4th ed., 38.

4. Bacon and Ferguson, "Guitar," *NGDJ*.

5. Ibid.

6. Mongan, *History of the Guitar in Jazz*, 29.

7. Richard Hadlock, *Jazz Masters of the 20s*, 127, quoted in Mongan, *History of the Guitar in Jazz*, 32; Stan Britt, *The Jazz Guitarists*, 52.

8. Gridley, *Jazz Styles*, 83–84; Britt, *Jazz Guitarists*, 47.

9. Pelote, liner notes, *Jazz Strings*.

10. Raymond Horricks, *Count Basie and His Orchestra*, 128.

11. Britt, *Jazz Guitarists*, 125.

12. Ibid., 31–32.

13. Gridley, *Jazz Styles*, 102.

14. Britt, *Jazz Guitarists*, 114.

15. Mongan, *History of the Guitar in Jazz*, 125.

16. Interview by George Clinton, *Guitar Player*, August 1976, quoted in ibid., 126–127.

17. Mongan, *History of the Guitar in Jazz*, 114.

18. Interview by Bill Lee, *Guitar Player*, October 1970, quoted in ibid., 115.

19. Mongan, *History of the Guitar in Jazz*, 118.

20. Interview by Lee, *Guitar Player*.

21. John Williams Handy, liner notes, *Catch Me*, Pacific Jazz record, LLJ-70041.

22. Mongan, *History of the Guitar in Jazz*, 156.

23. Ibid., 157.

24. Buddy McPeters, "Junior Barnard, Hard-Driving Soloist of Western Swing," *Guitar Player* 17 (September 1983): 44.

25. Ibid.

26. *The Bob Wills Anthology*, Collector's Series, CBS Special Products, compact disc A32416.

27. McPeters, "Junior Barnard," 49.

28. Mongan, *History of the Guitar in Jazz*, 133.

29. Jimmy Wyble, "Achieving Polytonality by Superimposing Scales," *Guitar Player* 14 (October 1980): 46, 48.

30. Jimmy Wyble, "Combining Scales to Expand Technique and Harmonic Awareness," *Guitar Player* 13 (July 1979): 82.

31. "Wyble, Jimmy" (unsigned), *NGDJ*.

32. *The Bob Wills Anthology*.

33. "Wyble, Jimmy," *NGDJ*.

34. Frankie R. Nemko, "Whether with Spade Cooley, Benny Goodman, or in L.A.'s Studios . . . He's Always Been Jimmy Wyble," *Guitar Player* 11 (June 1977): 22.

35. Ibid.

36. Townsend, *San Antonio Rose*, 118.

37. Ibid., 151.

38. Ibid., 152.

39. Ibid., 209.

40. Ibid., 210.

41. Cheryl Boyles, "Profiles in Western Swing: Tiny Moore," *Western Swing Society Music News* 1, no. 5 (June 1986).

42. Dunbar, *From Bob Wills to Ray Benson*, 73.

43. Ken Frazier, interview by author, November 26, 1994, Waco, Texas, personal notes, P.O. Box 1391, Hewitt, Texas 76643.

44. Ken Frazier, interview by author, June 25, 1992, transcript, Baylor University Oral History Institute.

45. Ibid.

4. The Steel Guitar in Western Swing

1. Hugh Davies, "Hawaiian Guitar," *The New Grove Dictionary of Musical Instruments*, ed. Stanley Sadie; hereafter cited as *NGDMI*.

2. Malone, *Country Music, U.S.A.*, 26.

3. Charles T. Brown, *Music U.S.A.: America's Country and Western Music*, 10.

4. Davies, "Hawaiian Guitar," *NGDMI*.

5. Tony Bacon, "Electric Guitar," *NGDMI*.

6. Tony Bacon, "Rickenbacker," *NGDMI*.

7. Tom Wheeler, *American Guitars: An Illustrated History*, 333–334.

8. Ibid., 131–132.

9. Davies, "Hawaiian Guitar," *NGDMI*.

10. Coffey, "Is Bob Wills Still the King?"

11. Wheeler, *American Guitars*, 293–294.

12. Ibid.

13. Mongan, *History of the Guitar in Jazz*, 82.

14. Milton Brown and His Musical Brownies, "Taking Off," recorded for Decca on January 28, 1935, Chicago; re-released on Rhino's *Texas Music*.

15. Leon McAuliffe, interview by David Stricklin, May 19, 1985, transcript, Baylor University Oral History Institute. Subsequent quoted remarks by McAuliffe in this chapter are from this interview unless cited otherwise.

16. Dunbar, *From Bob Wills to Ray Benson*, 7.

17. John Wooley, "Profiles in Western Swing: Leon McAuliffe," *Western Swing Society Music News* 3, no. 6 (June 1988).

18. *The Bob Wills Anthology*.

19. Bea Poling Perry, "Profile: Noel Boggs, 1917–1974," *Western Swing Society Music News* 5, no. 2 (February 1990).

20. Townsend, *San Antonio Rose*, 239.

21. Ibid., 241.

22. Dunbar, *From Bob Wills to Ray Benson*, 68–69.

23. Perry, "Profile: Noel Boggs."

24. Dunbar, *From Bob Wills to Ray Benson*, 68–69.

25. Perry, "Profile: Noel Boggs."

26. *The Bob Wills Anthology*.

27. *Spade Cooley*, Columbia Historic Editions, Columbia Records, cassette FCT 37467.

28. Griffis, liner notes, *Tex Williams and the Swinging Western Caravan*.

29. "Profile: Herb Remington," *Western Swing Society Music News* 9, no. 5 (May 1994).

30. *The Bob Wills Anthology*.

31. Herb Remington, *Pure Remington Steel*, Stoneway Records, cassette STY-138.

32. Tom Morrell and the Time Warp Tophands, *Pterodactyl Ptales: How the West Was Swung*, vol. 4, WR Records, cassette WR-0004.

33. Perry Jones, "Profile: Maurice Anderson," *Western Swing Society Music News* 6, no. 8 (August 1991).

34. Ibid.

35. O'Connor, liner notes, *Heroes*.

36. Jones, "Profile: Maurice Anderson."

5. The Western Swing Rhythm Section: Banjo and Bass

1. Gridley, *Jazz Styles*, 86.

2. Barry Kernfeld, "Beat," *NGDJ*.

3. Russell, *Jazz Styles in Kansas City and the Southwest*, 63.

4. Ibid., 81.

5. Gunther Schuller, *Early Jazz: Its Roots and Musical Development*, 294–295.

6. Schuller, *The Swing Era*, 8–9.

7. Leonard Feather, *The Book of Jazz: A Guide to the Entire Field*, 110.

8. Julian F. V. Vincent, "Banjo," *NGDJ*; Feather, *Book of Jazz*, 111.

9. Bill Russell, "St. Cyr, John Alexander," *NGDJ*.

10. Coffey, "Is Bob Wills Still the King?"

11. "Profile: Smokey Rogers," *Western Swing Society Music News* 9, no. 1 (January 1994).

12. Griffis, liner notes, *Tex Williams and the Swinging Western Caravan*.

13. "Profile: Smokey Rogers."

14. Feather, *Book of Jazz*, 119.

15. Alyn Shipton, "Double Bass," *NGDJ*.

16. Ibid.

17. Ibid.

18. Feather, *Book of Jazz*, 120.

19. J. Bradford Robinson, "Page, Walter (Sylvester)," *NGDJ*.

20. J. Bradford Robinson, "Blanton, Jimmy," *NGDJ*.

21. J. Bradford Robinson, "Pettiford, Oscar," *NGDJ*.

22. J. Bradford Robinson, "Brown, Raymond Matthews," *NGDJ*.

23. J. Bradford Robinson, "Stewart, Leroy Elliott (Slam)," *NGDJ*.

24. Loyd Jones, "Tribute: Billy Jack Wills," *Western Swing Society Music News* 6, no. 4 (April 1991).

25. Jack Rowe, *A True Life Story: 50 Years of Western Swing Music by the Seven Rowe Brothers and Sister Louise*, 5th ed., 4.

26. Ibid., 4–5.

6. The Western Swing Rhythm Section: Piano and Drums

1. Feather, *Book of Jazz*, 57.

2. Ibid., 59.

3. Billy Taylor, *Jazz Piano: History and Development*, 48–50.

4. Ibid., 39.

5. Ibid., 60.

6. Lawrence Koch, "Piano," *NGDJ*.

7. Taylor, *Jazz Piano*, 83.

8. Gridley, *Jazz Styles*, 63.

9. Feather, *Book of Jazz*, 61.

10. Ibid., 62.

11. Ibid., 65.

12. Gridley, *Jazz Styles*, 101.

13. Feather, *Book of Jazz*, 69.

14. Al Stricklin, *My Years with Bob Wills*, 12–13.

15. Ibid., 21.

16. Ibid.

17. Al Stricklin and W. E. "Smoky" Dacus, interview by David Stricklin, May 19, 1985, transcript, Baylor University Oral History Institute.

18. Ibid.

19. Stricklin, *My Years*, 83.

20. Ibid., 84.

21. Ibid., 142–143.

22. Guy Logsdon, "Profile: Clarence Cagle," *Western Swing Society Music News* 3, no. 12 (December 1988).

23. Ibid.

24. Ibid.

25. Sometimes spelled "Curly."

26. T. Dennis Brown, "Drum Set," *NGDJ*.

27. Feather, *Book of Jazz*, 124.

28. Gridley, *Jazz Styles*, 82–83.

29. Brown, "Drum Set," *NGDJ*.

30. Gridley, *Jazz Styles*, 90–91.

31. Brown, "Drum Set," *NGDJ*.

7. The Rest of the Western Swing Band: Horn Players and Vocalists

1. "Profile: Milton Brown, 1903–1936, Posthumous 1989 Western Swing Society Hall of Fame Nominee." *Western Swing Society Music News* 4, no. 10 (October 1989).

2. Coffey, "Is Bob Wills Still the King?"

3. Townsend, *San Antonio Rose*, 227.

4. "Tribute/Profile: Laura Lee Owens McBride," *Western Swing Society Music News* 4, no. 6 (June 1989).

5. Dallas Williams, interview by author, July 27, 1993, transcript, Baylor University Oral History Institute.

6. "Profiles in Western Swing: The McKinney Sisters," *Western Swing Society Music News* 3, no. 7 (June 1989).

7. Ibid.

8. Ibid.

9. Norma-Lee, "Profile: Truitt Cunningham," *Western Swing Society Music News* 7, no. 5 (May 1992).

Works Cited

Books and Articles

Boyles, Cheryl. "Profiles in Western Swing: Tiny Moore." *Western Swing Society Music News* 1, no. 5 (June 1986).

Britt, Stan. *The Jazz Guitarists*. Poole, Dorset, U.K.: Blanford Press, 1984.

Brown, Charles T. *Music U.S.A.: America's Country and Western Music*. Englewood Cliffs, N.J.: Prentice-Hall, 1986.

Casey, Betty. *Dance across Texas*. Austin: University of Texas Press, 1985.

Coffey, Kevin. "Is Bob Wills Still the King?" *Fort Worth Star Telegram*, March 9, 1992, E2.

Dunbar, Tom. *From Bob Wills to Ray Benson: A History of Western Swing*. Austin, Tex.: Term Publications, 1988.

Feather, Leonard. *The Book of Jazz: A Guide to the Entire Field*. London: Arthur Barker, 1959.

Fehrenbach, T. R. *Seven Keys to Texas*. El Paso: University of Texas Press, 1983.

Gridley, Mark C. *Jazz Styles*. 4th ed. Englewood Cliffs, N.J.: Prentice-Hall, 1991.

Hadlock, Richard. *Jazz Masters of the 20s*. New York: Collier Books, 1974.

Horricks, Raymond. *Count Basie and Orchestra*. London: Citadel Press, 1957.

Jones, Loyd. "Tribute to Billy Jack Wills." *Western Swing Society Music News* 6, no. 4 (April 1991).

Jones, Perry. "Profile: Maurice Anderson." *Western Swing Society Music News* 6, no. 8 (August 1991).

Kernfeld, Barry, ed. *The New Grove Dictionary of Jazz*. New York: Macmillan, 1988.

Logsdon, Guy. "Profile: Clarence Cagle." *Western Swing Society Music News* 3, no. 12 (December 1988).

Malone, Bill C. *Country Music, U.S.A.* Austin: University of Texas Press, 1968.

McPeters, Buddy. "Junior Barnard, Hard-Driving Soloist of Western Swing." *Guitar Player* 17 (September 1983): 44.

Mongan, Norman. *The History of the Guitar in Jazz*. New York: Oak Publications, 1983.

Nemko, Frankie R. "Whether with Spade Cooley, Benny Goodman, or in L.A.'s Studios . . . He's Always Been Jimmy Wyble." *Guitar Player* 11 (June 1977): 24–25.

Norma-Lee. "Profile: Truitt Cunningham." *Western Swing Society Music News* 7, no. 5 (May 1992).

Perry, Bea Poling. "Profile: Noel Boggs, 1917–1974." *Western Swing Society Music News* 5, no. 2 (February 1990).

"Profile: Bobby Boatright." *Western Swing Society Music News* 8, no. 6 (June 1993).

"Profile: Herb Remington." *Western Swing Society Music News* 9, no. 5 (May 1994).

"Profile: Milton Brown, 1903–1936, Posthumous 1989 Western Swing Society Hall of Fame Nominee." *Western Swing Society Music News* 4, no. 10 (October 1989).

"Profile: Smokey Rogers." *Western Swing Society Music News* 9, no. 1 (January 1994).

"Profiles in Western Swing: The McKinney Sisters." *Western Swing Society Music News* 3, no. 7 (June 1989).

Richardson, Rupert N., Ernest Wallace, and Adrian N. Anderson. *Texas, the Lone Star State.* 3d ed. Englewood Cliffs, N.J.: Prentice-Hall, Inc., 1970.

Rowe, Jack. *A True Life Story: 50 Years of Western Swing Music by the Seven Rowe Brothers and Sister Louise.* 5th ed. Irving, Tex.: Jack Rowe, 1990.

Russell, Ross. *Jazz Styles in Kansas City and the Southwest.* Berkeley: University of California Press, 1971.

Russell, Tony. *Blacks, Whites, and Blues.* New York: Stein and Day, 1970.

Sadie, Stanley, ed. *The New Grove Dictionary of Musical Instruments.* London: Macmillan, 1984.

Schuller, Gunther. *Early Jazz: Its Roots and Musical Development.* New York: Oxford University Press, 1968.

————. *The Swing Era: The Development of Jazz, 1930–1945.* New York: Oxford University Press, 1989.

Stricklin, Al. *My Years with Bob Wills.* With Jon McConal. Burnet, Tex.: Eakin Press, 1980.

Tarver, Glen. "Profile: Johnny Gimble." *Western Swing Society Music News* 6, no. 6 (June 1991).

Taylor, Billy. *Jazz Piano: History and Development.* Dubuque, Iowa: Wm. C. Brown Co., 1982.

Tirro, Frank. *Jazz History.* 2d ed. New York: W. W. Norton, 1993.

Townsend, Charles R. *San Antonio Rose: The Life and Music of Bob Wills.* Urbana: University of Illinois Press, 1976.

"Tribute/Profile: Laura Lee Owens McBride." *Western Swing Society Music News* 4, no. 6 (June 1989).

Western Swing Society Music News 9, no. 1 (January 1994).

Wheeler, Tom. *American Guitars: An Illustrated History.* New York: Harper and Row, 1982.

Willoughby, Larry. *Texas Rhythm, Texas Rhyme: A Pictorial History of Texas Music.* Austin, Tex.: Tonkawa Press, 1990.

Wooley, John. "Profile: Leon McAuliffe." *Western Swing Society Music News* 3, no. 6 (June 1988).

Wyble, Jimmy. "Achieving Polytonality by Superimposing Scales." *Guitar Player* 14 (October 1980): 46, 48.

———. "Combining Scales to Expand Technique and Harmonic Awareness." *Guitar Player* 13 (July 1979): 82.

Interviews

Transcripts of all interviews listed below are in the Texas Collection, Baylor University Oral History Institute, Baylor University, Waco, Texas.

Anderson, Maurice. Interview by Jean A. Boyd, June 2, 1990.

Beasley, Louise Rowe. Interview by Jean A. Boyd, July 30, 1991.

Boatright, Bobby. Interview by Jean A. Boyd, June 23, 1993.

Boyd, Jim. Interview by Jean A. Boyd, June 13, 1992.

Brewer, Clyde. Interview by Jean A. Boyd, August 13, 1991.

Briggs, Billy. Interview by Jean A. Boyd, June 23, 1993.

Bruce, Bobby. Interview by Jean A. Boyd, July 29, 1993.

Bruner, Cliff. Interview by Jean A. Boyd, August 14, 1991.

Cagle, Clarence. Interview by Jean A. Boyd, July 6, 1993.

Cunningham, Truitt, and Dean Moore. Interview by Jean A. Boyd, July 23, 1993.

Cuviello, Johnny. Interview by Jean A. Boyd, July 25, 1993.

Dacus, W. E. "Smoky." Interview by Jean A. Boyd, July 30, 1992. *See also* Al Stricklin

Duncan, Glynn. Interview by Jean A. Boyd, July 29, 1993.

Elkins, Cliff "Skeeter." Interview by Jean A. Boyd, July 23, 1993.

Ferguson, Joe Frank. Interview by Jean A. Boyd, June 10, 1992.

Frazier, Ken. Interview by Jean A. Boyd, June 25, 1992.

Garcia, Benny, and Tommy Perkins. Interview by Jean A. Boyd, July 7, 1993.

Gimble, Johnny. Interview by Jean A. Boyd, June 7, 1990.

Hollingsworth, Ray "Curle." Interview by Jean A. Boyd, August 9, 1992.

Hubbard, Carroll, and Ora Mae Hubbard. Interview by Jean A. Boyd, January 20, 1993.

Lewis, Curly. Interview by Jean A. Boyd, July 6, 1993.

McAuliffe, Leon. Interview by David Stricklin, May 19, 1985.

Montgomery, Marvin "Smokey." Interview by Jean A. Boyd, June 1, 1992.

Moore, Dean. *See* Truitt Cunningham

Morrell, Tommy. Interview by Jean A. Boyd, June 29, 1993.

Murrell, Bob. Interview by Jean A. Boyd, July 18, 1991.

Perkins, Tommy. *See* Benny Garcia

Rausch, Leon. Interview by Jean A. Boyd, June 2, 1990.

Ray, Buddy. Interview by Jean A. Boyd, June 22, 1993.

Remington, Herb. Interview by Jean A. Boyd, August 14, 1991.

Rhees, Glenn. Interview by Jean A. Boyd, July 6, 1993.

Shamblin, Eldon. Interview by Jean A. Boyd, July 21, 1992.

Stricklin, Al, and W. E. "Smoky" Dacus. Interview by David Stricklin, May 19, 1985.

Thomason, Jimmy. Interview by Jean A. Boyd, July 27, 1993.

Williams, Dallas. Interview by Jean A. Boyd, July 27, 1993.

Wills, Luke. Interview by Jean A. Boyd, July 21, 1993.

Recordings

Boatright, Bobby. *Among My Souvenirs*. Cassette. Garland Recording Studio, Garland, Texas, 1993.

The Bob Wills Anthology. Collector's Series, CBS Special Products. CD A32416. 1973.

Gimble, Johnny. *Still Fiddlin' Around*. Compact disc MCAD-42021. MCA Records, 1988.

Griffis, Ken. Liner notes. *Tex Williams and the Swinging Western Caravan*. Record AFM 711. American Folk Music Archive and Research Center, 1981.

Handy, John Williams. Liner notes. *Catch Me*. Record LLJ-70041. Pacific Jazz, n.d.

Hubbard, Carroll. *Carroll Hubbard Swings*. Cassette. Hubbard Entertainment, n.d.

Hubbard, Carroll, and Ora Mae Hubbard. *Side by Side*. Cassette. Hubbard Entertainment, n.d.

Morrell, Tommy, and the Time Warp Tophands. *Pterodactyl Ptales: How the West Was Swung*. Cassette WR-0004. WR Records, Box 248, Hunt, Tex. 78024, n.d.

Morthland, John. Liner notes. *Texas Music: Western Swing and Honky Tonk*. Compact disc R2 71782. Rhino Records, 1994.

O'Connor, Mark. *Heroes*. Compact disc 9 45257-2. Warner Brothers, 1993.

Pelote, Vincent. Liner notes. *Jazz Strings*. Record 29/30-31/32. Greatest Jazz Recordings of All Time. Institute of Jazz Studies Official Archive Collection, Franklin Mint Record Society, 1983.

Remington, Herb. *Pure Remington Steel*. Cassette STY-138. Stoneway Records, 1990.

Spade Cooley. Cassette FCT 37467. Columbia Historic Editions, Columbia Records, 1982.

Wakely, Jimmy. Liner notes. *Spade Cooley*. Cassette FCT 37467. Columbia Records, 1982.

Index